# LABOR AND POLITICS IN PANAMA

The Torrijos Years

Sharon Phillipps Collazos

Westview Special Studies on
Latin America and the Caribbean

# Labor and Politics in Panama

# Labor and Politics in Panama

## The Torrijos Years

Sharon Phillipps Collazos

Westview Press

BOULDER • SAN FRANCISCO • OXFORD

HD
8173.5
P47
1991

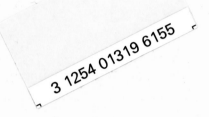
3 1254 01319 6155

*Westview Special Studies on Latin America and the Caribbean*

This Westview softcover edition is printed on acid-free paper and bound in library-quality, coated covers that carry the highest rating of the National Association of State Textbook Administrators, in consultation with the Association of American Publishers and the Book Manufacturers' Institute.

Copyright © 1991 by Westview Press, Inc.

Published in 1991 in the United States of America by Westview Press, Inc., 5500 Central Avenue, Boulder, Colorado 80301, and in the United Kingdom by Westview Press, 36 Lonsdale Road, Summertown, Oxford OX2 7EW

Library of Congress Cataloging-in-Publication Data
Phillipps Collazos, Sharon.
    Labor and politics in Panama : the Torrijos years / by
Sharon Phillipps Collazos.
      p.   cm.—(Westview special studies on Latin America and the
Caribbean)
    Includes bibliographical references and index.
    ISBN 0-8133-8115-0
    1. Labor policy—Panama—History—20th century.  2. Labor laws and
legislation—Panama—History—20th century.  3. Panama—Politics and
government—1946-1981.  4. Panama—Politics and government—1981-
5. Panama—Economic conditions.  I. Title.  II. Series.
HD8173.5.P47   1991
331.12′042′097287—dc20                                          90-21689
                                                                    CIP

Printed and bound in the United States of America

   The paper used in this publication meets the requirements
∞  of the American National Standard for Permanence of Paper
   for Printed Library Materials Z39.48-1984.

10    9    8    7    6    5    4    3    2    1

# CONTENTS

# TABLES AND FIGURES

## TABLES

## FIGURES

# ACKNOWLEDGMENTS

The story of the making and reversal of labor policy in Panama during the 1970s could not have been told without discussing the many different perspectives of those involved in this historical process. The persons I interviewed all provided invaluable information and deserve a special acknowledgment. They are listed in the appendix. There are many others not mentioned who in some way or another helped in the reconstruction of the period by providing details or insights, adding color to the picture. The missing view is that of the principal protagonist. Omar Torrijos died in a plane crash a few days before I was to interview him, so his side of the story has to be left untold.

An important insight afforded by this study is that of the fragility of Panamanian societal institutions, be they economic, political, or civic. The country's social structures are incipient or atrophied. The level of consciousness of Panamanian society regarding rights and duties is low. The research was also enlightening because it provided a glimpse of how Panamanian society really functions. When I was growing up, it was always puzzling to hear categorical explanations about why and how things happened in the country, always from the point of view of those I have called the "private sector" in these pages. Looking at Panamanian society at a time when that sector was not in control provided a rare opportunity to map the strategies of businessmen as they wove their way in and out of different positions. During an interview with a well-known member of the sector, he acknowledged that what hurt him the most about the Torrijos years was that Torrijos "had robbed him of his right" to a prominent political position. I asked what he would do with that position but was rebuffed and told that that was beside the point.

This study was carried out with a grant from the Social Science Research Council, for which I am very grateful. I owe special thanks to Peter Evans, Robert Fiala, Karen Remmer, and Nelson Valdés, for their helpful comments and patience, and especially to Gilbert Merkx, who has always been there with encouragement and support. Several economists were kind enough to discuss different issues with me or to read parts of the manuscript and offer helpful suggestions. I wish to thank Peter Gregory from the University of New Mexico, Albert Berry from the University of Toronto, and Adalberto Garcia from El Colegio de Mexico. I have also had the helpful comments and insights of Miguel Antonio Bernal, Carlos Castro, Marco Gandásegui, Arturo Hoyos, Richard Koster, and Gerardo Maloney. Perhaps most supportive over the years has been Steve Ropp, who was always willing to discuss an issue, to share information, or to provide another angle. Finally, Sam Adamo was a faithful and encouraging friend who shared many insights into methodological questions while we both concluded our studies. The interpretation of the facts and any errors are entirely my responsibility.

The manuscript has been greatly improved through the expert editing of Peg Sutton and Diane Hess, and it owes its present form to the help and patience of Victor Bandeira de Mello, Mark Lawrence, and Neil Ribeiro da Silva. Barbara Ellington and Diana Luykx from Westview Press have also been very helpful and supportive. To all, I offer my most heartfelt gratitude.

Finally, I owe much to my friends and family, who were there to offer comfort and encouragement during the difficult hours of writing and rewriting. But my greatest debt is to my children for their patience and tolerance during the endless times when working on the manuscript came before doing something "normal or fun." To them, then, Marc, Daniel, and Andrés, I dedicate this study.

*Sharon Phillipps Collazos*

# ACRONYMS

| | |
|---|---|
| AFL | American Federation of Labor |
| AIFELD | American Institute for Free Labor Development |
| APEDE | Asociación Panameña de Ejecutivos de Empresa (Panamanian Association of Business Executives) |
| BDA | Banco de Desarrollo Agropecuario (Agricultural Development Bank) |
| CADE | Conferencia Anual de Ejecutivos (Annual Conference of Business Executives) |
| CAPAC | Cámara Panameña de la Construcción (Panamanian Construction Chamber) |
| CATI | Central Auténtica de Trabajadores Independientes (Authentic Central of Independent Workers) |
| CIT | Central Istmeña de Trabajadores (Isthmian Workers Central) |
| CNTP | Central Nacional de Trabajadores de Panamá (National Central of Panamanian Workers) |
| CONATO | Consejo Nacional de Trabajadores Organizados (National Council of Organized Workers) |
| CONEP | Consejo Nacional de la Empresa Privada (National Council of Private Enterprise) |
| CPTT | Central Panameña de Trabajadores del Transporte (Panamanian Central of Transportation Workers) |
| CSS | Caja de Seguro Social (Social Security Bank) |
| CTRP | Confederación de Trabajadores de la República de Panamá (Confederation of Workers of the Republic of Panama) |
| CUT | Central Unica de Trabajadores (Singular Workers Central) |
| DIGEDECOM | Dirección General para el Desarrollo de la Comunidad (Agency for Community Development) |
| ESCANAP | Escuela Nacional de Capacitación Política (National School for Political Capacitation) |
| FENACOTA | Federación Nacional de Conductores de Taxi (National Federation of Taxi Drivers) |
| FEP | Federación de Estudiantes de Panamá |

|  | (Federation of Panamanian Students) |
|---|---|
| FER | Federación de Estudiantes Revolucionarios |
|  | (Federation of Revolutionary Students) |
| FITC | Federación Istmeña de Trabajadores Católicos |
|  | (Isthmian Federation of Christian Workers) |
| FSTRP | Federación Sindical de Trabajadores de la República de Panamá (also known as Federación Sindical) |
|  | (Trade Union Federation of the Republic of Panama) |
| IFARHU | Instituto para la Formación de Recursos Humanos |
|  | (Institute for the Development of Human Resources) |
| IFE | Instituto de Fomento Económico |
|  | (Institute for Economic Development) |
| ILO | International Labour Organization |
| IMA | Instituto de Mercadeo Agropecuario |
|  | (Institute for Agricultural Marketing) |
| INDESA | Investigación y Desarrollo, S.A. |
|  | (Research and Development Company) |
| IRHE | Instituto de Recursos Hidráulicos y Electrificación |
|  | (Hydraulic Resources and Electricity Institute) |
| JCD | Juntas de Conciliación y Decisión |
|  | (Decision and Conciliation Boards) |
| MICI | Ministerio de Comercio e Industrias |
|  | (Commerce and Industry Ministry) |
| MIDA | Ministerio de Desarrollo Agropecuario |
|  | (Ministry for Agricultural Development) |
| MIPPE | Ministerio de Planificación y Política Económica |
|  | (Planning Ministry) |
| MITRAB | Ministerio de Trabajo y Bienestar Social |
|  | (Labor Ministry) |
| PDC | Partido Demócrata Cristiano |
|  | (Christian Democratic Party) |
| PP | Partido del Pueblo (Communist Party) |
|  | (People's Party) |
| PRD | Partido Revolucionario Democrático |
|  | (Democratic Revolutionary Party) |
| PREALC | Programa Regional del Empleo para América Latina y el Caribe |
|  | (Regional Employment Program for Latin America and the Caribbean) |
| SIP | Sindicato de Industriales de Panamá |
|  | (Panamanian Industrialists Union) |
| SITRACHILCO | Sindicato de Trabajadores de la Chiriquí Land Co. |
|  | (Union of Workers of the Chiriqui Land Company) |
| SUNTRACS | Sindicato Unico de Trabajadores de la Construcción |
|  | (Singular National Union of Construction Workers) |
| UEU | Unión de Estudiantes Universitarios |
|  | (Union of University Students) |

# 1

# INTRODUCTION

In 1968, the National Guard of Panama deposed the newly elected president and took control of the country. That was not the first time that the Guard had acted beyond its constitutionally established bounds. But contrary to other such incidents, it was the first time that the National Guard did not return power to civilian hands once it had things under control. In former incidents of National Guard takeovers, the Guard had acted primarily as a broker among the factions of the ruling elite and restored power to the faction that offered them the best deal.

Another first was that the regime that emerged, under the leadership of Omar Torrijos, perceived its mission as a reformist one and aimed at restructuring society by incorporating new sectors, introducing redistributive measures, and changing the balance of power in Panamanian society.

This was the first time since Panama's independence from Colombia in 1903 that power was not in the hands of a small group of entrepreneurs, who were part of and represented primarily the interests of the private business community. This group was politically dispossessed from 1968 until 1989, when Noriega was deposed by U.S. invading forces. But it was during the first part of the Torrijos regime, roughly from 1970 to 1975, that the regime enjoyed autonomy to enact policy quite contrary to these former rulers' interests. During that period, an agricultural reform was instituted, a new constitution and a new labor code enacted as well as laws regarding housing and social services, and negotiations started for a new canal treaty with the United States. In some ways, the negotiations regarding the Panama Canal and the Labor Code became the two most important issues for the regime.

A new treaty favorable to Panama would settle once and for all the thorny issue of a foreign power having sovereign rights over part of the country's territory. And the Labor Code was a means of incorporating a large sector into society and symbolically clipping the wings of the business community, or former rulers.

What ensued after the enactment of the Labor Code and other progressive measures of the period provides a glimpse of the capacity and limitations of authoritarian states in politically underdeveloped societies and of the resources and tactics that the various interested actors can and do employ to protect their turf. All this unfolded under the constraints of a situation in which external forces, totally outside the control of the actors, had an overriding influence on the internal situation. In this case, the changes in the world economy severely affected Panama's situation and presented the first limitations to the autonomy of the Torrijos regime. Subsequently, during the Canal Treaty negotiations, the ability of the Panamanian business community to influence U.S. policy-makers to take a stand against the Torrijos regime presented another limitation to the regime and brought Torrijos to his knees regarding the Labor Code.

This is a study of the relationship between regime type, policy enactment, and policy implementation. It is also a study of the impact of policy on social sectors and on the changes in the relationship among the affected sectors. The regime type studied is one characterized as inclusionary authoritarian, and the specific case is the one of Omar Torrijos, in power from 1968 to 1981 in the Republic of Panama. The policies analyzed are the three main labor laws enacted by the Torrijos regime: the 1972 Labor Code, its amendment through Ley 95 in 1976 and Ley 8a in 1981 (that, while failing to restore the Labor Code to its original form, eliminated the harshest aspects of Ley 95). Apart from the regime itself, the significant actors affected by the policies under study are the private business sector and the labor force. A significant aspect of this study is that the three policy changes were enacted by the same regime.

The Torrijos regime came into power after the Panamanian ruling elite suffered a loss of hegemony and lost control of the political system. During its first years in power, the regime enjoyed enough autonomy to enact policies contrary to the interests of the former ruling group. Among the new policies, the 1972 Labor Code had a special significance for the regime, both symbolically and in real terms. The Labor Code was a clear statement that the regime represented a break with the past and that it was reformist and wished to single out new groups for preferential treatment. But the Labor Code was also the most direct and effective way to incorporate a sector formerly excluded, a sector that would give the regime support and lend it a measure of legitimacy.

After the Labor Code's enactment, the private sector attributed to it most of the economic woes it experienced during the decade. Arguments against the code centered around the cost increases due to higher wages and benefits as well as to strikes, labor litigations, absenteeism, and to loss of productivity. Also attributed to the Labor Code was the deteriorated employment situation as well as the alarming number of closures of small businesses. Once Ley 95 was passed, employers asserted that productivity went up, the economic situation stabilized, and loss of revenues due to union activities such as strikes and labor litigations were considerably reduced.

The findings of this study do not support those claims. Wages as a percentage of value added for the manufacturing sector did not increase with the enactment of the 1972 Labor Code; also, wages could not keep up with inflation, and measures outside the control of the labor and business sectors had to be used by the government to guarantee workers their livelihood. Cost increases due to union activities such as participation in seminars and protection through the *fuero sindical* (union privilege), strikes, and labor litigations also proved to be negligible. And although no direct correlation could be detected between the level of productivity and the labor laws in question, productivity went down in the period after the Ley 95 amendment to the Labor Code, which invalidated the claims of the positive effect of Ley 95 on productivity and on the economy as a whole.

The argument that the stability clause prevented the efficient running of businesses, because it made it impossible to reduce the work force, also did not prove true. During the recessionary period of 1974-1976, the work force in Panama was reduced by 8 percent. Neither could any correlation be found between the labor laws and the well-being of small enterprises. Their performance was found to conform to the macro-economic trends affecting the country, so that between 1975-1977, when the rate of increase of GDP was lowest, requests for licenses for new businesses were lowest, and closures were at their highest. As for employment, factors such as the slow growth of GDP and the lack of coherence of governmental policy regarding economic development had a far greater effect than the Labor Code. The International Labour Organization's PREALC (Programa Regional de Empleo para América Latina y el Caribe) concluded that the Labor Code forced Panamanian employers to treat their workers in an institutionalized and rational manner—they were used to dealing with them in a paternal-istic, non-systematic way—and that this was the underlying factor that prompted the vehement campaign against the Labor Code.

The enactment of the 1972 Labor Code acted as a catalyst for the private sector by providing them with a reason to coalesce and act as a united force against the regime. The coming together of the private sector—and their manipulation of their considerable economic assets at the same time they maintained a fierce anti-government campaign both in Panama and abroad—was aided by the economic recession of the mid-1970s and by the efforts of the regime to conclude treaty negotiations with the United States regarding the Panama Canal.

Ley 95 had an effect on labor similar to that the 1972 Labor Code had had on the private sector. Ley 95 provided the rallying point around which labor would unite and fight for its rights and also provided an opportunity for labor to grow in strength and class consciousness. The enactment of Ley 8a in 1981 was a compromise by the Torrijos regime with both labor and the private sector. That law signaled the loss of autonomy of the regime vis-à-vis labor, just as five years before Ley 95 had signaled the loss of autonomy of the regime vis-à-vis the private sector. Ley 8a marked the completion of a cycle for labor from excluded sector to an actor with power to play in the political game of demand-making. It also marked the end of a phase for the Torrijos regime from complete autonomy at the outset of its tenure to loss of autonomy to both the former dominant class and the subordinate labor sector.

## PREOCCUPATIONS IN THE LITERATURE ON LATIN AMERICAN REGIME TYPE AND POLICIES

In their seminal work that inspired the study of dependent development, Cardoso and Faletto posited that the manner in which a country is inserted into the world market produces specific class configurations and political arrangements.[1] Beginning with O'Donnell, theoretical attention has shifted from the broad outlines of dependency itself to a more specific concern with regime types in general and authoritarian regimes in particular, with specific reference to the "projects" or policies implemented by such regimes.[2]

O'Donnell defined bureaucratic-authoritarian regimes as "excluding" and non-democratic, with a dominant coalition of high-level technocrats (military and civilian) working in close association with foreign capital.[3] O'Donnell argued that bureaucratic-authoritarian regimes are a typical response to popular mobilization and that they are characterized by policies designed to demobilize popular sectors and to favor private enterprise. Through such measures, bureaucratic-authoritarian regimes attempted fundamental restructuring of society.

More recent work has drawn attention to other authoritarian regimes that engage in pre-emptive mobilization and the channeling of popular support for the regime in conjunction with redistributive measures. Peru in 1968 is a case in point, with Mexico under Cardenas, Brazil under Vargas, and Argentina under Peron viewed as precursors. Because of the mobilization of a mass base through the enactment of policy and other measures, these regimes have come to be labeled "inclusionary authoritarian regimes." Work on Peru in particular but also on the other cases, has suggested that these inclusionary authoritarian regimes have drastically altered the political landscape in countries where they have been in power.[4]

[1] Fernando Henrique Cardoso and Enzo Faletto, *Dependencia y desarrollo en América Latina*. Mexico: Siglo Veintiuno, 1969.
[2] Guillermo O'Donnell, *Modernization and Bureaucratic Authoritarianism: Studies in South American Politics*. Berkeley: University of California, Institute of International Studies, 1973.
[3] David Collier, "Overview of the Bureaucratic-Authoritarian Model," in *The New Authoritarianism in Latin America*, edited by David Collier. Princeton: Princeton University Press, 1979, p. 24.
[4] Evelyne Huber Stephens, "The Peruvian Military Government, Labor Mobilization, and the Political Strength of the Left," *Latin American Research Review*, 18:2:(1983) 57-93; and

In both exclusionary and inclusionary regimes, labor policy is critical in defining the regime's goals and in achieving its ends. In all the inclusionary regimes mentioned above, reform of labor legislation has been an important element of the regime's effort to mobilize the support of popular sectors and to control and channel that support. Labor policy is therefore a key to analyzing regime dynamics, particularly in the case of inclusionary regimes, and may be important for understanding both the long-run failure of past inclusionary regimes and the long-term impact that they have had on political landscapes.

## The Significance of the Panamanian Case

The interaction between regime type and dependency on the one hand and regime type and policy on the other are of particular theoretical interest in the case of the Torrijos regime in Panama because of the extreme dependency that characterizes Panamanian economy and society. In addition, the Torrijos regime (along with Peru's) is one of the few recent cases of an inclusionary authoritarian regime. Labor policies are of special interest in this case because they were the focus of much of the regime's attention, generated much controversy, and were the subject of some major reverses in policy.

## Panama as a Case of Extreme Dependency

Within the world system of nations, Panama is a country with a peculiar history and a very particular role determined by its geographical location and configuration and by the need of the United States to control the waterway it constructed to link the Atlantic and Pacific oceans. These two factors have shaped Panama's history and substantially determined its role in the international economic system. It is not by accident that Panama is probably one of the most dependent countries in the world, with an extremely open economy, no currency of its own, and no control over external factors that affect its internal situation.[5] It is also not by accident that Panama owes its existence to the United States and as such is widely considered an appendage of that country.[6]

The country's economy has been based on a service-providing infrastructure that arose out of the needs and opportunities offered by the canal and the transit area. Thus, a large percentage of Panama's foreign exchange

Evelyne Huber Stephens, *The Politics of Workers Participation*. New York: Academic Press, 1980.

[5] Herbet de Souza, "Notas acerca de la situación socio-política de Panamá," *Tareas*, no. 35 (1976): 7-42.

[6] Goran Therborn, "The Travail of Latin American Democracy," *New Left Review*, nos. 113-114 (1979): 85.

comes from the services and labor provided to the Canal Zone as well as from the assemblage and resale of goods through the Colon Free Zone and the processing and selling of goods to passing ships. An index constructed by Richardson to measure dependence in Latin America based on the amount of foreign trade, investment, and aid for the period between 1950 and 1973 ranked Panama highest in dependency. According to Richardson, this is the result of the "extraordinary and continuous quantities of new private investment capital pumped into operations associated with the Canal Zone."[7]

## From Dependency to Hegemony

Panama became independent from Colombia in 1903, with the aid of the United States. The United States wanted to build a canal, and the Panamanian elite saw independence and alliance with the United States as their opportunity to enhance the emporium-like development they envisioned for Panama, which would also enhance their private fortunes. That elite, which remained in control of the political apparatus until the 1968 National Guard takeover, controlled and governed the country primarily in terms of their particular private interests.

The traditional ruling elite was highly dependent on foreign capital and foreign interests.[8] Although it held political power, its economic sustenance came from external sources. Because its interests veered toward external conditions and alliances rather than toward internal ones, the ruling elite saw no need to build the nation from within. Consequently, the ruling class never bothered to build up a political machinery or to institutionalize political values and practices that would lead to the development of a strong polity and a politically capable citizenry.

The alliance of the national bourgeoisie and foreign capital provided the local elite with enough security to maintain the status quo without a felt need to change or find solutions to problems caused by a rapidly changing society and an increasingly complex social and economic situation. One outcome of this is that Panama, with one of the highest per capita incomes in Latin America as well as the highest ratio of foreign investment, also had one of the most skewed income distributions of the continent.[9]

---

[7] Neil R. Richardson, *Foreign Policy and Economic Dependence*. Austin: University of Texas, 1978, pp. 103-106.

[8] The traditional ruling elite in Panama is made up of a small group of families that also control the economy of the country. Although there are factions, it is a rather homogeneous group in terms of interests and goals. Because of its size and homogeneity, I refer to it indistinctly as the ruling elite, the national bourgeoisie, or the private sector. A detailed analysis of this sector is given in Chapter 2.

[9] Gian Sahota, "Public Expenditure and Income Distribution in Panama," Report prepared for MIPPE, Panama, 1972.

The country's internal situation during the 1960s deteriorated so thoroughly due to the weakness and division among the traditional political forces that it reached a point of stagnation, which peaked during the Robles administration (1964-1968). The Panamanian governing elite reached what Poulantzas has termed a "representational crisis," which resulted in its loss of hegemony.[10] This loss of hegemony provided the grounds for the National Guard takeover.

The notion of hegemony as set forth by Gramsci implies a consolidation of the bourgeois rule in regimes in which force is not necessary to maintain the social organization because the values of that group are accepted by the lower strata.[11] A "representational crisis" occurs when there is disorganization or a rupture in the dominant class that will lead to the loss of hegemony of that class. A representational crisis can result in an exceptional form of state, which can take three forms: a fascist state, a bonapartist state, or a military dictatorship. In the case of Panama, the regime that emerged under Torrijos had the characteristics of a bonapartist state, and arose at a moment of stagnation of the political factions.

Bonapartism has been described as a semi-competitive system characterized by a strong executive, the lapse of control by the ruling classes, and the painless demobilization of the subordinate and the dominant social strata. In such systems, the repressive level is moderate and the reforms set forth do not threaten the dominant property system. A bonapartist state is unified by an ideology of "exalted nationalism." This type of regime exhibits a high degree of centralism maintained by the state bureaucracy.[12]

The characteristics of bonapartist states correspond to those of inclusionary authoritarian regimes as defined by pluralist political analysts. Both pluralist and marxist analyses agree on the conditions that allow the emergence of these regimes and the role played by the leaders of such regimes, usually populist or reformist leaders not constrained by the status quo. But while marxist analysts dwell more on the class alliances and the social conditions that precede bonapartist states, pluralist analysts have placed more emphasis on the types of policies enacted by the regimes under study and on the consequences to the political landscape of those policies.

---

[10] Nicos Poulantzas, *Fascism and Dictatorship*. London: Verso Editions, 1979, pp. 313-319.
[11] Antonio Gramsci, *Selections from the Prison Notebooks*. New York: International Publishers, 1980, pp. 57-61.
[12] Alain Rouquie, "L'Hypothèse 'bonapartiste' et l'émergence des systèmes politiques semi-compétitifs," *Revue Française de Science Politique*, 25:5(1975): 1099-1109. The classic bonapartist model, analyzed by Marx in *The Eighteenth Brumaire*, represented a situation in which social order needed to be restored in France and the bourgeoisie were incapable of accomplishing this. They gave up their control of the state apparatus and allowed Louis Bonaparte to create a strong executive and restore the order needed to regain economic domination and social power. Karl Marx, *The Eighteenth Brumaire of Louis Bonaparte*. New York: International Publishers, 1963.

I will refer to the Torrijos regime as an inclusionary authoritarian regime following O'Donnell's classification but will in addition subsume the characteristics of bonapartism for enhanced explanatory power.

The regime that emerged in Panama in 1968 fits the inclusionary authoritarian type of regime described by O'Donnell as an "incorporating political system" that seeks to activate the popular sector and to allow it some voice in the national political system.[13] Inclusionary authoritarian regimes tend to arise in societies with low levels of social differentiation and political activation, low levels of industrialization, and a prevalence of foreign capital in their export sector.[14] The case used by O'Donnell to exemplify this type of authoritarian state is that of Peru under Velasco Alvarado, although O'Donnell also includes the populist periods of Vargas's Brazil and Peron's Argentina in this classification. The case of Panama under Torrijos has many similarities with these prior cases. The main difference lies in Panama's economic thrust, which instead of relying on the expansion of domestic markets based on increased industrialization, relies on an increased service infrastructure designed to attract foreign capital.

Other important characteristics of inclusionary authoritarian states according to O'Donnell are the weakening of the traditional ruling sectors, the expropriation of the most visible foreign symbols, and the incorporation of previously unincorporated sectors "from above" while maintaining tight control over them.[15] In Panama, the ruling class, although removed from power, did not lose its economic power; that power, however, was weakened considerably by the regime's increased encroachment into the economic sphere as a direct competitor to private interests. As for foreign symbols, early on the foreign-owned utilities companies were expropriated, and the government engaged in a long dispute with United Brands, which culminated in a new arrangement with that company. For Panama however, the most important symbol of foreign penetration and domination is the Panama Canal. Shortly after the National Guard takeover, the government engaged in an all-out effort to renegotiate with the United States the treaty governing that waterway. Although a careful study of the Torrijos-Carter treaties signed in 1977 and ratified in 1978 would show those treaties to be not very advantageous to Panama, at face value they

---

[13] O'Donnell, *Modernization*, p. 55. Following Cardoso, the term "regime" is used to refer to the formal rules that link the main political institutions, as well as the political nature of the ties between citizens and rulers—in other words, the system of governance. "State" is defined as the basic alliance that exists among the social classes and the norms that guarantee their dominance over the subordinate strata. Fernando Henrique Cardoso, "On the Characterization of Authoritarian Regimes in Latin America," in *The New Authoritarianism*, p. 38.

[14] O'Donnell, *Modernization*, p. 111.

[15] O'Donnell, *Modernization*, p. 111.

were a victory for Torrijos, primarily because they set an acceptable date for the return of the canal to Panama.

Following Poulantzas's analysis, once an exceptional form of state is in power, it can attain a large degree of "relative autonomy" from the former dominant group, which will allow it the leeway to enact policy directly opposed to the interest of the former ruling elite.[16] One of the most important considerations regarding relative autonomy in an exceptional state form is the fragility of the state due to the unstable situation that allowed it to emerge and the constant threat of inroads by the forces formerly in control, which will undermine the state and contribute to its demise.

In order for the state to attain a degree of relative autonomy that will allow it the leeway to act independently and carry out social restructuring plans, some conditions must be present. According to Stallings, two important conditions that must be present are state organizational capacity and state access to financial resources.[17] In Panama, the regime was able to keep the most innovative officials of the former administration in the government. Together with the pro-Torrijos factions and under the cunning leadership of Torrijos, these officials were able to restructure the bureaucracy and provide the organization needed to carry on. And, most important, Torrijos was able to secure backing with foreign capital, which provided the resources needed to finance the government's programs.

The previous negates the argument that foreign capital is detrimental to peripheral countries and that it will not be forthcoming to progressive regimes. The relative autonomy the Torrijos regime enjoyed was aided by the availability of foreign capital, which helped sustain it and facilitated many of its programs. The Panamanian situation is similar to the one described by Stallings regarding the Velasco regime in Peru.[18] Relative autonomy of the state is facilitated in situations in which the previous

---

[16] The arguments about the "relative autonomy of the state" were first discussed in marxist literature following Marx's *The Eighteenth Brumaire* and Gramsci's *Selections from the Prison Notebooks* (notes 11 and 12). Poulantzas developed the concept in *Fascism and Dictatorship* (note 10) and in *Political Power and Social Classes*. London: New Left Books, 1973. Other marxist discussions include Ralph Miliband, *The State in Capitalist Society*. New York: Basic Books, 1969; and "The Capitalist State: Reply to Nicos Poulantzas," *New Left Review*, 59(1970): 53-60; Non-marxist discussions using the concept of relative autonomy include Stephen Krasner, *Defending the National Interest*. Princeton: Princeton University Press, 1978; Ellen Kay Trimberger, *Revolution from Above: Military Bureaucrats and Development in Japan, Turkey, Egypt and Peru*. New Brunswick: Transaction Books, 1978; and Eric Nordlinger, *On the Autonomy of the Democratic State*. Cambridge: Harvard University Press, 1981. An excellent review of studies on the state is Peter Evans et al., eds., *Bringing the State Back In*. New York: Cambridge University Press, 1985.

[17] Barbara Stallings, "International Lending and the Relative Autonomy of the State: A Case Study of Twentieth-Century Peru," *Politics & Society*, 14:3(1985): 260.

[18] Stallings, "International Lending," pp. 263, 275-280.

dominant class is weakened due to internal or external crisis. Relative state autonomy is also facilitated by an alliance of the state with subordinate groups as a means of confronting the dominant class. A third condition that can facilitate state autonomy is the degree of cohesion and unity within the factions of the state.[19] Although Hamilton in no way implies that all those conditions that facilitate state autonomy have to be found together for a state to achieve a period of relative autonomy, in Panama after the National Guard takeover and once Torrijos consolidated his power, all three of these conditions were present. The dominant class was in crisis and had lost hegemony. The state tried to restructure society by enacting laws that incorporated groups previously outside the power structure. By enhancing the position of sectors formerly dispossessed, the state entered into an alliance with subordinate groups that lent it support. Even so, this was an unequal alliance, with the state in control of the newly incorporated sectors through a series of mechanisms of inducements and constraints to insure that these sectors would only act within the expected bounds. The subordinate sectors, however, recognized the state as a benefactor and supported its programs.

The third condition Hamilton singles out that facilitates state autonomy regards the degree of cohesion among the factions within the state. During the initial period, from 1969 or 1970 until about 1975, the Torrijos regime had several factions, including one with ties to the deposed private sector, but there is no doubt that the pro-Torrijos factions were in complete control.[20] And even the individuals with ties to the former ruling groups were committed to Torrijos's programs. It was not until the economic situation began to deteriorate, placing the government on very shaky grounds, that private-sector interests began making inroads and that those sector's demands began to be heeded by the administration. During the most intensive period of reform and incorporation, however, the internal cohesion of the factions within the regime was high, a condition that greatly facilitated its autonomy.

[19] Nora Hamilton, *The Limits of State Autonomy*. Princeton: Princeton University Press, 1982, pp. 25, 281-282.

[20] Apart from the National Guard, which did not play a very visible role at the higher governmental levels, Pereira has singled out four other groups that held key posts during the period: one made up of bureaucrats and technicians left over from previous administrations, with ties to the former ruling elite; one of individuals of rural middle-class origins who up to then had had no role in politics; one of individuals of leftist tendencies active in socialist and communist organizations; and one of Torrijos's relatives and close friends. There was considerable overlap among the last three groups. Renato Pereira, *Panamá: Fuerzas armadas y política*. Panamá: Ediciones Nueva Universidad, 1979, pp. 143-145.

## LABOR POLICY AS AN AREA OF KEY IMPORTANCE
## TO THE TORRIJOS REGIME

Perhaps one of the most important characteristics of inclusionary authoritarian regimes is their incorporation of previously excluded sectors of society. This incorporation is accomplished "from above." It provides the government with legitimacy and popular support while also allowing it to maintain tight control over the newly mobilized population. The classic group to incorporate is labor because it usually has a certain degree of organization and structure and a role in the political spectrum. By incorporating the labor sector according to specific directives and carefully controlled measures, the regime can maintain labor as a source of support that can be used effectively at the will of the government.

The control of labor is achieved through the provisions of inducements and benefits that will co-opt it and through the use of mobilization tactics such as the allusion to nationalism, which will allow the government to activate or demobilize labor by heightening or reducing the stimulating factor. The shrewd use of such tactics, with the proper shifting and balancing of inducements and constraints, can keep a newly incorporated sector under tight control of the state for an indeterminate amount of time. Collier and Collier have made a distinction between benefits that may be granted to labor with no strings attached and pro-labor laws that contain a set of inducements as well as constraints. Pro-labor laws provide significant gains for labor and have built-in mechanisms for keeping labor under control.[21] Both Vargas and Peron used pro-labor legislation as well as the allocation of government resources to gain control of and manipulate organized labor. In the case of Panama, the 1972 Labor Code served the same purpose as did other measures established to strengthen organized labor such as early recognition of new unions, financial assistance to unions, extension of the right to negotiate collective agreements, and the granting of political prominence to certain labor groups.

The 1972 Labor Code had a special significance for the Torrijos regime, both symbolically and in real terms. The Labor Code was a clear statement that the regime represented a break with the past, that it was reformist and wished to single out new groups for preferential treatment. Just as the new canal treaty became the regime's most important external symbol, the 1972 Labor Code became its strongest statement of internal changes. And, just as changing the rules of the game in conducting negotiations with the United States was, according to Torrijos, a redress to the colonialist situation experienced up to then by Panama, shifting the balance of power among the existing social forces signified a reduction of the internal

---

[21] David Collier and Ruth Berins Collier, "Inducements versus Constraints: Disaggregating 'Corporatism,'" *American Political Science Review*, 73(1979): 967-986.

colonialism suffered by Panamanian society. In this respect then, the 1972 Labor Code was the most powerful symbol of the regime's stance vis-à-vis the internal social structure.

But for the Torrijos regime, passage of the Labor Code also had very concrete meanings. As previously mentioned, the Labor Code was the most direct and effective measure for incorporating a previously unincorporated sector. This incorporation in turn served as a tool for securing popular support for the regime, which also lent the regime a measure of legitimacy. The Labor Code represented a break with the past and the beginning of a new era. It had important implications both for labor and for the economic elite, as it dramatically changed the balance of power between those sectors.

## Major Stages in the Evolution of Labor Policy

Important changes introduced in the 1972 Labor Code were job stability after two years of employment; collective bargaining at the request of the union; union dues collected of all workers covered by a collective agreement; a bonus after 10 years of employment; and the right to strike. But above all, the most important aspect of the Labor Code was its explicit pro-labor tenor.

The Labor Code was introduced at the same time as other measures that aimed at restructuring society and providing the legal framework for institutionalizing Torrijos's "revolutionary process." The other measures included a new constitution that legalized the enhanced role of the National Guard and strengthened the executive; representational structures based on the smallest local units such as a National Assembly of Representatives and *juntas comunales* and *juntas locales*; and a series of social laws, which aimed at improving the lot of the popular sector.

Barely four years after the 1972 Labor Code became law, it was amended through Ley 95 by the same government of Omar Torrijos. Ley 95 took away the most important benefits conceded to labor by the 1972 Labor Code— some temporarily, such as the right to negotiate collective agreements, and others permanently, such as stability of employment and the right to organize factory committees. Then in 1981, Ley 95 was replaced by Ley 8a, which restored some of the benefits lost through Ley 95 but fell short of returning the Labor Code to its original form.

This study analyzes the three major labor policy changes that were brought about by the Torrijos regime in Panama. It looks at the conditions in the country in general and as they regard labor and labor policy in particular before the 1972 Labor Code was enacted into law. The ways in which the Labor Code affected or modified the various sectors involved are also considered. Furthermore, the study analyzes the 1976 reform of the Labor Code through Ley 95 and the consequences of this change for labor, for the private sector, and for the regime. Finally, it looks at the partial recovery of labor in 1981 through the enactment of Ley 8a and at the prevailing conditions that led to that law, as well as its consequences for the regime and for society. The study is divided into three parts. In the first, a careful analysis is made of the principal actors involved: the private sector (and its brand of traditional politics), organized labor, and the Torrijos regime. In the second part, the study deals with the labor policies in question and tries to present an accurate portrayal of the interaction among the various forces that led to the enactment of labor policy (1972 Labor Code), to its reform (Ley 95), and to the code's partial recovery (Ley 8a). The third and last section is a careful and detailed analysis of the economic outcomes of each of these policy changes and assesses the validity of the arguments put forth by those in favor of or against these policies. That part is of special interest because one of the principal reasons for undertaking this project was the constant and unrelenting lamentations heard in Panama regarding the noxious effects of the Labor Code on the economy. A rather intriguing puzzle was how one piece of legislation could have such a far-reaching effect. The issues brought up regarding the Labor Code were so diverse and their effects so all-encompassing, according to the rhetoric of the groups affected, that the curiosity of this researcher was piqued, resulting in this study.

To summarize, the rise to power of the Torrijos regime was directly attributable to the dependent condition of Panama as a country and to the weakness of its societal institutions. The relationship of the national bourgeoisie with external interests, which allowed them both the resources they needed and a secure position vis-à-vis other social groups, did not provide incentives for the ruling elite to promote the development of strong political institutions. When the ruling elite lost hegemony, a crisis situation ensued and presented the opportunity for a new regime to emerge with a different type of leadership and a different political agenda. The inclusionary authoritarian regime that arose, headed by a populist reformist leader, enjoyed "relative autonomy" during its first years in power, enabling it to enact laws and promote measures to restructure society. Of all the measures enacted during that period of relative autonomy, the 1972 Labor Code was one of the most important because it allowed for the incorporation of the labor sector, lent legitimacy to the regime, and was the tool used by the regime to shift the balance of power in Panamanian society.

# 2

# THE PRIVATE SECTOR AND
# TRADITIONAL POLITICS

Until the National Guard took power in 1968, Panama's political system and its economy were in the hands of a small group of families, some of which dated back to pre-independence days. The interests of these families lay in exploiting (primarily for their personal benefit) the country's location and the unique services Panama provides the world mercantile system. The commonality of interests shared by these families precluded the need for them to promote the development of political parties with strong platforms and clear-cut lines of class representation. Instead, the party system was based on small parties representing particular individuals, which arose during elections only to fade away once their candidate was out of power. Nor were these families compelled to promote the development of a viable political system with well-defined political institutions, because their interests lay with international capital and concerns external to the country. The political system and the governmental bureaucracy functioned in order to sustain the economic interests of these families, who had little concern for their social obligations to the nation. This ruling elite, with interest primarily in business and commercial endeavors, had unchallenged hegemony over the social forces operating in their society.[1]

The situation began to change in the early 1960s, when Panama entered a growth phase of import substitution industrialization at the same time that it experienced a rapid population growth, an expansion of its workforce, and the growth of its middle and lower-middle class, who were excluded from the power structure. The country's social and economic situation increased in complexity and could not be accommodated with the old and tried formulas that the traditional ruling elite had used up to then. Conflict emerged within the ruling elite that led to its loss of hegemony and

---

[1] Antonio Gramsci, *Selection from the Prison Notebooks*. New York: International Publishers, 1980.

prompted a "representational crisis."[2] This crisis situation provided the conditions for the National Guard takeover in 1968 and the emergence of the Torrijos regime.

## THE MAKING OF THE ELITE

Panama's historical development is inextricably linked to its geographical position, which made it a natural passageway between the Atlantic and Pacific oceans. Not long after Panama's discovery and colonization, Charles V of Spain dreamed of building a canal to bring together those two oceans. Even though the canal was not built until much later, Spain and its Pacific Coast colonies traded by transporting goods overland through Panama throughout the colonial period. For six weeks every year, a commercial fair was held in Portobelo to exchange goods and supplies between Spain and its colonies. These fairs provided the livelihood for the inhabitants of Portobelo and Panama City.

From the end of the Portobelo Fairs in 1739 until gold was discovered in California in 1848, Panama's economy stagnated. The people survived mainly through a *situado* of 250,000 pesos, provided first by Lima and later by Nueva Granada, to protect the isthmus. A brief respite came in 1809 when Spain relaxed its regulations on commerce and allowed Panama to engage in trade with the British colonies. The wars of independence also relieved Panama's economic situation for a brief period, because the bulk of the merchandise and passengers bound for Peru had to be rerouted through the isthmus.[3]

A local elite emerged in the isthmus during colonial times and in the nineteenth century. It was based on the occupancy of government posts or on commercial and service enterprises catering to the transit zone. During that time, there was a steady commercial flow between Panama and the Pacific Coast ports of South America as well as with the British Caribbean colonies, primarily through Kingston, Jamaica.[4] The individuals who made up the upper class were distinguished by being white and by having connections through blood or marriage to other upper class families. After independence from Spain in 1821, the bureaucratic opportunities were expanded to include legislative office and high administrative positions in the Colombian government. Between 1821 and 1850, Panama had 11 governors. All but one were native-born members of leading families.[5]

---

[2] Nicos Poulantzas, *Fascism and Dictatorship*. London: Verso Editions, 1979, pp. 313-319.
[3] Omar Jaén Suárez, *La población del Istmo de Panamá del siglo XVI al siglo XX*. Panamá: Impresora de la Nación, 1978, pp. 170-171.
[4] Alfredo Figueroa Navarro, *Dominio y sociedad en el Panamá Colombiano (1821-1903)*, 2d ed. Bogotá: Ediciones Tercer Mundo, 1980, p. 33.
[5] The one exception was a Frenchman, married into a local family. Figueroa Navarro, *Dominio*, p. 205.

Pressed by the depression that ensued at the termination of the Portobelo Fairs, some urban families moved to the interior and settled in the central provinces. This ruralization of a small number of the Panamanian elite took place in the late eighteenth and early nineteenth centuries. The families who moved to the countryside maintained ties with their urban relatives and engaged in economic ventures with them as well as raised cattle to supply the capital city. But they left the purely agricultural endeavors to the peasants, of Indian and mestizo stock.

Panama gained its independence from Spain in 1821 and joined Colombia, first as a member of La Gran Colombia and later as a regular province. Although to Colombia Panama was just a backward and remote territory accessible only by sea, its importance to countries engaged in mercantile endeavors became increasingly obvious. Both the United States and Britain became concerned with unimpeded use of the transit area and with the fact that if one power controlled it, access to it might be denied the other. To insure against any such occurrence, they signed the Clayton-Bulwer Treaty in 1850.[6]

The first economic boom that Panama experienced in the nineteenth century became known as "La California" due to the discovery of gold in that westernmost state of the United States. It saw the arrival of a large number of adventurers, most just in transit, but some stayed to take advantage of the economic opportunities provided by that massive movement of people and goods across the isthmus. The boom lasted from 1849 to 1869. During this twenty-year period, the nature of the services provided changed dramatically, particularly after the completion of the Trans-Isthmian railroad in 1856. Before there had been a need for mule teams, carriers, and oarsmen, as well as for small lodges along the Cruces Trail. After completion of the railroad—which shortened the trip from 4 days to 6 hours and could carry 1,500 passengers and three steamship loads at once—services became localized in the two terminal cities and concentrated on lodgings and restaurants and on supplying provisions needed for the ocean voyages.[7]

By the time the railroad was completed in 1856, the established elite were primarily engaged in real estate, bureaucratic jobs, and the financing of some of the more profitable commercial endeavors. But they left the actual running of commercial enterprises to the newcomers and their less endowed compatriots. So the hostelries and the dry goods stores were managed by Colombians, Americans, and Frenchmen, as well as some Panamanians not as well connected or financially established. Small-scale commerce throughout this period was in the hands of a Chinese petit bourgeoisie, which had arrived during the California gold rush to build the Trans-Isthmian Railroad.

---

[6] Figueroa Navarro, *Dominio*, p. 267.
[7] Jaén Suárez, *La población*, pp. 318-322.

Within the next half century, two other projects would be undertaken by foreigners to take advantage of Panama's natural passageway. The second such project was the attempt by De Lesseps and the French Canal Company to build a sea-level canal. The third large project was the U.S. canal construction project that began in 1904.

The economic pursuits of the Panamanian ruling families were heightened during the French attempt to build a canal, when Panamanian endeavor was expanded to provide rentals for the French administrators and technical personnel as well as for the hordes of laborers brought in from Jamaica and Barbados. A high point in Panama's economy was attained during construction of the U.S. canal, when imported laborers numbered in the thousands.

A real anguish for the Panamanian elite had been Colombia's disinterest in their development. For the far-away central government, Panama was nothing more than a backward territory. Colombians did not share with the elite of their annexed province their view of the potentials of the isthmus, nor did they perceive its importance for world trade and transportation. While Colombia experimented with political models and engaged in bloody civil wars, the isthmian elite dreamed of converting Panama into a commercial emporium and welcomed the interest of Britain and the United States.[8] Even though they harbored plans of secession during the nineteenth century, oddly enough these did not envision a totally independent country. Most schemes included coming under the tutelage of one or all of the super powers—the United States, Britain, and France—by becoming their protectorate, while having the country's sovereignty guaranteed.[9]

It was probably the combined frustration of having some of the bloodiest battles of the Thousand Day War fought on its territory and of seeing their dreams of a canal shattered by Colombia's refusal to accept the Herrán-Hay Treaty that finally prompted the Panamanian elite to carry out their independence plans.[10] The action was taken with a measure of assurance of Panama's future. The United States promised to support the independence movement and to take over where the French had left off in building the canal.

---

[8] Colombia had a centralist government in the first half of the nineteenth century and a federalist one in the second half. During its federalist period it changed names and arrangements with its territories as follows: República de la Nueva Granada (1843-1858), Confederación Granadina (1858-1863), Estados Unidos de Colombia (1863-1886). After 1886 it became centralist again and took the name of Estados Unidos de Colombia. Figueroa Navarro, *Dominio*, p. 319.

[9] Figueroa Navarro, *Dominio*, pp. 333-334.

[10] The Thousand Day War was fought between 1889-1902, with over 100,000 casualties. Figueroa Navarro, *Dominio*, p. 352. The Herrán-Hay Treaty had been negotiated between the United States and Colombia to build a canal through Panama but was rejected by Colombia in 1903. The terms of that treaty were much more favorable to Panama than the Hay-Bunau Varilla Treaty negotiated by Panama after independence from Colombia. For instance in the Herrán-Hay Treaty the amount of territory ceded for the establishment of a canal zone was

The only stumbling block to this plan was Panama's reliance on the French engineer and stockholder of the New Panama Canal Company, Bunau Varilla, to negotiate a treaty on its behalf. The shameful outcome of that transaction has directed most Panamanian efforts during this century to redress what they perceived as an unjust agreement. The Hay-Bunau Varilla treaty signed between Panama and the United States in 1903 for the canal construction increased the area to be controlled by the United States from 5 kilometers to 5 miles on either side of the canal, and the agreement was made in perpetuity.[11]

On November 3, 1903, Panama became an independent nation. By 1904, the United States had purchased the holdings of the French Canal Company and resumed construction. The U.S. project, changed in design from a sea-level canal as the French had envisioned it to a lock canal that would raise ships through the continental divide, took ten years to complete and was put into operation in 1914. The era of construction was again one of massive importation of labor and machinery and of economic boom for the new nation.

The history of Panama after independence from Colombia and the construction of the U.S. canal has been one of attempts to recover the rights it lost through the Hay-Bunau Varilla Treaty. Because for many years this seemed out of reach, Panama concentrated its efforts on trying to improve commercial relations with the U.S.-controlled Canal Zone. Two treaties were successfully negotiated with the United States, one in 1935 and one in 1955. In 1935, the annuity paid by the United States was increased from $250,000 to $430,000 and several commercial agreements were reached. In 1955, the annuity was again increased to $1.93 million, and apart from commercial agreements, improved pay and benefits were agreed on for Panamanian workers in the Canal Zone. A treaty in 1967 was not acceptable to Panama, and finally the Torrijos-Carter treaties, signed in 1977 and ratified in 1978, set the year 2000 for the return of the canal to Panama.

Development in other areas of Panama has been slow and sporadic. A banana plantation established in the 1890s prospered during the early part of the century and then suffered a huge setback when the plants were attacked by disease. In 1927, the United Fruit Company began new plantations on the Pacific side and left the Atlantic ones to lie dormant for more than two decades. Some agricultural concerns controlled by local capital developed in the central

---

10 kilometers instead of 10 miles, and the United States only had rights to administrate in the Canal Zone; the Hay-Bunau Varilla Treaty gave the United States rights in the Canal Zone "as if it had sovereignty." Figueroa Navarro, *Dominio*, pp. 352-355.

[11] Regarding the 1903 Treaty, U.S. Secretary of State John M. Hay commented to Senator Spooner that "we have a very advantageous treaty for the U.S., and not so for Panama. You and I know very well how many points are in that treaty that every Panamanian patriot would object to." Quoted in Ricardo J. Alfaro. *Panamá 50 años de República*. Panamá: Edición de la Junta Nacional del Cincuentenario, 1953, pp.122-125.

provinces and Chiriquí, mostly in the production of sugar, rice, and coffee, but these were few and far between. The main thrust of the small rural elite was still raising cattle, now to supply the growing population of Panama City and the Canal Zone after the 1936 Treaty.

From "La California" on, we thus find upper-class Panamanians operating in official capacities or as financiers and new arrivals engaged in the still very profitable but much more demanding role of managing commercial and service enterprises. The upper class in Panama was not socially closed by any means and easily incorporated successful newer entrepreneurs through marriage and joint ventures. This elite group, which Gandásegui has called "Separatista" because of their involvement in the move for independence from Colombia, includes eleven families, of which the Duque, Vallarino, Arias Espinosa, and Chiari were the most powerful. The last family is the only one whose wealth was based on landed enterprises.[12]

A short listing of the controlling assets of some of these families can help elucidate their power and interrelations. The Chiari family owns the Compañía Azucarera La Estrella, the largest private sugar industry, started in 1926. It also owns the Compañía Ganadera de Coclé, the Compañía La Estrella Azul, a milk-commercializing concern, and was one of the founders of Compañía Azucarera Nacional, the second largest private sugar producer. It also owns a TV channel and a textile factory. In total, Chiari capital controls 14 enterprises. None of these companies is public. The Chiaris also control the Partido Liberal Nacional, the largest of the Liberal Party splinter groups. The Duque family made their money in the rental of tenement housing to the laborers of the Panama Canal. They founded the Panama Brewing and Refrigerating Company in 1909 to market beer and ice. In 1915 they founded another company, the Compañía Unida de Duque, with one million gold dollars. This company is still privately held. The Duque family also owns Panama's two oldest newspapers, *The Star & Herald* and *La Estrella de Panamá*. In 1939, along with several other families, the Duques expanded their beer company and renamed it Cervecería Nacional. Today, their capital is invested in nine of Panama's largest companies.

The scion of the Vallarino family, J.J. Vallarino, was a large investor in the Cervecería Nacional and in 1969 started another brewing company in Chiriquí, Cervecería del Barú. The family's interests are mostly in commercial enterprises and their capital is invested in eight of the largest companies studied by Gandásegui. They are majority stockholders in Industrias Panamá Boston and the Panamá Coca Cola Bottling Company. This family

---

12 Marco Antonio Gandásegui, "La concentración del poder económico en Panamá," in *Panamá, dependencia y liberación*, edited by Ricaute Soler, 2d ed., Ciudad Universitaria Rodrigo Facio, Costa Rica: EDUCA, 1976, p. 151. I will refer to these families as the pre-independence families. The information for this section on the families is from Gandásegui, "La concentración," pp. 148-174.

has always been very influential among the economic elite and has headed the most powerful forums of that group. Col. Bolívar Vallarino, commander in chief of the National Guard from 1952 to 1968, is a member of this family. The Arias Espinosas, another of Panama's most powerful families, are mostly engaged in real estate and commercial enterprises. In 1909, together with the Duques, they founded the Panamá Brewing and Refrigerating Company and in 1910, Manuel Espinosa was named the first president of the Compañía Internacional de Seguros. After President Remón was assassinated in 1955, Ricardo Arias Espinosa became president, and ran again unsuccessfully in 1960. In the late 1960s he was named ambassador to the United States.

Another elite group whose arrival coincided with the turn of the century was made up of British and Dutch subjects of Sephardic Jewish origin, who came from Curacao and the Antilles. This group, which engaged originally in commercial enterprises and later expanded into financial ventures, is very cohesive and basically closed. Counted among its members are the Maduro, Fidanque, Cardoze, Lindo, Motta, Del Valle and Eisenmann families, and Marcel Penso.

A later wave of important immigrants arrived during or shortly afterward the construction of the U.S. canal from Italy, Spain, and other European countries, as well as from the United States. These "post-canal" families invested in areas neglected up to then, such as the production of paper and construction material, bakeries, and simple food processing. They later became the core of the industrial elite. These families seem to be much more enterprising and innovative than the "old" elite, investing considerable capital and effort into new areas, especially for the supply of the internal market. Some of the most prominent among them are the Martinz, Canavaggio, Novey, Pascual, Garcia, Tagaropulos, Vázquez Corredeira, and Eleta families. They control about one third of the national economy and by now have become somewhat assimilated with the older pre-independence families through joint ventures and intermarriage.

A last group of entrepreneurs came from the Middle East and Turkey. They arrived after World War II and made their wealth through petty commerce. They control most of the commerce along Central Avenue in Panama City and have many outlets in the Colon Free Zone. Two families in this group have made inroads in industry, the Hararis in shoe manufacturing, and the Mizrachis in textiles.

In his study of the 120 most lucrative enterprises in Panama, Gandásegui found that 36 are controlled by three families; of the 60 most profitable companies, 45 are commercial ventures and only 15 are in manufacturing; and members of the families mentioned above have controlling interests in 99 of the 120 enterprises.[13] Because the number of families is so small—30

---

[13] Gandásegui, "La concentración," p. 100.

or 40 at most among the four elite groups described—and because the merging of capital and integration among them has been so thorough, labeling them under one rubric does not seem inappropriate, and they will be referred to as "the private sector" throughout this study. Today there seems to be little difference among these families regarding their interests, the driving force behind their efforts, or their ideology and goals. While members of the private sector represent a homogeneous block, political control has been primarily in the hands of the older, pre-independence families, with members of the newer families filling in posts in the government administration.

In 1964 the various organizations representing private-sector interests, under the leadership of the Chamber of Commerce, the Sindicato de Industriales (SIP), and the Asociación Panameña de Ejecutivos de Empresa (APEDE), formed the Consejo Nacional de la Empresa Privada (CONEP). The aim was to create a powerful lobby group or a ministry without portfolio to be consulted by the government prior to the enactment of laws that would affect the interests of the private sector.[14] CONEP's goals were easily fulfilled during the administration of Marco A. Robles, but its style was crimped once the National Guard took power. CONEP members were at the forefront of every move against the Torrijos regime and carried out constant and unrelenting campaigns against policies that they considered detrimental to their interests. These included most of Torrijos's progressive policies, but principally the Labor Code.

An interesting issue to look at in detail, because it set a precedent for CONEP's modus operandi and the role it cut out for itself, was CONEP's role in the attempt by the Robles administration to enact a tax reform. The position that CONEP took on this issue also explains its posture and many of its reactions during the Torrijos regime.

The tax reform had been recommended by the Alliance for Progress, based on an Inter-American Development Bank study of Panama's fiscal situation. That study pointed out that many of Panama's largest corporations had not been audited in the last 20 years, and that there were only 65 national entities (individuals and corporations) that paid more than $2,000 per year in income tax.[15] In 1964, the 65 most profitable national enterprises had paid a total tax of $2.5 million and the 20 most profitable foreign corporations paid taxes in the amount of $2.6 million.[16] Another remarkable fact brought to light by the fiscal study was that up to 1962, the Ministry of Finance had never levied a fine for tax evasion. One of the most serious tax loopholes was the allocation of special contracts (Contratos con la Nación),

---

[14] Consejo Nacional de la Empresa Privada (CONEP), *En pocas palabras... ésto es CONEP.* Panama: n.d.
[15] Gandásegui, "La concentración," p. 136.
[16] Seventy-five percent of that amount was paid by two companies, the United Fruit Company and the Compañía Panameña de Fuerza y Luz.

which provided many benefits and exemptions. In 1964, there were at least 251 enterprises with these special contracts and another 404 with special provisions and exemptions. It was calculated at that time that for each corporation with a special contract, the government lost at least $10,000 per year in revenues. That year, the government lost $4.9 million, or 13 percent of taxes due through these exemptions.[17]

The tax reform did not propose to cancel the special contracts but to increase the tax table and enforce payment of the income tax. CONEP gave lip service to the reform until its members realized that the first director of the Revenue Service, Dr. Rodrigo Núñez, was serious about implementing the reform. Núñez, a young Chicago-trained economist, had been the drafter of the new tax law. CONEP gave an ultimatum to President Robles, who got rid of Núñez barely two months after he had appointed him.[18] His successor, Félix Armando Quirós, another economist, lasted three months. After this, the tax reform lost its muscle and momentum, because it was clear that the president would not take a firm position against CONEP or stand by his own appointees.

## DEVELOPMENT OF THE POLITICAL SYSTEM

It is impossible to separate the discussion of the Panamanian elite from that of the development of the country's political traditions and institutions. During the Colombian period, Panamanians participated in the politics of that country in various ways. Some were elected to the legislature and traveled to Bogotá every year to represent their interests in the parliamentary debates of the National Assembly. Others filled official posts in the provincial governmental apparatus.

From independence until around 1912, the Colombian Partido Liberal and Partido Conservador continued to hold forth in Panama's political arena. After that, with little to differentiate the two parties and because Panama had been a liberal stronghold, the Partido Conservador ceased to exist and its members were assimilated by the Partido Liberal.[19] From then on, parties contesting elections were either splinters of the Partido Liberal or parties constituted just before an election to support a particular candidate. Neither the Partido Liberal, its splinter groups, nor the personalistic parties that emerged before elections ever established platforms or programs. If one were pressed to elaborate on an ideology that informed

---

[17] Gandásegui, "La concentración," p. 135.

[18] It seems that when Núñez returned to Panama to work on the tax reform he neglected to fill out the proper forms to take his car into the country. When CONEP exposed this as a tax fraud and the President did not support him, Núñez resigned.

[19] Sossa states that the *liberales* were predominantly representative of the urban oligarchy and the *conservadores* of the rural elite. This is a rather artificial classification, because the Chiaris, the most powerful rural oligarchic family have been the leaders of the Partido Liberal since the early decades of the century. José Antonio Sossa, *Imperialismos, fuerzas armadas y partidos políticos en Panamá*. Panamá: Ediciones Documentos, 1977, p. 36.

all these parties, it could be said that they stood for some loose ideal of liberalism and for laissez faire economic development.

The splintering and the regrouping of the Partido Liberal during the first three decades of the century was overwhelming. For example, the following groups emerged during that period: the Liberal Nacional (Chiarista), Liberal Doctrinario (it first supported Harmodio Arias and later Domingo Díaz), Liberal Demócrata (Jimenista), Liberal Renovador (Panchista, or supporter of Francisco Arias Paredes), and Liberal Unido (supporter of Belisario Porras). Splinter groups and new parties usually appeared right before elections. By election time, the number of candidates would be reduced through deals and realignments, yet the political payoffs would go to all the groups supporting the elected candidates, making it a rather costly enterprise for the winners.[20]

A peculiarity of the Panamanian electoral system, which made elections extremely confusing and winning teams highly unstable, was that candidates from different parties running under different tickets for president, vice president, and second vice president, could end up winning the election. The outcome of the election was determined strictly by the number of votes each candidate received for the position he ran for, which could mean that candidates from opposing parties could be elected to govern together. Even though this type of outcome may appear highly unlikely, often presidents and vice presidents from different parties were elected, because candidates campaigned individually and as "personalities." Throughout Panama's political history, this has been a source of much tension and political instability.

## ARNULFO ARIAS

While the powerful families described above have all shared in the spoils of politics, direct power has been primarily in the hands of the pre-independence families. Inroads have been made by a few other families, especially some from the post-canal period, but until 1968 the political machinery was still under control of the older families. The only threat to that control, which has lurked in the background of Panamanian politics since the 1930s, has been Arnulfo Arias.

Before the Torrijos era, Arnulfo Arias was by far the most anachronistic figure in the Panamanian political panorama. He and his brother Harmodio (president from 1932 to 1936)[21] began their political careers in 1923 with the formation of a semi-secret group called Acción Comunal,[22] made up of

---

[20] Sossa, *Imperialismos*, pp. 35-36.

[21] These Arias are not related to the Arias Espinosa family. Their father immigrated from Costa Rica and settled in Penonomé, a small interior town in the province of Coclé. Steve C. Ropp, *Panamanian Politics: From Guarded Nation to National Guard*. New York: Praeger, 1982, p. 22.

[22] This may have been influenced by Arnulfo Arias and Víctor Florencio Goytía, another prominent member, who were both Rosicrucians.

lawyers, doctors, and other professionals committed to the "defense of institutional truth."[23] They were highly nationalistic and extremely negative toward some foreign groups, especially Americans and Caribbean blacks, whom they saw as usurping from Panamanians their rightful economic opportunities and as defiling the national culture.[24]

In 1931, Acción Comunal deposed the elected president and prepared the way to run their own candidate, Harmodio Arias, in the 1932 elections. The Partido Liberal Doctrinario was formed to back Arias. During the 1936 elections Harmodio lost control of the party to his brother Arnulfo, who supported Juan Demóstenes Arosemena for the presidency, because he (Arnulfo) was too young to run himself. For the 1940 elections, the party changed its name to Partido Nacional Revolucionario and ran Arnulfo for president. Once elected, Arnulfo founded Panameñismo, the political force that backed him throughout his long political career. His followers were urban workers from Panama and Colón and peasants and small landholders from the interior. Panameñismo is the closest Panama has ever come to having a populist movement such as that of APRA in Peru. Arnulfo has also been the only real threat to the ruling elite, but he has not represented a great peril, because he never stayed in power very long.

After winning the 1940 presidential elections, Arnulfo wrote a new constitution in 1941, which contained many progressive measures, such as a social security system, a Patrimonio Familiar (family subsidy), an agrarian bank, the National Conservatory of Music, and the National Library. This constitution also gave women the vote, protected maternity, and established the legal equality of children, whether born in or out of wedlock. It established a civil service for government employees, provided annual paid vacations for workers, and for the first time spoke about the social function of private property. Another innovation was the government's right to intervene in conflicts between capital and labor.[25] Some negative aspects of the 1941 constitution were its racial and xenophobic overtones. Orientals and blacks of Antillean origin were declared "races of forbidden immigration" and a program was instituted to deport all illegal immigrants.[26]

Arnulfo's racial policies have been explained as an individualistic strain by most Panamanian authors, who point out that he was in Germany during the late 1930s when Hitler and the Nazi party were in their apogee. But many of the racist ideas that Arnulfo supported had been given

---

[23] The ambiguity of this statement is puzzling. Renato Pereira, *Panamá: fuerzas armadas y política*. Panamá: Ediciones Nueva Universidad, 1979, p. 11.

[24] Ropp, *Panamanian Politics*, p. 22.

[25] Sossa, *Imperialismos*, pp. 45-46. Ropp, *Panamanian Politics*, p. 30.

[26] The West Indians who had entered the country to work in the canal suffered the most, because Panama did not grant them citizenship and at the end of the construction project their countries of origin did not encourage their return. Pereira, *Panamá: fuerzas armadas*, p. 49.

prominence in the documents of Acción Comunal two decades earlier. Ropp stresses that these racist and anti-foreign overtones were sentiments shared by the middle and upper-middle classes, who were fearful of perceived threats to the national character and culture.[27]

The concern with racial purity and the constant preoccupation with their family origins is a given in the minds of most Panamanians. This may be a function of living in a country that has always been a passageway, in which much racial mixing takes place. Also, during this century Panama has been inundated by two large foreign groups that have been a constant source of alarm to Panamanians concerned with saving the national culture. The United States has had as many as 30,000 soldiers in the Canal Zone at any one time. The U.S. forces constitute a group that feels highly superior to the natives, does not learn Spanish, and basically sees the host country and its people as available for plunder. The Caribbean blacks, also a large group, kept themselves separate from Panamanians and identified with the Americans in the Canal Zone. The fact that Caribbean blacks did not speak Spanish or share a cultural heritage or religion with the host population created distrust in the minds of native Panamanians. These factors may help explain the intense racism and cultural chauvinism that is rampant in Panama and that is shared by Panamanians of all hues. It is not hard to understand, then, that the sentiments that Arnulfo stood for found a willing public who felt he spoke to their fears and needs and who have remained loyal to him through his long and often bizarre political career.

Arnulfo was deposed 13 months after he came into power, in October 1941, because the United States was alarmed by his pro-Nazi inclinations and the Panamanian elite by his social policies. The opportunity presented itself when Arnulfo left the country illegally to visit a mistress in Cuba. When he left from a Canal Zone airport on the Atlantic side, Panamanian officials were alerted and removed him from office.

In 1948 Arnulfo ran for president again and won but was prevented from taking office by José Antonio Remón Cantera, the chief of the National Police, in the name of the traditional elite.[28] In the political turmoil that ensued, in which the country had three presidents between 1948 and 1949 and the government was in a state of chaos, Remón relented. This time Arnulfo lasted 16 months in the presidency. He enacted laws to protect the incipient national industry, created provincial banks to stimulate the economy in the interior, founded the Casa del Periodista, and enhanced the Patrimonio Familiar (family subsidy) by giving property titles to landless

---

[27] Ropp, *Panamanian Politics*, p. 23. The quest to maintain the purity of the language prompted some comical situations. For instance, Arnulfo decreed that all advertisement had to be in Spanish. Johnny Walker scotch became "Juanito El Caminador," and for some time that became Arnulfo's nickname.

[28] Between Arnulfo's overthrow in 1941 and 1949, when he was given the presidency again, Panama had six presidents, one of which only lasted one day.

peasants.[29] However, he had only nine deputies in the National Assembly, which presented problems for his securing approval of programs. When Arnulfo announced plans to rewrite the constitution, he was deposed, tried, and lost his constitutional rights.[30] Since then and until the early 1960s, he was exiled to his coffee farm in Boquete, in the province of Chiriquí.

In 1960 Arnulfo made a deal with the Partido Liberal, specifying that in exchange for the Panameñistas' support of Chiari's candidacy, Arnulfo's constitutional rights would be restored. Once elected, Chiari kept his promise and Arnulfo, once again a citizen in good standing, gathered his forces and ran in the 1964 elections. By all accounts he won that election by a huge margin, but he was not allowed to take power. He ran again in 1968 and won. After taking office on October 1, he was deposed 11 days later by the National Guard.

## CRISIS AND STAGNATION, 1950-1968

In 1952, José Antonio Remón Cantera, first and only chief of the National Police since 1932, won the presidential elections backed by a new party, the Coalición Patriótica Nacional. Remón's presidency was peculiar in that he promoted some very innovative measures and yet was terribly repressive to selected groups.[31] He appeared to be very open, held press conferences often, toured the interior and was accessible to the people. He promoted industrialization, fought for better salaries for Panamanian workers in the Canal Zone and for an end to the injustices and discrimination to which they were subjected. He bolstered agricultural production and founded the Instituto de Fomento Económico (IFE) to make Panama self-sufficient in rice production and so reduce the importation of foodstuffs.[32]

But Remón's policies towards organized labor, students, and political parties that were not of his liking were extremely repressive. He enacted a law that political parties needed 45,000 registered voters as adherents, and only his party, the Coalición Patriótica Nacional, and the Partido Liberal Nacional filled this quota. Another law banned all "communist organizations," so the Federación de Estudiantes de Panamá (FEP), the Federación Sindical de Trabajadores de la República de Panamá (FSTRP), and the Partido del Pueblo (Communist party) were declared illegal and some of their leaders exiled.[33] Remón also fostered the creation of the Confederación de Trabajadores de la República de Panamá (CTRP), a pro-U.S. labor

---

[29] A newspapermen's guild. This included a building and an endowment.
[30] The Constitution of 1941, enacted by Arnulfo Arias, had been replaced by a new one in 1946.
[31] Remón was president for two years and was assassinated on January 2, 1955. He was the only president in the history of the republic to suffer such a fate.
[32] Sossa, *Imperialismos*, pp. 53-57.
[33] Pereira, *Panamá: fuerzas armadas*, p. 2.

organization with close ties to the AFL-CIO, as a counterbalance to the Federación Sindical (FSTRP).

Remón was assassinated in 1955, and his vice president, Ricardo Arias Espinosa, finished the term. In the 1956 elections, Ernesto de la Guardia Jr. won, supported by Remón's party. Then in 1960, Roberto F. Chiari, won the elections backed by a coalition of his party, the Liberal Nacional, with a number of others.[34] These included the Partido Republicano, led by the owners of Ingenio Santa Rosa, Eric and Max del Valle and Marcel Penso; Partido Acción Democrática of the González Ruíz brothers, from the Azuero Peninsula; Partido Panameñista, Arnulfo Arias's party; Partido de Liberación Nacional, a coalition of several small groups; and the Tercer Partido Nacionalista, founded by Gilberto Arias (son of Harmodio and nephew of Arnulfo) and Aquilino Boyd, a member of one of the old ruling families. The other candidate for president was Ricardo Arias Espinosa, supported by Remón's party and by the National Guard.[35] These are said to be the only clean elections Panama has ever had, on the promise made and kept by de la Guardia. And even though Chiari was not the candidate of the National Guard, he was allowed to take office after he agreed to respect the integrity of that military body.[36]

By 1964 the political fragmentation had reached chaotic proportions. During those elections there were seven presidential candidates, including Arnulfo Arias, and 19 contesting parties.[37] Robles, the official candidate, a cousin of the Chiaris, had been minister of government during the previous administration. Although Arias won the elections, Robles was declared the winner by 11,441 votes.[38] According to Pereira, Robles was defeated four to one in the urban areas, so he then stuffed ballots in the rural areas.[39]

The situation did not improve in the intervening years, although Robles brought into the government some highly trained technical personnel and tried to institute some changes. The administration's slogan was "La Reforma Va," which pertained to three different programs: a tax reform, an agrarian reform, and a new canal treaty. The agrarian reform that had

---

[34] His father, Rodolfo Chiari, had been president in the 1920s and since then his family had controlled that party.

[35] Arias Espinosa had been second vice president to Remón and had taken over the presidency after Remón's assassination when the first vice president was implicated in the murder.

[36] Pereira, *Panamá: fuerzas armadas*, pp. 28-29. It is interesting to note that even though Remón was a cousin of Chiari, his party supported Arias Espinosa.

[37] Seventeen of those parties were new or splinter groups, and the other two were the Coalición Patriótica Nacional and the Partido Liberal Nacional. Sossa, *Imperialismos*, pp. 62-63.

[38] Sossa, *Imperialismos*, p. 49. Arnulfo's party without the help of any coalitions poled 119,201 to Robles's 116,521. Víctor F. Goytía, *Los partidos políticos en el istmo*, quoted in Sossa, *Imperialismos*, p. 88.

[39] Pereira, *Panamá: fuerzas armadas*, p. 29.

actually become law during the previous administration was not implemented; the new canal treaty was not ratified; and the tax reform was thwarted by CONEP. The president was blocked in all directions and was incapable of exerting control over the various factions of the ruling elite. That administration reached such a low point that in addition to a motion to impeach the president brought about by the National Assembly, Robles tried to have the National Guard depose him so he could stage a counter-coup, forego elections, and keep his faction of the Partido Liberal in power.

In 1968, Arnulfo Arias ran again and won against the official candidate, David A. Samudio, who was supported by the Liberal Nacional and 11 parties grouped in two coalitions. A third candidate was Dr. Antonio González Revilla of the Christian Democratic party (PDC). During that election, there were an incredible number of realignments and last minute deals between the parties, the factions, the splinter groups, the candidates, and the commander-in-chief of the National Guard, so much so, in fact, that the situation became unworkable. After observing these elections, Zúñiga concluded that they provided the most spectacular proof yet of the crisis of the Panamanian oligarchy, which disqualified it for governing. He claimed that the parties and their leaders have not known how to find solutions or channel the hopes and concerns of Panamanian society.[40]

## CONCLUSION

The ruling elite of Panama, until 1968 in control of the political machinery of the country, never had to hone their political expertise, because they were never faced by opposition strong enough to threaten their position. This being the case, the ruling elite used the political machinery for their private needs and interests, and relied on their traditional approach to carry them through. The knowledge that they could always fall back on the United States if things got out of hand, exacerbated their complacency.

The changes experienced by Panama in the 1960s decade were such that the social fabric grew in complexity as the ruling elite became increasingly incapable of ministering to the pressing needs of the country. Faced by the incapacity to act effectively, the traditional ruling elite became more and more disorganized until they reached a point of stagnation and total impotence, with a consequent loss of hegemony. That loss of hegemony of the ruling class provided the perfect setting for an exceptional form of state such as the Torrijos regime to arise. In the following chapter, I will describe the regime that emerged after 1968, and the antecedents of the National Guard as well as its historical role in Panamanian society.

---

[40] Carlos Iván Zúñiga, "Las elecciones presidenciales de 1968." *Tareas*, no. 28(1974): 68-69.

# 3

# THE TORRIJOS REGIME

The regime that arose in Panama after the National Guard takeover in 1968 moved into the political vacuum left by the chaos and disorganization of the ruling elite. An exceptional form of state arose that for a period of time enjoyed relative autonomy from all other social forces and considerable leeway to enact progressive policy and to see to its implementation.

The regime, consolidated in the hands of Omar Torrijos after some internal power jousting among the officers of the National Guard had the characteristics that marxist analysts have labeled bonapartist and that pluralist political analysts call inclusionary authoritarian. Bonapartist states are characterized by a strong executive and the lapse of upper-class rule. The level of repression is moderate and the dominant property system is not threatened.[1] Populist authoritarian or inclusionary-authoritarian regimes are described by O'Donnell as incorporating political systems that seek to activate the popular sector and give it a role in the national political system.[2] Marxist analysts dwell more on the class configurations as well as the alliances and systemic imbalances that give rise to bonapartist regimes; pluralist analysts place more emphasis on the policies enacted by inclusionary authoritarian regimes and on the way such policies get implemented.

Both stress that these regimes are unstable because they arise under very particular circumstances that cannot be sustained for long periods. This is so, because as the societal balance of power changes, so will the forces acting for or against the regime. But for a period of time these regimes enjoy the necessary autonomy to enact progressive policies that will be in keeping with their populist project. This ability to maneuver is an important factor in the success of the regime because the type of incorporating policies they usually pursue

[1] Alain Rouquie, "L'Hypothèse 'bonapartiste' et l'émergence des systèmes politiques semi-compétitifs," *Revue Française de Science Politique* 25:5(1975): 1099-1109.
[2] Guillermo O'Donnell, *Modernization and Bureaucratic Authoritarianism: Studies in South American Politics*. Berkeley: University of California, Institute of International Studies, 1973, p. 55.

will be vehemently opposed by the traditional forces and could never be implemented if the regime did not enjoy autonomy to act. It is the enactment and implementation of incorporating policies that gives regimes like Torrijos's their most salient characteristics and that make them important to study in order to understand the process that such policies go through and their impact on society.

Torrijos took political control in 1968 and for a period of years had enough autonomy to enact and institute policies clearly bypassing the interest of the traditional ruling groups. At that juncture, Torrijos was able to establish a populist authoritarian regime, in which he aimed to incorporate the popular sectors, primarily peasants and workers, into an active role in society. There were two reasons for this. First, Torrijos perceived his mandate as one of instituting a "revolutionary process" to redress the injustices of the traditional Panamanian state. At the same time, he needed to garner support for his regime, which would give him legitimacy and enable him to stay in power.

Before Torrijos, Panama's political system had been in the hands of a small urban ruling elite whose wealth, based on commerce and services, was centered around the transit area. The new regime was made up of people of rural middle class and educated individuals of humble origins (*hijos del pueblo*), both types previously denied entry into the governmental apparatus. Until then, the Panamanian state, in the hands of the traditional ruling groups, had maintained a political system and a set of institutions solely to cater to their needs. The Torrijos regime, unhampered by such traditional needs and expectations, pursued two kinds of policies, those to provide social services to the masses and upgrade the life of the common people and those that would upgrade Panama's infrastructural base and enhance its position as a service provider in the world market economy.

Prior to 1968, the Panamanian state had been organized around small political parties controlled by members of the oligarchy. Among these, the Partido Liberal and its factions stand out, but during election years smaller parties appeared to advance the candidature of particular individuals. Elections were held every four years to chose a president, two vice presidents, and the deputies to the unicameral National Assembly. At those times, the trappings of a pluralistic democratic society would be put in evidence and a mock electoral campaign staged. The campaign would entail bargaining and arm-twisting among the parties and factions and the eventual selection of a candidate that either by consensus or by default would "win." The National Guard usually acted as a broker, allowing the candidate with strongest support of the controlling political faction to take power or denying the position to a candidate that was distrusted or feared by the ruling groups. The role of broker carried with it substantial payoffs in terms of financial benefits for the officer corps and the control of activities that would lead to profits.

The only threat to the existing political order prior to Torrijos had been Arnulfo Arias, who managed to attract a large popular following and to challenge the power of the oligarchy. He was elected to office three times and deposed by the National Guard the same number of times.[3] The first two times Arnulfo was deposed, the National Guard acted within tradition and passed power on to a civilian faction. Only in 1968 was the pattern changed, when the National Guard remained in control. After a short period of internal fighting, Torrijos surfaced as the victor, to remain in control until his death in 1981.

There are some similarities between Torrijos and Arnulfo Arias. Both were of rural middle-class origins, both adopted a populist stance and promoted policies with a social content in benefit of the popular masses, and both assumed a highly nationalistic posture. Both also tried to foster a pride in Panama that was introspective, that looked away from the canal and the transit area, from the urban and the urbane, and exhalted the land, the peasant, and the folkloric aspects of Panama's culture (*lo de uno*, that which is ours). Both also attempted to pursue policies independent of U.S. wishes and to secure recognition for Panama as something other than a U.S. appendage.

The regime that began in 1968 is difficult to characterize simply. Torrijos can been characterized as a bonapartist leader and his regime as populist or inclusionary authoritarian, but he also possessed many of the characteristics of the traditional *caudillo* and had the power to act like one. A more effective way of analyzing the regime would be as a progression through a series of phases: of power consolidation (1968-1971), of relative autonomy to enact independent policies and incorporate new sectors (1972-1976), and of loss of autonomy and reversal to a more traditional and conservative mode (1976-1981). What is obvious about this regime is that Torrijos genuinely saw himself as a reformist and that the reforms he attempted centered at the internal level on upgrading the masses and externally at attaining redress from the United States on the issue of the Panama Canal.

Apparent also is the fact that the regime followed no particular ideology, changing course if a given policy was not achieving the expected results. It is also obvious that the regime had no preconceived plan of action or specific goals in its 13 years. This allowed it a great degree of leeway to shift directions in relation to the specific aims pursued at a given time. This also gave rise to many incongruences within the various ministries and agencies and confusion among those outside the government who tried to anticipate its moves and actions. Perhaps the most fitting characterization of Torrijos is that of a pragmatist who took advantage of opportunities as he saw fit and who was not afraid to change directions if doing so seemed more expedient. But the fact that he mobilized the support of popular sectors clearly places the Torrijos regime in the constellation of inclusionary authoritarian regimes.

---

[3] Arias took office in 1940, 1948, and 1968. He also won the elections of 1964 and 1984 but was not allowed to take power then.

## THE NATIONAL GUARD BEFORE 1968

Torrijos was the third commander-in-chief of the National Guard and the first one not directly linked to one of the ruling families. Even though the National Guard was made up of citizens of humble origins, its first commander, José Antonio Remón Cantera, who held the post between 1931 and 1952, was an impoverished cousin of the Chiari family. His successor, Bolívar Vallarino, a member of one of the most important families of pre-independence days, held the post from 1952 to 1968.

Panama's need to protect its own territory ended with independence from Colombia and the relationship then established with the United States. The 1903 treaty between Panama and the United States stipulated in its first clause that the United States guarantee the independence of the new republic and in its Seventh clause that the United States had the right to intervene in the internal affairs of the state to "maintain the public order necessary" for the construction and running of the canal. These two clauses, reaffirmed in the Panamanian Constitution of 1904, rid Panama of any concerns regarding internal or external security.[4] The United States put pressure on Panama's leaders to dissolve the national army, which was done that same year.

After the Panamanian army was dissolved, the military tradition among the old ruling families came to an end. The police function, which symbolically remained in the hands of Panamanians, was looked upon with disdain by the upper class as well as by most of the urban popular sector. For a long time policemen were identified as "cholos," because most of the officers and the rank and file were of rural origin, either of middle-class or peasant extraction.[5] Toward the end of Remón's tenure, he actively recruited urban elements to the police force, and many individuals of Antillean descent joined its ranks then. The officers of urban origin were the sons of public employees, teachers, and small merchants.

The events that took place from the signing of the 1903 treaty to 1936, when a new U.S.-Panama Treaty—which greatly curtailed the interventionist role of the United States—went into effect, lead us to believe that the United States was more than pleased to be the watchdog and order keeper of the new republic. The United States oversaw elections, put down riots, maintained order during strike movements, and at one point occupied the city of David for two years to preserve public order.[6] Furthermore, the Panamanian police was disarmed in 1913, left only with

---

[4] Renato Pereira, *Panamá: fuerzas armadas y política*. Panamá: Ediciones Nueva Universidad, 1979, p. 2.

[5] This term, which is generally applied to mestizos, is generically used in Panama to denote all people of rural background, especially the peasants. Pereira, *Panamá: fuerzas armadas*, p. 112.

[6] This took place between 1918 and 1920. Tom Barry, *Dollars & Dictators*.Albuquerque: Resource Center, 1982, p. 145.

ornamental guns to be used in parades.[7] Until the early 1930s, the chief administrator of the Panamanian police was a U.S. officer.[8] With the enactment of the 1936 treaty, the United States relinquished its right to interfere in the internal affairs of Panama and the Panamanian government found it necessary to build up the police force to maintain internal order. Harmodio Arias, then president, entrusted José Antonio Remón Cantera with that task.[9]

By the 1940s, the power of the national police was so strong that it had assumed the role of chief arbiter in the political arena. In collusion with one or another faction of the governing elite it installed and removed presidents as it saw fit, ostensibly to maintain political order. Once a coup had taken place, the police never remained involved directly as a political actor but rather passed on the power from one faction to another of the ruling elite. In that respect, the police acted as a broker among the many political factions. An indication of this is that although the president was forcibly removed from office five times between 1931 and 1955, these crises were resolved according to constitutional provisions, and political power was passed on to those the police considered the rightful successors.[10] This is probably the reason that in 1968 the actions of the National Guard came as such a surprise. The ruling elite had always perceived the National Guard as a lackey to their interests and needs but never as a participant in the political forum.

As a direct outcome of the Cold War, the United States passed the Mutual Security Act of 1951 to upgrade and strengthen military organizations of friendly countries. In order to qualify for the benefits under the act, Remón upgraded the national police force in 1952 to a paramilitary organization to be known as the National Guard. This fell short of Remón's goal of a national army, since that was vetoed by the U.S. Southern Command based in the Canal Zone. The United States upheld the view that it was still its duty and prerogative to defend Panama from external aggression because of the canal, and therefore Panama did not need an army.

The level of professionalization of the National Guard did not increase until the 1960s. In 1959, of a total officer body of 192, only 35 had been trained in military academies, and the rest had come up through the ranks. The favored academies then were those of some of Panama's neighbors: Nicaragua, El Salvador, and Honduras. By the mid-1960s this trend shifted, and more recently, a great many

---

[7] The few arms the police had at the time, mostly Springfield rifles, were transferred to the Canal Zone. Pereira, *Panamá: fuerzas armadas*, p. 12.

[8] This, however, was not a unique situation, because many Panamanian public and private enterprises were headed by U.S. personnel, such as the Santo Tomás Hospital and the Fuerza y Luz (light company).

[9] Remón was the only Panamanian officer trained in a military academy. He had graduated as a cavalry lieutenant in Mexico and took over as chief of the Central Police Headquarters built in 1932 by the Harmodio Arias administration. Pereira, *Panamá: fuerzas armadas*, pp. 12-13.

[10] Steve C. Ropp, *Panamanian Politics*. New York: Praeger, 1982, p. 27.

officers attend military training in South America, primarily in Peru and Brazil. By the mid-1970s, of a total of 700 officers about 43 percent had been professionally trained at military institutions.[11] But the greatest impact on the National Guard was the School of the Americas, a counter-insurgency center run by the U.S. army in the Canal Zone. This institution has produced 34,000 graduates from the time of its founding in 1949 to the mid 1970s. Of those, 3,500, or the fourth highest number, were from the Panamanian National Guard. Torrijos took courses there and was proud of the training he received but once in power, he fought to have the school removed because he considered it a violation by the United States of the 1903 treaty. He called the School of the Americas a "great colonial encampment."[12]

## THE NATIONAL GUARD AFTER THE 1968 COUP

Immediately after the coup on October 11, 1968, that deposed Arnulfo Arias, it became clear that the officers who initiated the action had no preconceived program or defined goals. An indication of this was that the first cabinet they named was not markedly different from previous cabinets and included several well-known members of the ruling elite.[13]

A few days after the coup it became known that its leaders were junior officers in the National Guard. The names of Torrijos and Martínez were often mentioned. On October 15, the National Guard was restructured and a general staff named, with Torrijos as chief of staff and Martínez as second in command, "in recognition for the role" they had played in the coup.[14]

Before the coup, Boris Martínez had been the military commander in the Chiriquí Zone. He has been described as puritanical, intense, very impulsive, and in a permanent state of combat. He was also said to have strong anti-oligarchic feelings and blamed the deposed political leaders for the "communist tragedy" that the country was living.[15] According to one source, Martínez carried out the coup because of his perception of the political disorder existing in Panama and because of the amount of corruption, both civilian and military. He stated that he had prepared the coup to rid Panama of people like Torrijos, whom he considered corrupt.[16]

---

[11] Pereira, *Panamá: fuerzas armadas*, p. 150.

[12] Walter LaFeber, *The Panama Canal: The Crisis in Historical Perspective*. Oxford: Oxford University Press, 1979, p. 169.

[13] The minister for internal affairs, Eduardo Morgan, was related to the Chiaris, and his brother is married to a daughter of National Guard Commander Bolívar Vallarino. Henry Ford, appointed minister of finance, was at the time president of the Chamber of Commerce, and Rafael Zubieta, named minister of agriculture, commerce and industry, was president of the Cattlemen's Association. The junta also included as president Col. José María Pinilla Fábrega, second commandant of the National Guard since 1960 and Col. Bolívar Urrutia, third commandant of the National Guard since 1960.

[14] Pereira, *Panamá: fuerzas armadas*, p. 120.

[15] Pereira, *Panamá: fuerzas armadas*, p. 121.

[16] Robert H. Miller, "Military Government and Approaches to National Development: A Comparative Analysis of the Peruvian and the Panamanian Experience." Unpublished Ph.D. dissertation. Miami: University of Miami, 1975, p. 44.

Omar Torrijos Herrera, the son of middle-class teachers, was born in 1929 in Santiago de Veraguas and raised in that interior city. His background has been described as that of a small, ultra-nationalistic, ambitious, and anti-foreign middle class, mostly established in rural areas. Torrijos attended the Normal School through its first cycle and left at 17 to attend a military academy in El Salvador. The Normal School Juan Demóstenes Arosemena, located in Santiago, is the only teacher-training school in Panama and is considered "the focal point" for the formation of a radical rural intelligentsia, which has traditionally been extremely frustrated due to its marginal position in relation to the urban elite.[17] Torrijos's seven sisters and one of his three brothers were also graduates of the Normal School, as was Roberto Díaz Herrera, his cousin, who then received military training in Peru and became the executive secretary in the General Staff.[18]

Torrijos was characterized as more flexible and less militaristic than Martínez. From the beginning he talked of an understanding not with the old political leaders but with popular groups and with students. This was probably prompted by the isolation the National Guard found itself in after the coup, because the only group that rallied to its side was the Samudio faction of the Partido Liberal, who had no popular support.[19] During the early months after the takeover, Torrijos had no discernible group of followers within the National Guard.[20]

The first General Staff was in power from October 1968 to February 1969, when Martínez was ousted. This happened after a TV broadcast in which Martínez announced an agrarian reform. He further declared that from then on the Guard would not interfere in any type of civil unrest against the Canal Zone, a statement clearly made to enrage the United States. Four days later, Martínez and seven other officers were exiled or sent abroad on diplomatic missions. Torrijos's next consideration would be how to avoid antagonizing the United States to the point that they would instigate and support a coup against him.

## THE DECEMBER 15, 1969, COUP

Once rid of Martínez, Torrijos appeared to be in complete control and governed as such between February and December of 1969. Then, in the early morning of December 15, 1969, the heads of the provisional junta, José María

---

[17] Ropp, *Panamanian Politics*, p. 51.

[18] Another prominent member in Torrijos's cabinet who was a graduate of that school was Juan Materno Vásquez.

[19] Followers of David Samudio, the presidential candidate for the Partido Liberal Nacional in the 1968 elections. They supported the National Guard because many were in high positions in the state bureaucracy and wanted to keep those posts. Nevertheless, their support came conditioned by a demand that elections be held and political power returned to the traditional block.

[20] We only know about Martínez's group because they were exiled in 1969.

Pinilla and Bolívar Urrutia, announced that with the unanimous backing of the General Staff and the ranks of the National Guard, Col. Ramiro Silvera had been named commander in chief and Col. Amado Sanjur had been promoted to assistant commander. No mention was made of Torrijos, who was vacationing in Mexico. Although no specific reasons were given for the counter-coup, Silvera proclaimed that "they had had to take this decision because communists were taking over Torrijos's government.[21] The Consejo Nacional de la Empresa Privada (CONEP) immediately supported the coup and demanded that the military be replaced by a civilian junta and that elections be held in six months.[22]

Torrijos was alerted and flew back to Panama. But instead of going directly to Panama City, he landed in David, where Noriega, head of that military zone, had engaged the support of workers in the banana plantations of the United Fruit Company. These workers surrounded the city and in something similar to a state of siege, awaited Torrijos's return. Torrijos arrived on December 16, and after being assured the support of the heads of the military zones between Chiriquí and Panama provinces, he set out by land to Panama City. The banana workers went with him, and as his caravan passed through the interior, peasants and rural workers joined him. By the time Torrijos arrived in Panama City, he did so with a huge following, and according to one source, the march resembled a "truly popular fiesta."[23]

Torrijos had no problem regaining control. He then removed Pinilla and Urrutia from the Cabinet and Silvera and Sanjur from the General Staff. Demetrio Lakas, an engineer and former manager of the Caja de Seguro Social (CSS) who had been in Mexico with Torrijos, was named president, and Arturo Sucre, a lawyer, vice president. Of the post-Martínez General Staff four officers remained: Torrijos, Rodrigo García, Florencio Flores, and Rubén Darío Paredes (who had also been in Mexico with Torrijos). Four new officers were brought in at that time: Armando Contreras, Manuel Noriega, Luis A. Segura, and Manuel Araúz. Later on Luis A. Segura was removed and Armando Bellido, Gaspar Suárez, and Roberto Díaz Herrera (Torrijos's cousin) were given positions in the General Staff.

## TORRIJOS—POST-1969

After the attempts to remove him in December 1969, Torrijos remained in control of the government until his death in July 1981. As a political figure, Torrijos has remained enigmatic and difficult to characterize. On the surface, he seemed a rather uncomplicated individual, with a direct and simple style of speaking laced with colloquialisms. He portrayed himself as "el Cholo

---

[21] Col. Sanjur declared that 47 key posts in the Torrijos government were held by communists. Pereira, *Panamá: fuerzas armadas*, p. 129.

[22] Pereira, *Panamá: fuerzas armadas*, p. 131.

[23] Epica Task Force. *Panama: Sovereignty for a Land Divided*. Washington, D.C. 1976, p. 56.

Table 1    National Guard General Staff

| General Staff | Academy & Year | Position |
|---|---|---|
| Omar Torrijos | Salvador, 1952 | Commander in Chief |
| Rodrigo García | Salvador, 1955 | Deputy Commander |
| Florencio Florez | Nicaragua, 1955 | Chief of Staff |
| Rubén D. Paredes | Nicaragua, 1957 | G1, Personnel |
| Manuel A. Noriega | Peru, 1962 | G2, Intelligence |
| Armando Contreras | Nicaragua, 1958 | G3, Operations |
| Armando Bellido | No academy | G4, Administration |
| Gaspar A. Suárez | Salvador, 1950 | G5, Civic Action |
| Manuel A. Araúz | Nicaragua, 1957 | Traffic Control |
| Roberto Díaz Herrera | Peru, 1961 | Executive Secretary |

Source: Adapted from Renato Pereira, *Panamá: fuerzas armadas y política*, Panamá: Ediciones Nueva Universidad, 1979, pp. 146-147.

Omar" and presented an image of complete accessibility to the common man, to "the people." The oligarchy ridiculed him and portrayed him as some sort of bumbling hill-billy. Still, he had the support and backing of the most highly regarded Latin American leaders of his time and of many Third World leaders. He was also appealing to international literary figures of renown such as Graham Greene and especially Gabriel García Márquez, who became his confidant and ideological mentor.

Torrijos compared himself to Velasco Alvarado and characterized the National Guard as integrated by a new generation of reformist officers concerned with national development, akin to those of Peru. In a letter written to Senator Edward Kennedy, he offered some insight into how he perceived himself and the National Guard:

The seed sown at Punta del Este in 1960 by John F. Kennedy has born fruit in the creation of a new generation of young men, well prepared professionals with good intentions, that speak, think, and live the language of development, and who little by little are occupying key decision making positions in Latin American countries. I consider myself to be a product of this crop.

He went on to recount how the National Guard had always been used by the ruling class to put down students, workers, and peasants, who, he considered, had rightful demands. And because he had been close to violence so often, he said, he was a military man "convinced of peaceful changes to promote the replacement of old structures."[24]

A metaphor commonly used by Torrijos to explain the National Guard and the role of his government was of Panamanian society as a family in which

---

[24] Omar Torrijos, letter to Senator Edward M. Kennedy, reprinted in Omar Torrijos, *La Batalla de Panamá*. Buenos Aires: EUDEBA, 1973, p.103. Translation by Steve C. Ropp quoted in *Panamanian Politics*, p. 49.

members of the Guard were portrayed as "bastards" because they were not descendants of the old ruling families and had not been elected to office. But he reminded the people that it was usually "the illegitimate child who was the one who saved the honor of the family . . . that same honor that was blemished by the legitimate sons."[25] This allusion to illegitimacy, which was used to elicit support from the masses, was a felicitous one for Panama because it linked the complex dynamics of class structure and racial background. Panama's upper class, derogatorily called *rabiblancos* (white tail), sees its members as the true descendants of the original colonizers and as the legitimate offspring of the nation. The rest of the society, dark and of mixed parentage, is often illegitimate and definitely treated as such by the elite.[26] Torrijos appealed to this mass, always before on the outside, for support. It is unquestionable that Torrijos was extremely skillful in his use of persuasive appeals to attract these people, the peasants, the popular urban classes, and the educated middle sector. In this respect, he could be considered a charismatic leader, if not to all segments at least to those groups previously dispossessed of any important role in society.

Notable also was Torrijos's ability to survive, thanks to his shrewdness, to his skills in manipulating people, and to his ability to change directions when it seemed expedient to do so. This survival factor of Torrijos is one aspect that makes the Panamanian case stand out from other military regimes in Latin America. In the 1960s and 1970s, the regimes in Brazil, Peru, and Honduras changed course, but they also changed their leadership. By contrast, in Panama, although policies often changed abruptly, those changes took place under the control and leadership of the same man.[27] Another important difference between Torrijos and other military leaders is that he was not a tyrant as so many others in similar positions have been. He usually tried to accommodate or co-opt opponents and thus to win them to his side.[28] These skills help explain his regime's longevity.

Torrijos maintained control of the government by keeping a tight reign on the National Guard and by creating a network of trusted relatives and friends in key positions. He never allowed a politician to become too familiar or too entrenched in a position. High government officials were rotated frequently. The average tenure for a minister between 1968 and 1980 was 2.2 years and for minister of government, a position crucial to internal political control, 1.3 years.[29] Due to this shifting around, Panamanians referred to Torrijos's cabinet

---

[25] Omar Torrijos, "El que da cariño recibe cariño," in *La Batalla de Panamá.* p. 90.

[26] Panama has the fourth highest index of illegitimacy in the world and of women heads of households, after Guinea Bissau, Jamaica, and Grenada. Elise Boulding, et al., *Handbook of International Data on Women*. New York: Sage Publications, 1976, p. 201.

[27] Steve C. Ropp, "Leadership and Political Transformation in Panama: Two Levels of Regime Crisis," in Steve C. Ropp and James A. Morris, eds., *Central America: Crisis and Adaptation*. Albuquerque: University of New Mexico Press, 1984, p. 243.

[28] Ropp, "Leadership," p. 248.

[29] Ropp, "Leadership," p. 245.

as the "musical chair ministers." One observer surmises that this use of family
and friends made it impossible for the regime to have a "clear definition of
ideologies and political views."[30]

## THE TORRIJOS GOVERNMENT

While a few members of the National Guard held governmental posts, such
as Rubén Darío Paredes who was minister of agricultural development in 1975,
most officers stayed out of the daily running of the government. The civilian
component of the regime can be divided into four groups according to their
origins and their ideological orientations.[31]

The first group was made up of young, highly trained technicians, who had
been brought into the government during the Robles administration to direct
the reform efforts of that government. They owed their jobs to the Samudio
faction of the Partido Liberal and were strongly committed to the programs for
which they had been hired. The most salient example of this group was Nicolás
Ardito Barletta, who was head of the Planning Office under Robles. After
Torrijos upgraded the office to a ministry, Ardito Barletta was appointed the
first planning minister. In 1984 he became president of Panama.

Another group was composed of Torrijos's relatives and close friends.
About 30 members of the immediate Torrijos family held key positions in the
central government, autonomous agencies, and state enterprises. At one point
they controlled the Instituto para la Formación de Recursos Humanos
(IFARHU), the Ministry of Education, the Comisión de Reforma Educativa,
the Institute for Special Children, the Caja de Seguro Social (CSS), Cemento
Bayano, the National Lottery, and the national casinos.[32]

A third group was composed of individuals of rural, middle-class origins.
Prior to Torrijos's rule, they had not found an entry into any of the governments
of the ruling elite. People such as Marcelino Jaén from Coclé, who became a
member of the Comisión Nacional de Legislación, and Gerardo González from
Veraguas, who became minister of agricultural development and later vice
president, are representative of this group.

A last group was made up of individuals with leftist tendencies who had
been active in the Partido del Pueblo (Communist party) and various other
leftist organizations such as the Movimiento Estudiantil, the Partido Socialista,
and the Frente Patriótico de la Juventud. Some had been active in the Unión
de Estudiantes Universitarios (UEU) at a time when that organization was
closely allied to the Partido del Pueblo.[33] Included among these are Adolfo
Ahumada, president of the UEU in 1962, Eligio Salas in 1963, Oydén Ortega

---

[30] Miller, "Military Government," p. 5.
[31] Pereira, *Panamá: fuerzas armadas*, pp. 143-145.
[32] LaFeber, *The Panama Canal*, p. 196.
[33] José A. Sossa, *Imperialismos, fuerzas armadas y partidos políticos en Panamá*. Panamá:
Ediciones Documentos, 1977, pp. 39-42.

in 1965, and Ascanio Villalaz in 1966.[34] Eligio Salas became a member of the Comisión Nacional de Legislación, Ascanio Villalaz head of the Corporación Nacional de Bayano, Adolfo Ahumada labor minister in 1976 and presidential chief of staff in 1978, and Oydén Ortega labor minister in 1978 and minister of foreign relations in 1982.

Once Torrijos was in firm control, the influence of the Partido del Pueblo became very strong in various organizations founded or promoted by the government.[35] There are several reasons that the government courted leftist elements and gave them such prominence. First, after the December 1969 coup, the regime found itself in almost complete isolation, with only the Samudistas openly supporting it. CONEP had shown the true colors of the private sector, and it was obvious to Torrijos that he could not win them over. He also suspected them of masterminding the 1969 counter-coup in collusion with the CIA. So there was no hope and less desire to secure elements from that sector to help run the government. Second, the leftist organizations were the most politicized and possessed a high degree of cohesion and some organizational know-how that could be handy, especially in organizing popular support. Third, in terms of Torrijos's perception of his mandate and his goals, he was closer to the left ideologically than to the CONEP group. Fourth, since individuals of leftist leanings did not share the interests of the former ruling group, they were more likely to be supportive of the types of policies Torrijos wanted to enact and to remain loyal to the regime.

Members of the Torrijos government considered leftist, or as Pereira puts it, as having "nationalistic and popular ideological inclinations" included: Juan Materno Vásquez, presidential chief of staff from 1968 to 1971 and then president of the Supreme Court; Manuel Balbino Moreno, a financier who became minister of education; Damián Castillo, an economist who had been linked to the student and labor movements and held a high position in the Contraloría General de la República; Juan Antonio Tack, minister of foreign relations who negotiated with Kissinger most of the preliminary agreements for the 1977 canal treaties; Rómulo Escobar Bethancourt, minister of labor in 1969, then rector of the National University and later negotiator of the new canal treaties. Included in this group also are Rolando Murgas, who in 1972 became

---

[34] In 1967, the Partido del Pueblo through a commission made up of Ascanio Villalaz, Oydén Ortega, and Orniel Urriola tried to make a deal with Arnulfo Arias prior to the elections that in return for being allowed to run some candidates for deputy and for municipal posts they would support Arias. Arias rejected the proposal and the Partido del Pueblo then supported David Samudio, the official candidate representing the Liberal party under the same proposal. Sossa, *Imperialismos*, pp. 39-40.

[35] Organizations such as the Confederación Nacional de Asentamientos Campesinos (CONAC) founded in October 1970, the Frente Reformista de Educadores Panameños (FREP), the Federación Nacional de Mujeres Democráticas (FENAMUDE), the Unión Médica Panameña, and the Confederación Nacional de Trabajadores de Panamá (CNTP) founded in May 1970 were all controlled by members or former members of the Partido del Pueblo. Sossa, *Imperialismos*, p. 40.

minister of labor, and Luis Shirley, a former student leader who became vice minister of labor under Murgas.[36] Other leftist personalities were the Pérez Herrera and Díaz Herrera relatives of Torrijos, Ascanio Villalaz, Adolfo Ahumada, Ricardo Rodríguez, and Gerardo González.

Ministries and agencies in the Torrijos regime have also been divided into the conservative and the progressive, or leftist, ministries.[37] The ministries of Labor, Health, Education, and Agricultural Development were progressive, and those of Planning, Finance, and Commerce and Industry were conservative. The implication is that the conservative ministries tended to represent the interests of the private sector and the upper class, and the progressive ministries were controlled by and represented the interests of the popular sector. According to Ardito Barletta, former minister of planning, the "conservative group" wanted to promote education, health, rural development, and nutrition, but with economic growth. The leftist group leaned toward state enterprises, the regulation of private capital, of prices, and of housing. The leftist group was in control from the beginning of the decade to 1974 and the more conservative group from 1974 on.[38]

To simply point to the rise of leftists obscures important features of the political landscape at that time. Excepting the technicians, there was a great deal of overlap between the civilian groups involved in the government. Most of Torrijos's family, especially his sisters and the Pérez Herrera branch, are members of the disaffected rural "intelligentsia." And some are leftist or have connections with leftist groups.[39]

Apart from the four identifiable groups, there were many individuals who held important posts in the Torrijos government, who were of lower and middle-class background, and who for the first time gained entry into the governmental bureaucracy. This incorporation of new elements allowed the regime to have a broad democratizing effect on society, an effect with far-reaching repercussions. It also furthered the separation of the private economic sector from the realm of the public bureaucracy, giving the government more room to maneuver.

A real enigma is how Torrijos maintained control over the National Guard. This is especially puzzling since his "leftist" policies and the participation in the government of so many individuals of leftist leanings would seem very difficult for the rather conservative elements in the General Staff to accept. In part, improvements in salaries and benefits helped maintain the regime's control.[40] But the reasons for Torrijos's power and the dynamics of the situation

[36] Pereira, *Panamá: fuerzas armadas*, p. 136.
[37] Pereira, *Panamá: fuerzas armadas*, pp. 143-145.
[38] Interview with Nicolás Ardito Barletta, minister of planning 1971-1976, and president of Panama 1984-1985.
[39] Torrijos's sister, Nelva Torrijos de Soler, who was head of the Comisión de Reforma Educativa, is the sister-in-law of Ricaute Soler, probably one of the most prominent leftist intellectuals in Panama.
[40] LaFeber, *The Panama Canal*, p. 163.

are infinitely more complicated. One reason may have been the Guard's known tradition of supporting its commander. Another reason may have been Torrijos's close ties with the personnel of the National Guard. During his tenure, he maintained direct lines of authority to all military units and spent a considerable amount of time keeping in touch with the troops.[41]

Another explanation may have been the genuine efforts of Torrijos to upgrade the National Guard and give it a real veneer as a military institution. In 1974, the Escuela Nacional de Capacitación Política (ESCANAP) was established under the direction of Roberto Díaz Herrera. ESCANAP was modeled after the CAEM in Peru, and its purpose was to educate both officers and enlisted men through courses and seminars held with cabinet members, labor leaders, students, and politicians. Another important role of ESCANAP, according to Ropp, was to keep the military officers informed of policy changes and new directions the government was taking, because these changes and shifts occurred so often.[42]

All of these reasons together still do not seem convincing enough to explain the docility of the officers in the National Guard.[43] Torrijos's unchallenged authority could have been further enhanced by the level of graft and corruption, ensuring that the material benefits the officers were reaping were so substantial that they found it expedient to support Torrijos. In an interview after he was exiled, Martínez talked about the corruption in the National Guard before the 1968 coup. There is no reason to believe that this stopped after Torrijos took over.[44] The illicit goings-on that have been uncovered in the last few years would indicate that these activities did not stop but rather were intensified after 1968. The dealings of the Transit Corporation exposed in 1981 by *La Prensa* pointed out that high National Guard officers owned and controlled that company and charged a tax for goods entering and leaving the Colon Free Zone. The monthly "profits" of the company were reported in the millions of dollars.[45]

---

[41] Torrijos frequently participated in military exercises, marches, and informal talks, and no assignments were made above the lieutenant level without his approval. Ropp, *Panamanian Politics*, p. 43.

[42] Ropp, "Leadership," p. 34.

[43] The charges made by Martínez and his supporters, and later by the members of the provisional junta and Silvera, that Torrijos had leftist or "communist" leanings, were charges that could have been made at any time during his tenure. There were high government officials who had been identified with leftist groups, and many of the policies promoted and the postures adopted by Torrijos went against those traditionally accepted.

[44] Martínez pointed out that officers ruled their areas as mafia chiefs, getting large amounts of income from gambling, prostitution and other vices. He mentioned a scam that involved the printing of fake lottery tickets and said he had been offered about $20,000 per month to allow the circulation of these illegal tickets. Another scam entailed the introduction of large quantities of contraband Colombian coffee. He was offered $100,000 by coffee importers from Colón to ignore such activities. Miller, "Military Government," pp. 220-224.

[45] "Transit es del Estado Mayor: Controlan entrada y salida de mercancía en Zona Libre." *La Prensa*, December 14, 1981. Another exposé of the illicit dealings in the Colon Free Zone, many of which involved military officers, is detailes in Ezequiel Muhtar, *La Mordida*, Miami: Editorial Istmo, 1976.

Torrijos's family has also been implicated in scandals of this sort. For example, *La Prensa* did an exposé of the Caja de Seguro Social, whose director was a nephew by marriage to Torrijos and which was allocating contracts for the construction of low-cost housing, often without bids or without any actual plans for construction. These accusations reached Torrijos himself. While his brother was ambassador to Spain, he allegedly was investing money for Torrijos in that country in real estate.[46] Many members of Torrijos's family held high government positions through which it was especially easy to channel funds, such as the national lottery and the national casinos.

The only known direct link so far substantiated between high National Guard officers and this sort of corruption is the one regarding the Transit Corporation. There are, however, strong indications that this type of activity was common during the Torrijos years. This seems the most compelling explanation of why, with most of the higher officers of the National Guard so conservative and suspicious of "leftist" policies, they were nonetheless so docile and acquiescent through the years that Torrijos was in power.

Torrijos's ability to bring into the government new elements and to use the human resources of groups up to then outside the political locus is perhaps one of the most remarkable aspects of his regime. The successful interface between a rural middle class, an urban lower and middle class, and the technocrats of the previous administration make the Torrijos regime unique in Panamanian history. Also remarkable is the fact that his National Guard background did not stop Torrijos from allying with marxists and other leftists. This is even more surprising in light of the fact that the General Staff of the National Guard, who also supported Torrijos, was extremely conservative.

## NEW INSTITUTIONAL STRUCTURES

The regime made two basic changes in Panamanian institutions, which broke with every precedent. These changes, included in the 1972 Constitution, entailed the redefinition of the role of the National Guard and the strengthening of the executive.

### The 1972 Constitution

Until the 1972 Constitution was drafted, the military regime ruled by cabinet decree.[47] The 1972 Constitution marks the beginning of a new period

---

[46] That brother, Moisés Torrijos, was later implicated in drug trafficking. The real estate acquired in Spain included a castle once owned by Fulgencio Batista. LaFeber, *The Panama Canal*, pp. 195-196.

[47] Of those, probably one of the ones with more far-reaching consequences was Cabinet Decree no. 58 of March 3, 1969, which abolished all political parties and suspended the right to assembly in the cities of Panama and Colón. This suspension was maintained until the new constitution was approved.

in the Torrijos regime, which was to last until 1978. According to the Constitution, the government was "centrist, republican, democratic, and representative." (Art.1). Article 2 declared that, instead of the public force (National Guard) coming under the control and authority of the government as it had in all previous constitutions, "the three governmental branches are obligated to act in harmonious collaboration with the public force." Also, the president was not given the title of commander in chief of the National Guard and had no power to name or remove officers or in any way to interfere with that body's roster. Other changes regarding the presidency included extending the presidential period from four to six years; granting the president the right to delegate his powers, which had been expressly forbidden in all other constitutions; and eliminating popular and direct elections as a means of selecting the president.

The other unprecedented change was the subsuming of all governmental powers under the executive along with granting Torrijos the right to exercise these powers for a period of six years. Article 277 reads as follows:

General Omar Torrijos Herrera, Commander in Chief of the National Guard is recognized as Maximum Chief of the Panamanian Revolution.

In consequence, and to assure that the goals of the revolutionary process will be carried out, he is granted for a six year period, the right to the following functions: to coordinate all the work of the public administration; to freely name and change the ministers of state and the members of the Legislative Commission; to name the General Comptroller and General Sub-Comptroller of the Republic, the general directors of the autonomous and semi-autonomous agencies, and the justices of the Electoral Tribunal; to name the chiefs and officers of the public force, according to this constitution, the law, and the military roster; with the approval of the Cabinet Council, to name the Supreme Court Justices, the Attorney General, and the Administrative Attorney and their substitutes; to engage in contracts and loan negotiations, and direct foreign relations.

General Omar Torrijos Herrera will furthermore have the right of voice and vote in the meetings of the Cabinet Council and the National Legislative Council, and the right of voice in the National Assembly of Representatives, as well as in the Provincial Coordinating Councils and the Community Councils (Juntas Comunales).[48]

This article in effect removed all the checks and controls previously exercised over the executive through the Contraloría and through the National Assembly. Effectively, it granted Torrijos the faculty of unrestricted action.

---

[48] Organization of American States, *Constitution of Panama 1972*. Washington, D.C., 1972.

## Legislative Bodies

Other new structures introduced into the governmental apparatus were an Asamblea Nacional de Representantes de Corregimiento (small land measure), a national legislative council, a legislating commission, and an array of community and municipal governing bodies such as *juntas comunales, juntas locales,* and municipal councils, all under the direction and control of the Dirección General para el Desarrollo de la Comunidad (General Directorate for Community Development - DIGEDECOM).

The Asamblea Nacional de Representantes de Corregimiento was made up of one representative from each of the 505 corregimientos in Panama. The first election for this assembly was held in August, 1972, by popular vote.[49] The assembly met for one month every year and in reality had a very restricted role. It had no say in the control of public expenses, in the creation of public positions, or in the negotiations of contracts and loans. The only important function that the 1972 Constitution delegated to this assembly was that of choosing the president and vice president of the republic. In fact, however, on the two occasions when this was done, that function was usurped by Torrijos, who publicly indicated the individuals of his choice. The main role of this assembly seemed to be one of advocacy for the small rural areas that had a majority of representation.

Departing from the tradition of an unicameral legislative body, the Torrijos government introduced a two-body system. The National Assembly of Representatives dealt with local matters, and the National Legislative Council dealt with issues and problems at the national level. This council was made up of the president and vice president, the ministers of state, the president of the National Assembly of Representatives, and the members of the Legislative Commission. The members of the Legislative Commission were named by Torrijos at his discretion, because the Constitution did not determine the number or the type of persons that it should contain. Most were Torrijos's friends or high functionaries that had been removed from other posts. For this last reason the people referred to this commission as "El Valle de los Caidos" because it became a sort of dumping ground for ex-ministers and the like.[50] Ultimately, the National Legislative Council was just an advisory body to Torrijos.

Summarizing the situation of the legislative branch of the government, the National Assembly of Representatives had few if any powers and a window-dressing role and did not perform either of the roles of the previous National Assembly, i.e. watching over the executive and legislating. The National

---

[49] The five citizens of each corregimiento who secured more signatures from their neighbors in support of their candidacy could run as long as they had not been previously involved in "acts contrary to the electoral purity." Pereira, *Panamá: fuerzas armadas,* p.138.
[50] Dulio Arroyo Camacho, *El sistema de gobierno existente en Panamá luego de las últimas reformas a la Constitución Nacional.* Panamá: Litho-Impresora Panamá, 1979, p. 22.

Legislative Council, which was assigned by the executive to legislate, was also subsumed into executive.[51]

Another institution set up to guide and control the popular sector was the Direccion General para el Desarrollo de la Comunidad (DIGEDECOM). Established as an independent agency in 1969, it was placed under the control of the Ministry for Internal Affairs in 1974. The purpose of this agency was to direct and control the government's efforts to promote popular sector participation. It worked at five different levels: at the local level through the *juntas locales*; at the corregimiento level through the *juntas comunales*; at the municipal level with the municipal councils; at the provincial level with the provincial coordinating councils, presided over by the governors of each province. At the national level DIGEDECOM had the "delicate task of organizing and mobilizing the population of the Republic so that it could play a vital role in the revolutionary process."[52] This translated as mobilizing the masses when the government was in need of a show of popular support. DIGEDECOM was a source of employment for large numbers of people as well as a controlling governmental tool, because it reached down to the smallest communities and its officers had intimate knowledge of popular feelings and attitudes.

## PERIODS OF THE TORRIJOS REGIME

The Torrijos regime can be divided into three periods. The first runs from the early years until about 1972, the second from then up to 1976, and the third from 1976 until Torrijos's death in 1981. The first period is characterized by Torrijos's efforts to establish and maintain control. During that time, first the junta and then Torrijos on his own governed through decrees. There was a high level of uncertainty about the stability of the regime and feelings of expectation from the deposed elite, who tried at every turn to regain control of the political machinery. The regime suffered a great deal of isolation and began efforts to secure backing from new sources.

The second period, beginning in 1972 with the enactment of the Labor Code and the 1972 Constitution, is characterized by the effervescence of the government. It is as if the regime wanted to correct all the ills of the country and experiment with new policies and formulas all at once. In analyzing the period, one gets the feeling that there was a need to make up for lost time. It was possible to do this because the regime experienced a period of relative autonomy that gave it room to maneuver. During this period, apart from the Labor Code and the thrust to bolster the labor movement, enormous efforts were also made to promote an agrarian reform and improve the lot of the subsistence peasant. Concomitant with the push for agrarian reform, the government also made efforts to improve the rural infrastructure. Measures

---

[51] Arroyo Camacho, *El sistema*, p. 30.
[52] Everardo Tomlinson Hernández, *El poder político en Panamá*. Panamá: Tribuna Electoral, 1977, n.p.

in this direction concentrated mostly on feeder roads, aqueducts, and increased services in medicine and education. Although the urban areas also benefited by the infrastructural expansion and the increase in services, the impact was felt primarily in the rural countryside, which had been neglected in this regard by most previous administrations.

The government also engaged in agro-industrial ventures of a profitable nature, in direct competition with the private sector. Thus, it embarked on a sugar-producing program that included the building of four mills; it took over and rehabilitated an almost defunct citrus plantation; it created a state agency for the marketing of bananas; and it began operations of a cement plant. Construction of several hydroelectric plants also began at this time, and feasibility studies were undertaken for the construction of a pipeline to carry Alaskan oil from the Pacific to the Atlantic, for a container port, and for a deep-sea port to service the international tuna fleet.

Other developmental efforts focused on Panama's location and service-oriented economy. These projects promoted tourism and services of a financial and commercial nature. For instance, the government took over the bankrupt company that was developing Isla Contadora and began construction of a new airport and convention center in Panama City. It also gave substantial incentives for the construction of several luxury hotels. A series of banking laws were enacted to convert Panama into an international financial center, and the Colon Free Zone was greatly expanded.

While all of these projects were underway, Torrijos also kept up pressure on the United States to negotiate a new canal treaty. Through these efforts he became a figure of stature among leaders of Third World and non-aligned countries. Torrijos touted his accomplishments and promoted the cause of Panama so effectively that by the mid-1970s most Latin American countries and many other Third World countries were rallying to Panama's cause.

But by the middle of the decade the economic situation began to deteriorate and the government faced problems of over-extension and financial constraint. In 1974 Panama was badly affected by the oil price increase and the cycle of inflation and recession that this caused worldwide. In order to continue with some of its costly plans, the government had to borrow heavily and invest substantially more than it had done before. National private investment contracted to very low margins. It was then that the regime began to reformulate some of its initial policies and to have second thoughts about its less successful programs. In this third period, which runs roughly from the passage of Ley 95 at the end of 1976 to Torrijos's death, the nature of the regime changed toward a more conservative, or traditional, position. The reasons for this seem to be due to the unimproved economic situation, to pressures from the United States for a more "democratic appearance," and to the fact that the government was looking for a political formula to institutionalize the regime. The government courted the private sector, Torrijos "returned to the barracks," and political institutions with a semblance of "traditional pluralistic democracy" began to appear.

## END OF AN ERA

In 1978, Article 277 of the 1972 Constitution expired, and Torrijos, in the midst of much fanfare, returned to the barracks and ostensibly left the running of the government to the civilian component. Lakas and Sucre retired as president and vice president, and Aristides Royo and Ricardo de la Espriella were picked to replace them. The 1972 Constitution was reformed. The National Legislative Council was completely restructured, extending membership to 38 members of the National Assembly of Representatives. Free and direct provincial elections were proposed for 1980 to chose 19 or 20 of the National Assembly's members. After that date, this council was to become very similar to the pre-1968 National Assembly. Also in 1980 the Legislative Commission was abolished, and the role of the ministers of state was diminished, as they were no longer members of the National Legislative Council.

In a further effort to move the country closer to a seemingly democratic situation, but under strict controls, political parties were allowed again. However, parties had to have 30,000 supporters to qualify, ostensibly to prevent the mushrooming of parties and splinter groups.[53] The government started its own party, the Partido Revolucionario Democrático (PRD), modeled after the PRI in Mexico, with a labor sector, a peasant sector, and in a departure from the model, an entrepreneurial sector. For the PRD there was no problem in reaching the 30,000 membership mark because all employees of governmental, autonomous, and semi-autonomous agencies, as well as state enterprises, were forced to join. The course the regime was to follow for the remaining years of Torrijos's life was cast.

## CONCLUSION

The Torrijos regime provoked fundamental changes in Panama by shifting the locus of power from the traditional elite to a new coalition made up of a rural middle class and an urban middle and lower class. Unique also was the role played by the National Guard, which evolved from being a broker in the political arena to being a direct participant. This, coupled with the personalistic staffing of key governmental positions and the constitutional changes that enhanced the role of the National Guard and gave almost absolute power to Torrijos, single out this regime. A further important consideration was the successful blending of the National Guard with the new coalition and the maintenance of this relationship in the face of obvious incongruences. That the National Guard, with its extremely conservative officer corps, was able to share power with a highly nationalistic and ideologically leftist group of

---

[53] Stipulating a high number of adherents was not new. During the Remón years, he had passed a law that required 45,000 adherents for a party to be registered.

individuals is a remarkable achievement of Torrijos and of his ability to exert control and maintain power.

That Torrijos took power at a time when there was a crisis in the political system and that he was able to maintain it through the strengthening of the executive are some of the characteristics that would label him a bonapartist ruler. His ability to play different interests against each other, to keep the loyalty of an incongruous coalition, and to incorporate large numbers of the previously unincorporated masses into the system were skills of a populist leader.

The salience of the Torrijos regime rests primarily with the incorporating policies that it enacted and successfuly implemented, because those policies provoked a fundamental change in the country's social composition. So the degree of success that the regime had in the implementation of inclusionary policies measured the degree of permanent change it effected in the country.

It is in this context that the study of the 1972 Labor Code was undertaken. Labor policy is a fundamental tool that can be used to reach a large popular sector and transform its position in society. Often, however, very progressive labor policy exists without it having an impact, because such policy is not implemented. It is important, therefore, to study the process of implementing the 1972 Labor Code and the power play that took place between the regime, the private sector, and labor, in order to determine how the various social forces influence the degree of success of progressive policy.

By careful analysis of the various factors that contributed to the success or lack of success of the policy, we gain an understanding of the process that inclusionary authoritarian regimes go through and of the effect that obstacles and facilitating agents have in their capacity to make a permanent impact on society.

# 4

# LABOR RELATIONS IN PANAMA

Until the Torrijos regime singled out the working class as a sector to bestow attention upon, labor had been dispossessed of power and status in Panamanian society. The meager gains that individual labor groups made had been achieved at a very high cost both to their membership and to the working class in general. Prior to Torrijos's ascent to power, active labor groups had a reputation for feistiness and for ruthless labor agitation but gained no consideration or recognition from those in political control.

Within a few years of Torrijos's takeover, labor groups were at the forefront of the regime's supporters. This was achieved by the Torrijos government through a series of measures that brought labor's strength and participation to a level of significance and converted the sector into a strong supporter of the government. This sudden change in status and power was achieved through the organization of the Ministry of Labor (Ministerio de Trabajo – MITRAB), the enactment of the very progressive 1972 Labor Code, and several other dispositions that enhanced organized labor. These measures insured the quick transformation of the labor sector into a strong supporter of the regime, which gave it a preferential position in the social system.

Panama has traditionally had a weak labor sector, which has had little or no success in directing the events that have affected it. The primary reasons for this lie in the composition of the working class and in the historical development of the country's economy. The labor sector is divided between a native group, which shares a cultural and racial heritage, and a group of recent immigration, of a different racial composition and background, imported to work in the canal construction. As for the economy, the main thrust of its development has been the commercial and service sectors, which do not require a well-trained work force or are capital intensive instead of labor intensive. Few enterprises employ a large or highly trained work force, and under these circumstances it has been difficult for organized labor to grow in strength and develop common bonds between its two component groups. Although some activist unions emerged, especially in the 1940s and 1950s, which on occasion achieved some benefits for their affiliates and the working class in general, it was not until Torrijos took power and made concessions to the working class that labor achieved a prominent, and controversial, position in Panamanian society.

Since the eighteenth century the working class of Panama has included a highly fluid population in the transit area, with many adventurers and fortune seekers as well as ordinary laborers. This last group was in a constant state of flux, and there were great opportunities for social mobility. During the second half of the nineteenth century into the early years of this century, large numbers of workers were imported to work on the Trans-Isthmian Railroad, the French canal, and the U.S. canal, as the local population proved to be insufficient for such large enterprises. For the last two projects over 140,000 workers were imported, mostly from Barbados and Jamaica.[1]

Besides the canal itself, Panama inherited from its construction the divided labor force that continues to characterize labor in Panama today and that has given rise to many of the problems and weaknesses that Panama presently confronts. On the one hand, the indigenous laboring class, although racially dark, is Spanish speaking and shared its Latin heritage and Catholic religion with the Panamanian upper class. The other group made up of Caribbean blacks, is English speaking, Protestant, and is composed of British subjects raised under an Anglo-Saxon value system. Once the canal was built, most of these people remained in the country because their countries of origin did not encourage their return. The majority continued working for the U.S.-run Panama Canal Company.

Historical factors contributed to the formation of a weak and divided labor force, which prior to the advent of Torrijos had no role in Panamanian society. The division of the labor sector between a native and an imported human resource, different in background and upbringing, was fundamental in preventing the formation of a strong labor sector. Another division between the opportunities and activities of the transit area versus the rest of the country also contributed to the lack of cohesion of the labor sector. A third factor was the development of the country as a service provider, with emphasis on commerce and tertiary sector activities and a very small and rudimentary industrial sector, neither of which requires a large or well-trained work force. These factors were fundamental in shaping the labor sector and placing it in the role of a weak and excluded sector prior to the Torrijos regime.

---

[1] For the construction of the railroad about 7,000 workers were imported. Then, between 1881-1903, over 105,000 workers were imported by the French, the majority from Jamaica. For the construction of the U.S. canal, 45,000 workers were imported, 68 percent from the English-speaking Caribbean and 26 percent from Europe. Omar Jaén Suárez, *La población del Istmo de Panamá*. Panamá: Imprenta de la Nación, 1978, pp. 451-460.

[2] Andrés Achong, *Orígenes del movimiento obrero panameño*. Panamá: Centro de Estudios Latino Americanos "Justo Arosemena" (CELA), 1980, pp. 13-17.

## EARLY LABOR ACTIVITIES

Before the second decade of this century, the only political activities involving the working class took place in the transit area and were directly linked to the foreign groups operating there. There were strikes against the Pacific Mail Steamship Company in the 1850s related to demands for better salaries.[2] Workers went on strike against the Trans-Isthmian Railroad Company five times between 1868 and 1895, also for better salaries, and there are also records of two strikes against the French Canal Company in 1881 and in 1896.[3] Besides better salaries, the strikers demanded better food and freedom to leave the housing camps on Sundays.

After the United States took over the construction of the canal in 1904, there were a series of strikes and work stoppages, with demands for better pay, better food, and better treatment. These actions were supported by the lodges, churches, and mutualist societies that the Caribbean workers had established along similar lines to those prevalent in their own countries.[4] Among the many irksome problems confronted by the Caribbean workers was a highly discriminatory system maintained by the United States, in which employees were classified into a "gold" or "silver" roll. All laborers belonged to the second, named as such because they were paid in silver currency. Separate housing as well as eating and bathroom facilities were maintained for each roll classification. And within the silver roll, there were different pay scales, with workers of European origin earning higher salaries for the same tasks as black workers from the Caribbean.[5]

Labor unrest in the transit area grew in size and frequency after the U.S. canal had been completed. Between 1916 and 1920, there were at least six strikes involving workers in the Canal Zone. The most serious of these took place in February 1920 and involved over 17,000 laborers, almost the entire silver roll.[6] The strike was called by the United Brotherhood of Maintenance Way, and the demands reflected concern not only with better salaries, but also with the status of workers regarding housing privileges and other benefits. This strike was the first within the Canal Zone in which the government of Panama openly intervened, first by trying to mediate and then by demanding that the U.S. authorities keep the strikers within the Canal Zone area and out of Panamanian territory. One outcome of the strike was the deportation of 2,000 blacks, including their leaders.[7] Those who remained realized the precariousness of their situation because they had no legal

---

[3] Marco A. Gandásegui et al., *Las luchas obreras en Panamá (1850-1978)*. Panamá: Centro de Estudios Latino Americanos "Justo Arosemena" (CELA), 1980, pp. 28-31.

[4] Two of the most prominent were the Colour Progressive Association and the West Indian Protective League, which published a newspaper entitled *The Workman*. Jorge Turner, *Raíz, historia y destino de los obreros panameños*. Mexico: UNAM, Instituto de Investigaciones Sociales, 1970, p. 22.

[5] Hernando Franco Muñoz, *Movimiento obrero panameño 1914-1921*. Panamá: n.p., 1979, p. 15.

[6] Franco Muñoz, *Movimiento obrero*, p. 20. Gandásegui et al., *Las luchas*, pp. 40-43.

[7] Gandásegui et al., *Las luchas*, p. 43.

status in Panama and all the privileges they received in the Canal Zone—housing, schools, medical attention, and far better pay than in Panama—were contingent on the benevolence of their employers and on acquiescence to these employers' authority.

The only labor organizations founded in the Republic of Panama prior to the 1920s were guilds and mutualist societies of a highly incipient nature.[8] One of the most progressive, the Sociedad Hijos del Trabajo, was instrumental in organizing the first workers' federation, the Federación Obrera de la República de Panamá, founded in 1921. Several anarcho-syndicalists who had arrived from Spain during the previous years, such as José María Blázquez de Pedro and his brother Martín, were its driving force.[9] The Federación Obrera followed no political persuasion according to its statutes, and its main goal was to fight for the rights of workers and for their economic and social well-being. The American Federation of Labor strongly endorsed the Federación Obrera, and in 1924 Samuel Gompers visited Panama and was warmly welcomed by its members.[10]

The more progressive members of the Federación Obrera formed a Grupo Comunista in 1921, and shortly afterward conflict between the two groups developed when it became obvious that the first prized the approval of the American Federation of Labor (AFL) and adhered to the tenets of that U.S. labor organization.[11] Wishing to promote more forcibly the ideas emanating from the Russian Revolution and the Third International, the Grupo Comunista broke off with the Federación Obrera late in 1924 and formed the Sindicato General de Trabajadores.[12]

Although the Sindicato General de Trabajadores was short-lived, it was responsible for the first massive labor protest led by Panamanian workers. In 1925, the government announced an increase in real estate taxes to take effect

---

[8] Some of the most important were the associations of butchers, bakers, typographers, barbers, carpenters, trolley car-conductors, tailors, and blacksmiths. Franco Muñoz, *Movimiento obrero*, p. 31.

[9] The Blázquez de Pedro brothers were two of a group of exiles who had arrived in Panama from various countries and who played an important role in the incipient labor movement. The Spaniards and Sara Gratz, a Polish refugee, were anarcho-syndicalists; Luis Francisco Bustamante, Nicolás Terreros, Esteban Patlevitch (Peruvians), and Carlos Manuel Céspedes (from Colombia) were socialists. Alexander Cuevas, *El movimiento inquilinario de 1925.* Panamá: Centro de Estudios Latinoamericanos "Justo Arosemena", 1980, p. 21. Franco Muñoz has called José María Blázquez de Pedro the "father of Panama's labor movement," and its most influential figure from about 1917 until he was deported in 1925. Franco Muñoz, *Movimiento obrero*, p. 45.

[10] Franco Muñoz, *Movimiento obrero*, pp. 33, 38-45.

[11] Among the Panamanians prominent in the Grupo Comunista, some, such as Domingo H. Turner, Diógenes de la Rosa, and Jorge E. Brouwer would remain active in the labor movement for decades. They also founded the Communist party (Partido del Pueblo) in 1930 and the Socialist party two years later. Franco Muñoz, *Movimiento obrero*, pp. 45-48.

[12] Iván Quintero, *El Sindicato General de Trabajadores.* Panamá: Centro de Estudios Latinoamericanos "Justo Arosemena", 1979, p. 14.

in November of that year. By June the slum landlords, mostly upper-class Panamanians, had passed on the increase to their tenants, in many cases doubling their rent. The Sindicato General de Trabajadores organized a Liga de Inquilinos and promoted a boycott on rent payment. The organizers also called for a mass demonstration to be held in October. In mid-September the government jailed all foreign labor leaders, including José María Blázquez de Pedro, and later deported them. They also denied a permit for the mass meeting, which was held nevertheless, leaving a toll of four dead and many injured.[13] Fearing popular reprisals, the government requested the United States to intervene. U.S. troops occupied the cities of Panama and Colón until the unrest had subsided. Mass arrests and many more deportations followed.[14]

By 1926, the government decided to curtail any activities in which labor groups were involved.[15] Thus workers were not allowed to parade on May Day between 1926 and 1929, and there are few records of labor activities in this period. This suppression of labor was to last until the Second World War.

The founding of the Federación Obrera and the Sindicato General de Trabajadores set the parameters within which organized labor would evolve during the remainder of the century. The Federación Obrera considered itself the representative of a labor movement that followed Western democratic ideals, and its sphere of action was a capitalistic economic system. The purpose of the Federación Obrera was to seek better economic and working conditions for its members. The leaders of the Sindicato General de Trabajadores were marxists and socialists who saw organized labor from a different perspective. For them, there were inherent structural problems in the social and economic systems, which generated intense conflicts between the laboring class and the capitalist class, restricting the attainment of even the most basic benefits for workers. While in the wake of violent governmental repression—the Federación Obrera and the Sindicato General de Trabajadores seem to have disappeared around 1930—the organizations that emerged in the 1940s and 1950s maintained their predecessors' ideological perspectives as well as the concomitant cleavages within the labor movement.

THE REEMERGENCE OF LABOR—1940-1968

Labor organizations experienced a resurgence in the mid-1940s due in large part to the effects of the Second World War, which prompted some development of Panama's industrial sector through import substitution and caused services to the canal to expand very rapidly.

The reemergence of the labor movement was reflected in the formation of a number of very militant unions, organized largely through the efforts of the

---

[13] Cuevas, El movimiento, pp. 11-21.
[14] Quintero, El Sindicato, p. 17.
[15] Quintero, El Sindicato, p. 19.

socialist and communist leaders who had begun their careers in the 1920s.[16] These unions, which were primarily organized around trades, formed the Federación Sindical de Trabajadores de la República de Panamá (FSTRP) in 1945, which subsequently played a major leadership role in the Panamanian labor movement and developed a style of action that permeated all labor activities for the next three decades.

From its inception in 1945 until 1960, the Federación Sindical or one of its member unions was to be involved in most of the acts of labor agitation in Panama, which included two large strikes and two general movements to protest against increases in the cost of living and low wages.[17] In response to the first protest movement in 1950, the government enacted a renter's law and a price-control law and set up kiosks throughout poor neighborhoods for the sale of basic foodstuffs at cost. A second and similar movement, the Marcha del Hambre y la Desesperación (Hunger and Desperation March), took place in 1959. Throngs of underemployed and unemployed workers walked from Colón to Panama to protest the rising prices and high unemployment.[18] This march brought about a new renter's law, in addition to the first minimum-wage law in Panama, which established hourly wages at 40 cents per hour for the cities of Panama and Colón.[19]

Apart from involvement in the most notable labor protests of the times, the Federación Sindical and its member unions were instrumental in other activities significant to labor and to the popular sectors. During 1946 and 1947,

---

[16] These unions included the Sindicato Nacional de Trabajadores de la Industria de la Confección de Ropa y Anexos de Panamá, the Sindicato de Trabajadores del Mueble de Panamá, the Sindicato de Trabajadores de la Industria del Calzado y Similares, and the Sindicato de Tipógrafos y Trabajadores de las Artes Gráficas. Turner, *Raíz, historia*, p. 43.

[17] The first, called in 1946 by the seamstresses and tailors demanding higher wages from a shop that made uniforms for the U.S. army, lasted 38 days and then was declared illegal by the government. Marta Matamoros, "Huelgas ilegales: cuando las huelgas siempre eran ilegales." Mimeo. Panamá: n.d., p. 6-17. The second was a strike of the Sindicato de Choferes y Anexos in 1956 to demand a reduction of the gasoline tax. Several days before it began, close to 60 labor leaders were jailed. The strike ended after the cities of Panama and Colón were paralyzed for four days, and the drivers won a 5-cent reduction in the gasoline tax. Gandásegui et al., *Las luchas*, p. 62.

[18] The Marcha del Hambre y la Desesperación was called by the Unión Sindical de Trabajadores de Oficios Mixtos de Colón. Among the workers' demands were a minimum salary of at least 50 cents per hour, a 50 percent rent reduction, and an agrarian law to protect subsistence peasants. Eugenio Barrera, *La Marcha del Hambre y la Desesperación*. Panamá: Centro de Estudios Latinoamericanos "Justo Arosemena", 1980, p. 8. The purpose of the march was to present to the National Assembly the list of demands. But when the marchers reached their destination, the assemblymen fled, and the leaders of the march were jailed. A participant in that march said that the assemblymen were in such haste to escape and avoid a confrontation with the marchers that many fell in the pond in front of the National Assembly building. Interview with Marta Matamoros, founding member of the Federación Sindical de Trabajadores de Panamá (FSTRP), which later became the CNTP.

[19] Barrera, *La Marcha*, pp. 8, 13.

several of the Federación's members formed part of the Labor Code Commission, named by the government to elaborate Panama's first labor code, which was approved in 1947.[20] Female members of the Federación Sindical were successful in pressuring the commission to include clauses benefiting pregnant and nursing women.[21] The Federación Sindical also played a major role in the 1947 move to get the Filós-Haines treaties rejected by the National Assembly.[22]

Members of the Federación Sindical were also active in the formation of neighborhood associations in shantytown areas. In the early 1950s, the government attempted to remove squatters from various parts of Panama City. One of the rationales for doing so was esthetic. In addition, the land on which the squatters lived had appreciated substantially in value. The Federación Sindical was successful in staving off evictions in neighborhoods such as Boca la Caja and Panamá Viejo and in pressuring the government to buy land from private owners and subdivide it among the squatters in San Miguelito.[23]

For the most part, organized labor in this period was controlled by a core of highly disciplined and determined leaders who were not willing to compromise and acquiesce, as had previously been the case. The government, embodied in the figure of José Antonio Remón, who was chief of police until 1952 when he became president, had no qualms about using the full force of the police against demonstrators and brutally persecuting labor organizers.[24] Bolívar Vallarino, who succeded Remón as chief of police and remained in that position until the Torrijos takeover in 1968, shared Remón's views and continued his policies. Remón passed a law against communist organizations, and the Federación Sindical and the Federación de Estudiantes de Panamá (FEP) were banned. Labor leaders were singled out and persecuted, and in the midst of much red-baiting and witch-hunting, many had to go underground or into exile.[25]

It is not hard to understand why active unions were considered communist. Many of them had been affiliated with the Federación Sindical, and their leaders were known to have communist and socialist inclinations. However, it is a stigma that labor has not been able to rid itself of to this day, providing rhetorical grounds for the private sector to oppose most measures that will benefit labor. Whenever the business community wants to oppose a labor measure or to squelch a legitimate labor concern, it accuses the movement of being communist-inspired or led. This attitude on the part of business leaders

[20] Lorenzo Mora, "Síntesis histórica del movimiento obrero panameño." Mimeo. Panamá: Instituto Superior de Estudios Sindicales, 1979, p. 11.

[21] Interview with Marta Matamoros.

[22] These treaties proposed a 20-year lease extension for the 13 bases the United States had occupied outside of the Canal Zone territory during the Second World War. Renato Pereira, *Panamá: fuerzas armadas y política*. Panamá: Ediciones Nueva Panamá, 1979, p. 16.

[23] Interview with José Meneses, secretary general of the CNTP.

[24] Larry LaRae Pippin, *The Remon Era: An Analysis of a Decade of Events in Panama (1947-1957)*. Stanford: Institute of Hispanic American and Luso-Brazilian Studies, 1964, p. 94.

[25] Pereira, *Panamá: fuerzas armadas*, p. 23.

has tended to preclude dialogue between the private sector and organized labor.

The other significant event related to labor in the 1950s was the founding of the Confederación de Trabajadores de la República de Panamá (CTRP) in 1956. This confederation was formed with the blessing of the Remón government, under pressure from the United States, to counterbalance the unions under the aegis of the Federación Sindical. The CTRP remained the only labor confederation in Panama until 1970 when Torrijos upgraded the Federación Sindical to a confederation, the Central Nacional de Trabajadores de Panamá (CNTP). Apart from government approval, the CTRP enjoyed strong support from the AFL-CIO and from the American Institute for Free Labor Development (AIFELD). Included among its largest unions were the locals servicing the U.S. army and the Panama Canal Company, as well as the Federation of Hotel and Restaurant Workers.

During the 1960s the labor movement continued to grow, and the cleavage between the ideological tendencies represented by CTRP and the Federación Sindical became more pronounced. The decade also witnessed four major movements of labor unrest involving the banana and sugarcane workers and the typographers' union.

The first of these movements began in November 1960, when workers of the United Fruit Company went on strike in Bocas del Toro. The strike quickly spread to Puerto Armuelles and ended two weeks later with a new collective agreement setting wages at 36 and 37 cents per hour. Labor unrest on the banana plantations was not a new phenomenon. From the late 1930s, the plantation workers had tried to organize in both of the areas where the plantations are located, Bocas del Toro on the Atlantic Coast and Puerto Armuelles on the Pacific. Each time, the company (United Fruit, later known as United Brands) engaged in massive firings. One tactic often employed, especially in the Pacific Coast area, was to load the "rabble-rousers" with their families and belongings into trains, take them deep into the grasslands of Chiriquí, and abandon them.[26] In the early 1950s, the United Fruit Company allowed the formation of a company union, or *sindicato amarillo*,[27] and in 1955 the company and the union negotiated the first collective agreement in Panamanian labor history.[28] Salaries were established between 16 and 25 cents per hour, and workdays ran 12 to 16 hours.[29] The company preferred to pay by piecework, which made salaries even lower. This, coupled with terrible

---

[26] Carlos J. George, "La conciliación y el arbitraje en materia laboral y su vigencia en Panamá," Tesis de Licenciatura. Panamá: Universidad de Panamá, 1972, p. 206.

[27] Humberto E. Ricord et al., *Panamá y la Frutera*. Panamá: Editorial Universitaria, 1974, p. 40.

[28] Dimas Espinosa y Jorge E. Vissuetti, "Movimiento reinvidicativo del Sindicato de Trabajadores de la Chiriquí Land Company - Sección de Puerto Armuelles, 1960," Tesis de Licenciatura. Panamá: Universidad de Panamá, 1978, pp. 35-36.

[29] George, "La conciliación," p. 210.

working conditions, created widespread discontent. Morale was lowest in Bocas del Toro, on the Atlantic Coast, where the labor force included large numbers of Indians who were given the worst tasks and were often cheated out of their meager salaries.[30]

The most significant gain of the 1960 strike was the right to form independent unions, and thus the Sindicatos de Trabajadores de la Chiriquí Land Company (SITRACHILCO) of Bocas del Toro and of Puerto Armuelles were established.[31] The Bocas del Toro union affiliated with the CTRP and the one in Puerto Armuelles with the Federación Sindical. In 1964, a new strike erupted in Puerto Armuelles, lasting over a month. The strikers protested the indiscriminate use of herbicides and the lack of protective gear for the workers engaged in this dangerous work.[32]

Another large strike involved the sugarcane workers affiliated with the CTRP, who went on strike to demand the company's compliance with a newly enacted law raising rural salaries to two dollars per day. In March 1965, the union, Sindicato Industrial de Trabajadores del Azúcar, Sus Derivados y Afines, asked for a new collective agreement to raise salaries to the level set by the new law. The company, Azucarera Nacional, tried to stretch negotiations so that the new salary would not go into effect until after the harvest.[33] The workers took their case to the local labor office, which ruled in favor of the employer. About 300 workers went on strike and began a 130-mile walk on the Pan-American Highway to Panama City to elicit support from the government and from the urban masses.[34]

Upon their arrival in the city, the president tried to mediate, but to no avail. A 24-hour general strike was called in the City of Panama, carrying the threat by organized labor that if an agreement favorable to the cane workers was not reached, the sympathy strike would be prolonged indefinitely. Two days later Azucarera Nacional agreed to renegotiate the collective agreement, reinstate 70 percent of the striking workers, and pay them their back salaries.[35] In this case, even though the workers won, it was at a cost of 30 percent of their jobs.

The last labor unrest of any significance in this period, and the most devastating to the working class, involved the typographers, a militant and well-organized union of the FSTRP, which had a collective agreement with the Cámara Nacional de Artes Gráficas. In 1965, a worker was fired from one of the printing companies, allegedly for economic reasons. The union went on strike, and the strike was declared illegal because of procedural violations,

---

[30] Espinosa y Vissuetti, "Movimiento reinvidicativo," pp. 33-34.
[31] George, "La conciliación," pp. 217-219.
[32] Interview with José Nemo Herrera, former labor leader of SITRACHILCO and labor director for Chiriquí Province, Ministry of Labor.
[33] This would save the company a considerable amount of money because only about one third of the labor force in the sugar industry is employed full time and the other two thirds are employed only during harvesting.
[34] George, "La conciliación," pp. 223-230.
[35] Gandásegui et al., Las luchas, p. 66.

which meant that all striking workers could be fired for participating in an illegal strike. Over 350 workers lost their jobs. The union appealed to the Superior Labor Tribunal, which upheld the verdict of the illegality of the strike. This incident was a grave setback not only for the typographers but for the entire labor sector.[36]

These sporadic outbursts of labor unrest that took place during the 1950s and 1960s serve to illustrate the condition of organized labor and the maneuvers it had to engage in to achieve the most meager gains. The working class had no status or power, and the organizations representing workers had to engage in heroic antics just to get the attention of those in power. Because of the above, when labor groups acted, they usually engaged in desperate measures to publicize their plight. This gave them a reputation for being ruthless and tough. One public official described the unions as being "mean" (bravos).[37] These desperate tactics were necessary to obtain very modest results, as the outcomes of the conflicts described previously demonstrate.

The degree of success of these protest movements depended on the size of the group protesting and on the support it could wrest from other labor groups and from the popular sector. The more dramatic the appeal, the greater the degree of success. Thus the marches with large numbers of workers, either on the Trans-Isthmian Highway in the case of the Marcha del Hambre y la Desesperación or along the Pan-American Highway in the case of the sugar-cane workers, drew a great amount of media coverage and much popular support, which in turn influenced the results. Second, the more general the issue under appeal, the greater the support of the public and the chances for success. Thus, protests for renters' laws, minimum wages, and the reduction of food or gasoline prices had a greater degree of success than those for wage increases within a union or for the illegal firing of union members. Third, the results always fell far short of the demands. The precedent established during these years provided a pattern that unions would continue to follow, even in better times for labor. When collective agreements were mandated through the 1972 Labor Code, one of the complaints of the private sector was that union demands were always highly exaggerated. Union leaders knew from experience that unless they presented inflated demands, they would end up with little. As one labor leader said "if you want a 5 cent raise and you ask for 5 cents, you end up with one cent."[38]

## FROM 1968 TO THE PRESENT

During the first months after the National Guard takeover, several labor leaders were jailed along with student leaders and leftists. After Torrijos was

---

[36] George, "La conciliación," pp. 241-252.
[37] Interview with Fernando Manfredo, former presidential chief of staff, and highest ranking Panamanian in the Panama Canal Commission.
[38] Interview with José Meneses.

in control, he set free many of the leftist elements and the politicians held in jail.[39] By early 1969, with power firmly in his hands, Omar Torrijos tried to develop support that would lend legitimacy to his regime. This effort had major implications for labor, because that was one of the groups Torrijos turned to for support and popular backing. The growth of organized labor was promoted and mechanisms were established to both foster and control its future evolution. Among many innovations, a labor ministry was set up, and Rómulo Escobar Bethancourt, a former student activist and controversial political figure, was named labor minister. With Escobar Bethancourt at the helm, Torrijos tried to make unionization mandatory and to force labor into one organization, the Central Unica de Trabajadores (CUT), as the most expedient means of achieving his goals of strengthening labor and making it a viable political force.

The Central Unica de Trabajadores was seen as a fitting mechanism for the enhancement of the labor sector. Escobar Bethancourt, in his book on the Torrijos regime, asserted that the weakness of labor vis-à-vis the business sector prompted the idea of establishing forced unionization and one central. This seemed the only way of obtaining in a short time "a change in the panorama of the unions."[40] Organized labor as a unified group could be a powerful force and could serve many purposes for a government that had no strong societal backing.

However, both the CTRP and the Federación Istmeña de Trabajadores Católicos (FITC, which later became the Central Istmeña de Trabajadores - CIT) strongly opposed the idea of the CUT. The CTRP, with its strong ties to U.S. labor, claimed that this was against ILO agreements ratified by Panama regarding freedom to unionize and against basic human rights.[41] It may be that Torrijos was weary of antagonizing the United States, given the fact that his position was still not very strong, and that he backed off due to the intractable position of the CTRP regarding the CUT. This may be the reason why the idea of the CUT was abandoned and new tactics had to be found to strengthen labor.[42]

On Labor Day (May 1) 1969, Torrijos attended the celebrations of the banana workers' SITRACHILCO union in Puerto Armuelles. This was his first real contact with a large proletarian mass (the union had a membership of over 6,000 workers), and the event left a lasting impression on him. The lushness of the setting together with the open and direct approach of the workers must have provided a real contrast to Torrijos's life in the barracks and among

---

[39] Among those set free were Carlos Iván Zúñiga, who had made his name as a lawyer for the banana workers and had been elected by them to the National Assembly in 1964, and Efigenio Araúz, a banana union leader. Pereira, *Panamá: fuerzas armadas*, p. 127.

[40] Rómulo Escobar Bethancourt, *Torrijos: Colonia Americana, No!* Panamá: Carlos Valencia Editores, 1981, p. 94.

[41] Interview with Philip Dean Butcher, former secretary general of the CTRP.

[42] In 1975, the idea of one labor central again surfaced with the same results.

politicians in the city. The bond that was established that May between Torrijos and the banana workers was cemented in December 1969 during an attempted counter-coup against him, when these workers took over Puerto Armuelles and then marched to David to await Torrijos's arrival from Mexico. The workers then followed Torrijos to Panama, and what had almost been his demise became a triumphal reassertion of his control. The tie established then between Torrijos and the banana workers became indelible.

Many observers claim that it was the banana workers who pushed for a new Labor Code.[43] It was among them that Torrijos announced the enactment of the law for the thirteenth-month salary. From the march on Panama City in December 1969 until he returned to the barracks in 1978, Torrijos maintained close contact with these workers, gave many of his famous speeches to them, and attended their celebrations. The workers had easy access to him. Conversely, people claim that whenever Torrijos wanted to think over some new measure, especially if it pertained to labor or the popular sectors, he would go to Puerto Armuelles and talk it out with the workers.

Once Torrijos was forced to abandon his idea of the CUT, he began to concentrate on a new labor code. Along with the code and the organization of the Labor Ministry, other measures were instituted to improve the position of organized labor. The Labor Code provided for the formation of the Consejo Nacional de Trabajadores (CONATO), a consultative body made up of the heads of the confederations and centrals to look after labor matters. Because of the ideological split among the labor organizations, CONATO was not very effective in its actions because its members had difficulty reaching consensus. However, in 1980 and 1981, organized labor was able to coalesce and work for a common cause, and CONATO provided the leadership for the campaign against Ley 95.

Another approach of the government after the rejection of the CUT was to strengthen and upgrade the Federación Sindical. This move was apparently taken to win an ally well versed in organizational techniques and mass demonstrations and to create a counterweight to the U.S.-dominated CTRP. Since 1956, the CTRP had been the only labor confederation in existence in Panama.[44] In 1970, the Federación Sindical became the Central Nacional de Trabajadores de Panamá (CNTP).

Throughout the decade there were many occasions when the CNTP appeared to receive preferential treatment from the government. In 1973, the

---

[43] Interview with Carlos Iván Zúñiga, lawyer for the SITRACHILCO Union and highly respected socialist politician.

[44] There are four types of unions in Panama: unions representing a particular enterprise; unions representing a guild; mixed unions; and industrial unions representing a particular industry or sector. A union must have 50 members to be recognized. Two or more unions can form a federation, and two or more federations can form a central or confederation. The government has given recognition to the centrals and confederations as the highest representatives of labor by forming CONATO, which is made up of the secretary generals of all such organizations.

CNTP Congress was held in the National Assembly building.[45] Also in 1973, the two large unions of banana workers—SITRACHILCO of Puerto Armuelles, which had previously been independent, and SITRACHILCO of Bocas, which had been a CTRP affiliate—became affiliated with the CNTP. Many union leaders and businessmen declared in interviews that unions seeking recognition would gain it much more quickly if they affiliated with the CNTP rather than another group.[46] Clearly, CNTP membership grew very rapidly. In 1973, the first year for which there are figures, the CNTP had about half as many affiliates as the CTRP, whereas in 1978, the two organizations had about an equal number of affiliates.

Table 2    Union Membership, 1950-1978

| Years | Economically active population | Unions | Union members | Percentage |
|-------|-------------------------------|--------|---------------|------------|
| 1950 | * | 6 | 6,386 | * |
| 1960 | * | 19 | 17,247 | * |
| 1970 | 299,400 | 67 | 21,614 | 7.2 |
| 1975 | 231,634 | 217 | 80,550 | 17.6 |
| 1978 | 499,240 | 192 | 69,522 | 13.9 |

*data not available.

Source: Ministerio de Trabajo, Sección de Estadísticas Laborales, Las organizaciones sindicales en Panamá. Panamá: MIPPE, 1978, p. 27; Ministerio de Trabajo, Asesoría de Programación Sectorial, Estadísticas laborales 1975-1978. Panamá: MIPPE, 1979, p. 26.

Although the CNTP seemed favored in these regards, the picture is complicated by the many developments related to organized labor in the 1070s. In 1970, the government named José de la Rosa Castillo, a labor leader from Local 900 and the CTRP, as minister of labor.[47] During his tenure, De la Rosa Castillo was responsible for the law establishing the internal regulations of the MITRAB. At about the same time, Philip Dean Butcher, a prominent member of Local 900 and subsequently secretary general of the CTRP, was named ambassador to Jamaica.[48] Although symbolic, these two appointments had enormous repercussions not only within labor but to the society at large. They were important because they marked the first time that a government had given public recognition to someone from the popular sector. Both of these appointees, it should be noted, were members of the CTRP. If the government had been truly partial to the CNTP, it is improbable that members of the CTRP would have been selected for such recognition.

[45] "Clausuró Congreso de Trabajo con sendos acuerdos," Matutino, September 10, 1973.
[46] The figures provided by the MITRAB are aggregates and one cannot ascertain the affiliation of the unions given official recognition, nor do we know the number of members that each union has.
[47] Pereira, Panamá: fuerzas armadas, p. 134.
[48] Interview with Philip Dean Butcher.

Torrijos also encouraged the formation of labor groups other than the CNTP and the CTRP. In 1971, the Central Istmeña de Trabajadores (CIT), representing the Christian line of organized labor, was recognized officially. The Central Nacional de Trabajadores del Transporte (CPTT), organized in 1975, brought together all unions dealing with public transportation into one body where they would be easy to control. The labor groups most affected by this were the CTRP and CIT, who each lost an entire federation to the new central. Table 2 shows the growth of organized labor from the 1940s on.

A lesson not lost on politicians was how easy it was to paralyze the cities of Panama and Colon and what a powerful group the public transportation drivers could be. Along with organizing the CPTT, the government also organized the private bus lines into co-ops, helped owners buy new buses, and curtailed independent drivers. The CPTT became the allocator of new licenses to operate taxis and buses and the purchaser of subsidized gasoline. The leaders of the CPTT were close to prominent government officials. When the government party, the PRD, was formed in 1978, some of the CPTT leaders, such as Secretary General Nageli Herrera, were to occupy prominent positions within it.

The CPTT was later to feel the wrath of the government for not toeing the line. In 1979, the Federación Nacional de Conductores de Taxi (FENACOTA) went on strike to protest rises in gasoline and basic staples prices. The government warned the CPTT that there would be repercussions if they took any such action. During the strike, the police went into the parking lot of FENACOTA and destroyed about 40 taxis.[49] For the mass demonstrations against Ley 95 held in January 28-29, 1980, the CPTT was very careful to declare that it would not strike. However, it could not control its membership. By the second day, public transportation was paralyzed, contributing to the success of the strike.

Although the pro-labor measures enacted by the government seemed very progressive, they had many constraints built into them. MITRAB became an omnipotent presence in labor issues. It was empowered to grant official recognition to new labor organizations. Although the Labor Code spells out a simple formula for gaining recognition, this can be withheld whenever the government finds it expedient.[50] The Central Auténtica de Trabajadores Independientes (CATI), formed in 1976 from two federations that had split off from CIT and from an independent federation, was not granted recognition until 1981. The reason appears to be that CATI is a true independent central

---

[49] "Huelga de transportes colectivos," *Diálogo Social*, June 1973.

[50] Article 352 of the Labor Code states that if the request for recognition of a new organization meets all the requirements, the MITRAB has 30 non-prorrogable days in which to grant recognition. If at that time it does not do it, the organization can send the request to the president of the republic, who has two months to respond. At the end of the two months if no objection or rejection is made, the organization is considered registered (Article 356).

with no affiliations and was perceived as being difficult to control. The Sindicato Nacional de Bancarios (SINABAN) has been asking for recognition since the early 1970s, taking every opportunity to demand it and to embarrass the government for its violations of the Labor Code. The government apparently gave its word to the banking community that in order to prevent disruptions from labor unrest it would not allow a union of banking workers.

MITRAB controls other important union matters in addition to granting official recognition to unions. The books on which meeting minutes are kept, as well as those containing the accounting and the membership lists, have to be authorized by MITRAB and carry its seal on every page. Each union must send the ministry a list of its members every year, inform it of changes in its board of directors within two weeks, and have its minutes and its account books inspected by the ministry every six months. MITRAB also has some input on the use of funds. For instance, MITRAB has to approve the courses offered with the money from the educational tax. This tax is explained in Chapter 5. Also, the financial settlements resulting from labor demands have to go through MITRAB before reaching the worker. Initially, MITRAB also handled the Fondo de Garantía for the construction sector. At the end of a job, the lists of workers to receive the 6 percent from the fund were processed at MITRAB, with the worker receiving a voucher to have the money released by a bank. Following many protests by the construction union SUNTRACS over the slowness of the process, this is now handled between the construction companies and the union directly.

Some of these measures are very similar to those used in other Latin American countries to secure the alliance of organized labor. For Peru under Velasco Alvarado, Stephens mentions the formal recognition of unions, the siding with labor in wage settlements, the co-optation of labor leaders by offering them minor government positions, and financial assistance to labor groups as measures to secure the backing of labor. Stephens also lists ways in which the government maintains its control of labor. These include the division and co-optation of labor groups and leaders, the favoring of new organizations when problems arise with older ones, control of labor through legal provisions, and the exertion of selective repression. All of the above were also used in Panama by the Torrijos regime.[51]

Altogether 120 new unions with a total membership of 19,700 were recognized between 1970 and 1977. These unions represented 57 percent of the total number of unions, and their membership represented 30 percent of all unionized workers. The number of organized workers as a percentage of all workers in Panama had grown from an estimated 7.2 in the 1960s to 13.9 percent by 1978. The sectors most affected by increased unionization were the manufacturing sector, transportation and communication, and the utilities companies. The figures in Table 3 are not completely reliable. For instance, the

Table 3    Union Membership by Branch of Economic Activity, 1978

| Economic activity | Economically active population (EAP) | Union members | Percentage |
|---|---|---|---|
| Manufacturing | 48,640 | 28,368 | 43.3 |
| Transportation, warehousing | | | |
| & communication | 27,480 | 8,631 | 31.4 |
| Electricity, gas, water | 6,980 | 3,069 | 44.0 |
| Commercial activities | 65,920 | 13,197 | 20.0 |
| Social & personal services | 141,510 | 6,000 | 4.2 |
| Financial institutions, real estate | | | |
| and other services | 19,450 | * | * |
| Agriculture, forestry, | | | |
| hunting & fishing | 144,260 | 5,275 | 3.7 |
| Canal zone | 18,300 | * | * |
| Mining | 920 | * | * |
| Construction | 25,720 | 4,983 | 19.4 |
| Total | 499,240 | 69,522 | 13.9 |

* Data not available.

Source: Ministerio de Trabajo, Asesoría de Programación Sectorial, Estadísticas laborales 1975-1978. Panamá, 1979, p. 26 .

Union of Construction Workers SUNTRACS claimed a membership of 17,000, which would place the construction sector in first place, with 85 percent of its work force unionized, but SUNTRACS membership is not included in the official statistics provided by the Labor Ministry.

A further indication of the growth of organized labor is the number of collective agreements signed. Between 1970 and 1980 this number totaled more than 800, whereas before 1970, only 30 such agreements had been negotiated. Disregarding 1977 and 1978, when collective agreements were frozen due to Ley 95, an average of 92 agreements were negotiated each year of the decade.

By 1979 there were five centrals and several independent federations and unions. Of the independent unions the most important one is the Sindicato Unico Nacional de Trabajadores de la Construcción y Similares—SUNTRACS, which played as important a role in organized labor and in the life of the country toward the end of the 1970s decade as the SITRACHILCO unions had done up to then. Table 4 presents the figures for the affiliation and number of unions in each of the different centrals, for 1975 and 1978. Union membership had an impressive growth up to 1975, with 217 unions and 17.6 percent of the work force unionized. By 1978, the rate of growth of unions had decreased, and unionized workers dropped from 80,550 to 69,522, while the percentage of the work force in unions dropped to 13.9 percent. As stated before, these figures are not very reliable. For instance, because the government has never recognized the Union of Bank Workers (SINABAN), it does not include those workers. Another example of exclusion is the membership for CATI, because that central did not receive recognition until 1981.

Table 4    Labor Organizations and Membership

|  | 1975 (1) | | | 1978 (2) | | |
|---|---|---|---|---|---|---|
|  | Unions | Members | %* | Unions | Members | %* |
| CTRP | 70 | 19,916 | 24.8 | 60 | 24,756 | 35.6 |
| CNTP | 27 | 12,926 | 16.0 | 38 | 21,044 | 30.3 |
| CIT | 22 | 7,311 | 9.1 | 23 | 4,635 | 6.7 |
| CPTT | 10 | 5,262 | 6.5 | 22 | 5,233 | 7.5 |
| Indep. federat. | 4 | 14,030 | 17.4 | 4 | 2,556 | 3.7 |
| Indep. unions | 68 | 21,105 | 26.2 | 29 | 11,298 | 16.3 |
| CATI (3) |  |  |  |  | 4,000 |  |
| Totals: |  |  |  |  |  |  |
| Organized  Labor |  | 80,550 | 100.0 |  | 69,522 | 100.0 |
| EAP |  | 231,634 | 17.6 |  | 499,240 | 13.9 |

* Percentage economically active population.
Sources: (1) Ministerio de Trabajo, Asesoría de Programación Sectorial, Estadísticas laborales, 1974-1978, Panamá: MIPPE, p. 25; (2) Ministerio de Trabajo, Asesoría de Programación Sectorial, Estadísticas laborales, 1975-1978, Panamá: MIPPE, p. 22; (3) Interview with CATI officials.

## GROWTH AND DIVISION: THE LABOR MOVEMENT

There is no doubt that the labor movement grew in size and strength during the Torrijos years. Not only did organized labor grow but it also experienced some qualitative changes. Labor became more conscious of the potential it had for effectively advocating its rights. The changes brought about by the Labor Code and other labor laws made workers realize that the time was past for solving their problems on a one-to-one basis and for depending on the patrón's benevolence for improvements to their lives. Consciousness of the commonality of problems—of a working-class ideology—rose considerably, and workers began to use the mechanisms at their disposal to redress their problems. The various factions of organized labor were also able to unite on occasion to strive for common goals, such as the repeal of Ley 95.

All of this notwithstanding, the Panamanian labor movement continues to suffer from several structural problems that have been almost insurmountable and that weaken its position. One is the fact that the labor movement remains divided along ideological lines and the suspicion among labor groups is such that it negates their newly acquired working-class consciousness. This ideological division not only affects the two large centrals but also the smaller ones. According to many labor leaders, the CIT has had one of the most divisive roles within organized labor in the 1970s. CIT prevented any concerted actions by CONATO by vetoing its proposals and played a negative role in its dealings with the government and with the private sector. CIT is distrusted by the other labor groups, and in proportion to its size it has had a very detrimental impact on labor issues during the decade.

A result of the divisiveness of the labor sector is that in an effort of each central to promote its particular line and to play one group against another, several large segments of labor have been kept on the outside. Thus, SUNTRACS is not a member of CONATO because it is a union and not a central, although it represents about three times more workers than the two smaller centrals. The CPTT is also outside CONATO because it is integrated to include owners of vehicles as well as regular hired drivers. Although the government only recognizes a membership of approximately 5,000 for the CPTT, that organization claims to have at least 23,000 members. If that is the case, it is a group too large not to take into account.

Another problem of organized labor is the atomization and splintering of labor groups. Because the number needed for recognition of a union is small (50 members), disputes lead to splits and the formation of new groups. This contributes in great measure to the weakness of the unions and the lack of cohesiveness of organized labor.[52]

Probably one of the most serious problems for organized labor in Panama throughout its history has been the existence of the Canal Zone, with its attractive job market and much higher pay scale. The Canal Zone labor force represents the elite of Panamanian labor. Until the canal installations reverted to Panama, there was hardly a need for the two segments to mix. That picture has changed, and the hope is that the effects of the Canal Zone labor contingent on Panamanian labor will help strengthen it and improve its organization and its manner of operating.

Another real problem for labor is the attitude of the private sector toward it. This is part and parcel of a set of values held by businessmen and industrialists, which see their role as one of paternalistic benefactors and the work force as composed of childlike and irresponsible people who must be kept under tight control. Even though the labor laws have been complied with, they are challenged constantly and have not been accepted by private enterprise, which does not recognize labor demands as legitimate. This, coupled with the fact that the private sector sees labor organizations as communist and so is ready to destroy them at the first opportunity, precludes any possibility of dialogue and makes the situation an extremely difficult one. If the private sector would at some point accept the demands of labor as legitimate ones and be willing to negotiate with labor organizations, then there would be room for improvements. But as long as the private sector maintains its traditional attitude against labor, if power reverts to their hands, they will eliminate all benefits labor achieved under Torrijos. Considering that labor will not back down willingly to conditions before 1972, if the power reversal takes place (and there is every indication that it will) then Panama is headed for what Zúñiga has termed a class war.[53]

---

[52] According to Eduardo Ríos, the secretary general of SUNTRACS, in 1981 there were 31 unions representing petty commerce workers.
[53] Interview with Carlos Iván Zúñiga.

Torrijos's singling out labor as a group to incorporate and upgrade, and doing so through the various labor laws enacted in its favor, was a shrewd move on his part to gain the support he needed to legitimize his regime. But while the government secured improvements for organized labor, it also set in place the mechanisms to maintain a tight control on its actions and its development. It did so through the role it assigned to MITRAB through the increased benefits to labor as a sector and through the buying and co-opting of labor leaders.[54]

In the relation between the Torrijos regime and labor, the 1972 Labor Code was the centerpiece policy that provided the legal framework for the changes envisioned for the labor sector. The 1972 Labor Code, then, was instrumental in the development of the labor sector during the 1970s decade and in the changes brought about in the political landscape by the Torrijos regime. In the next chapter, we will discuss the implications of the 1972 Labor Code as well as the most important modifications introduced through its enactment of progressive policy such as the 1972 Labor Code.

---

[54] Articles 379 and 380 are perfect examples of the role given MITRAB and of the state paternalism exercised by the government. They read: "The Panamanian state through the MITRAB is obligated to promote the establishment of unions, in the areas or sectors where they are lacking, respecting the right of workers to form the type and number of unions they deem conventient (Art. 379)." And, "The MITRAB must provide to the social organizations [unions] the technical assistance they need, and will organize programs, courses, and seminars dealing with union capacitation and labor education." (Art. 380).

# 5

# THE 1972 LABOR CODE

The enactment of the 1972 Labor Code was the single most important act engaged in by the Torrijos regime to incorporate the labor sector in order to gain popular backing as well as legitimacy for the regime. The Labor Code served as the ideological métier that defined the regime as reformist, inclusionary, and populist. The enactment of that labor policy set into motion a series of measures that brought about a change in the balance of power of the country's social structure. This was accomplished by singling out a sector previously dispossessed of power and by providing it with an enhanced position in the socio-political landscape.

The working class, along with subsistence peasants, was one of the sectors chosen by Torrijos for incorporation. These two groups make up the bulk of Panamanian population and their support would provide a strong popular base to the regime. In the rhetoric of the early days Torrijos spoke of "hacer patria," by which he meant the building up of a country through the incorporation of Panamanians previously outside the mainstream of social and economic life. The inclusion of wage earners and peasants would bring into the forefront the main components of Panamanian society, which would fulfill the goals of Torrijos's "revolutionary process."

Subsistence peasants were approached through a variety of measures, most importantly through an agrarian reform with emphasis on collectivization through *asentamientos campesinos* (agricultural settlements) and cooperative programs, the creation of the Banco de Desarrollo Agropecuario (BDA), the strengthening of the Ministerio de Desarrollo Agropecuario (MIDA), and later on, the establishment of various state enterprises related to agricultural pursuits. Many large infrastructural projects also had direct effect on the peasant population, such as hydroelectric projects that allowed the expansion of the electric network into the countryside, irrigation projects, construction of feeder roads, the creation of the Corporación Nacional del Bayano, and the expansion of the medical and the educational systems.

For labor other measures were specifically instituted to strengthen its position and promote it as a viable alternative political force to the private sector. Most important among these were the creation of the Ministerio de Trabajo y Bienestar Social (MITRAB) in 1970 and the enactment of a new Labor Code in 1972. The 1972 Labor Code helped define the nature of the Torrijos regime as quite different from the traditional political approach of the former ruling elite. The Torrijos regime was able to enact such policy because at that particular moment it enjoyed relative autonomy from all other societal forces, which gave it ample room to maneuver. The 1972 Labor Code, then, was a direct outcome of the relative autonomy enjoyed by the Torrijos regime during its first years in power.

The alliance of the state with subordinate groups such as labor strengthened the position of the regime and at the same time provided the means for incorporating a sector that would act as an ally and would provide the change in the balance of power of the social structure. This chapter will analyze the 1972 Labor Code, the main changes it introduced, and the significance of those changes.[1]

## ANTECEDENTS TO THE 1972 LABOR CODE

The first important laws regarding labor issues enacted in Panama after its independence from Colombia were Ley 6a of 1914, which established an eight-hour workday for laborers and employees in commercial enterprises, and laws 17 and 42 of 1916, concerning work injuries. Another law of some importance, directly concerned with workers' benefits, was Ley 8a of 1931, which established a system of retirement pensions for which employers were to be responsible.[2] This law also granted one month of paid vacation per year to each worker.[3]

In 1941, a second constitution was passed that included numerous social rights and some basic norms regulating worker-employer relations. This constitution espoused such principles as work as a social obligation to be protected by the state, the regulatory capacity of the state in the relations between capital and labor, the right to strike, and others. These norms and other existing labor laws were then compiled in Law Decree no. 38 of 1941, which was the first effort to systematize the existing labor laws. Law Decree no. 38 contained 112 articles that pertained to issues such as length of the

---

[1] Although the code was enacted into law in December 1971, it went into effect in April 1972, so it will be called the 1972 Labor Code. The previous labor code was enacted into law in November 1946 and became operational in March 1947 and is known as the 1947 Labor Code.

[2] The retirement pensions were only awarded those workers with over 30 years of service; those who had accrued between 10 and 20 years received one month salary for each year of service at the time of retirement.

[3] Humberto E. Ricord, "El código de 1972: cambio radical en la legislación laboral panameña," *Revista Jurídica Panameña*, no. 2(1974): 140.

workday, compensation for work risks, and vacations. It also addressed the judicial problems arising from labor relations.[4]

The 1941 Constitution was replaced in 1946 by a new one, Panama's third. This constitution included a Third Chapter related to labor issues with 14 articles, which included items such as minimum salary (which was unembargable and had to be adjusted periodically), right to unionize, maximum workdays of 8 hours and 7 hours for night shifts, a maximum workweek of 48 hours, special protection for women and children, non-renunciability of workers' rights, regulation of the work contract, maternity benefits, and others.[5] These labor-related issues included in the 1946 Constitution were based on those contained in the Cuban Constitution of 1940.[6]

On November 11, 1946, by Law Decree no. 67, Panama's first labor code was approved. The code went into effect in March 1947, and according to Panamanian labor experts, it was a carbon copy of Costa Rica's 1943 Labor Code.[7] The Costa Rican code was based on the Ley Federal Mexicana de Legislación del Trabajo of 1932, U.S. labor laws of the late 1930s, and some of the International Labor Organization (ILO) convention agreements ratified by that country. The Panamanian code also included several articles from Colombian labor law.

Although this first Panamanian labor code contained many clauses regarding the protection of workers, its tenor was clearly on the side of the business sector. It stated that the role of the state was to "regulate the relations between capital and labor, placing them on a base of social justice . . . without harming [perjudicar] either part." The Labor Code should "guarantee the worker the necessary conditions for a normal existence, and capital a just compensation for its investments."[8]

The 1947 Labor Code recognized the right to strike. This was simply a *proforma* recognition, because the clauses governing strikes were so stringent and complicated that it was almost impossible for a strike to meet the requirements for legality. The code also recognized the *fuero sindical* (union privilege) for a reduced number of labor leaders, but it had no provisions for enforcing its compliance. And although the code included an article on

---

[4] Rolando Murgas T., "Panamá," in *La intervención del estado en las relaciones industriales en la década de los 80*. Madrid: Instituto de Estudios Sociales, 1982, p. 1.

[5] José A. Sossa, "Relaciones obrero-patronales y situación del sindicalismo." Mimeo. Panamá: n.p., 1981, pp. 16-17.

[6] Humberto E. Ricord, "Lecciones de derecho laboral panameño," in *Apuntes de derecho del trabajo*, edited by Jorge Fábrega. Panamá: Escuela de Derecho, 1976, p. 21.

[7] Although by 1946, the Costa Rican Code had been modified and those changes that tended to be progressive were not included in the Panamanian version. Dr. Humberto Ricord calls Panama's first Labor Code a *ad peddem litterae* of the one from Costa Rica. "Lecciones," p. 20. Lic. Jorge Fábrega has written a monograph comparing both codes, clause by clause. Interview with Lic. Jorge Fábrega, president of the 1972 Labor Code Commission.

[8] Ricord, "Lecciones," pp. 31-32.

minimum wage, it took 12 years and a massive protest movement by organized labor before the first minimum wage law was put into effect in Panama.[9] Even though Article 73 of the 1946 Constitution could be interpreted as establishing a system of employment stability, the 1947 Labor Code established an opposite system, giving the employer the unilateral right to fire a worker as long as he paid an indemnization, or *preaviso*, for an amount of up to two months salary.[10]

Complaints about the 1947 Labor Code were frequent among organized labor, but it wasn't until the mid-1960s that they were finally heard by those in power. After two devastating strikes by the banana workers in 1960 and 1965, another large strike by the sugarcane workers in 1964, and one by the typographers' union in 1965, the government decided to update the 1947 Labor Code. In 1967, during the administration of President Marco A. Robles, a commission was named to elaborate a new labor code. The final document was presented to the National Assembly in January 1968, but by that time, it was too late to discuss it in that session of the legislature.[11] After the presidential elections held in May of 1968, and before the new National Assembly had time to convene, the government of newly elected President Arnulfo Arias was overthrown, and the Labor Code Project was temporarily shelved by the military officers who took power.

One of the first steps taken by the Torrijos government in its effort to promote the growth and strength of the labor sector was to upgrade the Labor Relations Section from a simple department in the Ministerio de Trabajo, Previsión Social y Salud Pública, to ministerial level, thus creating the Ministerio de Trabajo y Bienestar Social (MITRAB) in January 1969.[12] Dr. César Martans, a young labor lawyer who had attained prominence in his dealings on behalf of the banana workers, was appointed first labor minister. Martans was soon replaced by Dr. Rómulo Escobar Bethancourt, a former student activist and lawyer of leftist leanings, whom Torrijos chose to make prominent in his cabinet.

Through Escobar Bethancourt, the government presented the idea of forced unionization of all workers and the establishment of one labor central, the Central Unica de Trabajadores (CUT). There was an immediate negative reaction to this proposal from most unions, especially those in the Confederación de Trabajadores de la República de Panamá (CTRP) and the unions of the Federación Istmeña de Trabajadores Católicos (FITC). The CTRP claimed that the forced formation of a single union was against ILO

---

[9] That was the Marcha del Hambre y la Desesperación of October 1959.

[10] In 1959 the *preaviso* scale was improved, although the maximum paid was six months salary after 25 years of employment. Ricord, "Lecciones," p. 21.

[11] Two ILO technicians, Dr. Jose Segadas Vianna from Brazil and Dr. Aníbal Aguilar Peñarrieta from Bolivia, advised the commission during the elaboration of the project.

[12] Cabinet Decree no. 2 of January 15, 1969.

agreements of freedom to unionize and that it also violated the principles of human rights.[13] This issue cost Escobar Bethancourt the ministry and he was replaced by José de la Rosa Castillo, a former labor leader.[14]

Another measure favorable to workers enacted by the Torrijos government early on was a law governing work-related injuries, or *riesgos profesionales*.[15] Before this law was passed, as established in the 1947 Labor Code, all workers had to be insured against work-related injuries. But the insurance was handled through private companies and no mechanisms were established to monitor adherence or to penalize employers who did not comply with it. The new law stated that "all state and private workers must be insured against professional risks and coverage will be regulated by the Caja de Seguro Social (CSS)." Because the establishment of an integrated social security system had been a frequent demand of Panamanian unions, using the Caja de Seguro Social to handle all cases of injuries was a first step toward establishing some type of system of socialized medicine.[16]

## THE 1972 LABOR CODE

In April 1971, the government named a commission to revise the Labor Code Project elaborated in 1967 during the Robles administration.[17] The commission was presided over by Lic. Jorge Fábrega and comprised Dr. Rolando Murgas, Lic. Luis A. Shirley, Lic. Rosario Oller de Sarasqueta, and Lic. Américo Rivera as principal members and Dr. Arturo Hoyos and Lic. Jaime Jované as adjunct members. Several aspects regarding the members of this commission warrant attention. Lic. Jorge Fábrega and Lic. Rosario Oller de Sarasqueta had been members of the 1967 commission, which had elaborated the project under discussion. These two lawyers, along with Lic. Américo Rivera were well-known representatives of the private sector in labor issues and were highly respected lawyers. The other members of the commission were extremely young and dynamic and known for their concern with social issues.[18] Murgas had just returned from completing doctoral studies on labor law in Italy, and along with Shirley and Hoyos,

---

[13] Interviews with Dr. Rolando Murgas, member of the 1972 Labor Code Commission and minister of labor (1972-1975), and Mr. Philip Dean Butcher, former secretary general of the CTRP.

[14] Leader of Local 900, the union of civilian employees in the Canal Zone. Renato Pereira, *Panamá: fuerzas armadas y política*, Panamá: Ediciones Nueva Universidad, 1979, p. 134.

[15] Cabinet Decree no. 68 of March 31, 1970.

[16] Humberto E. Ricord, "El sistema panameño de riesgos profesionales," *Revista Jurídica Panameña*, no. 1 (1973): 119.

[17] "Designada la Comisión del Código de Trabajo," *Matutino*, April 16, 1971.

[18] At the time the code was being elaborated they were all in their mid- to late twenties.

went on to hold important posts in the Ministry of Labor after the code was enacted into law.[19]

The commission was given ample leeway by the government in preparing the code, with only some guidelines of what must be incorporated and some parameters to follow. Torrijos kept close tabs on the work of the commission and met often with the codifiers to discuss different aspects of the labor code under elaboration. One issue on which he and the commission disagreed concerned the percentage of foreign-born employees that firms would be allowed to have. Fábrega wanted to "nationalize management" but Torrijos did not agree, given the nature of private enterprise in Panama. Another area of disagreement was the length of the workweek. Although Torrijos wanted it reduced to 40 hours, Fábrega felt that that would have a negative impact on productivity.[20] Among the points the government expected the new labor code to incorporate were the following:

1. Include workers excluded in the previous Labor Code, such as fishermen, bus and taxi drivers, street vendors working for a company, and artists.
2. Make collective agreements mandatory.
3. Stipulate that all workers benefiting from a collective agreement must pay union dues to the union that negotiated the agreement.
4. Provide workers with some type of stability of employment.
5. Modify the clauses that empowered the employer to unilaterally change the working conditions, or *jus variandi*.
6. Protect the salaries of workers.
7. Control the amount of overtime a worker can be forced to work.
8. Establish a seniority bonus, or *prima de antigüedad*.
9. Provide added protection to pregnant women.
10. Insure workers the right to their vacations.
11. Establish controls for piecework (*trabajo a destajo*).
12. Establish regulations so that strikes can be declared legal.[21]

Although all of the above were important, perhaps the most important point as far as the government was concerned was to force employers to negotiate collective agreements at the request of the union, because this was one of the most direct ways of fostering the growth of unions and of collectivizing labor relations. One issue that generated tremendous negative repercussions concerned stability of employment. The private sector

[19] Murgas became vice-minister under de la Rosa Castillo and then minister until late 1975. Shirley became Murgas's vice-minister and Hoyos national director of employment.
[20] Interviews with Dr. Rolando Murgas and Lic. Jorge Fábrega.
[21] Interview with Lic. Jorge Fábrega.
May 9, 1971.

was vehemently opposed to such guarantees and launched a relentless campaign against it.

For the elaboration of the 1972 Labor Code, the *codificadores* (members of the labor code commission) used the 1947 Labor Code and the 1967 Labor Code Project, as well as the Mexican Labor Law of 1970—in particular the part regarding special contracts. They also drew on labor law precedents from Panama, aspects of fair labor practice from U.S. law, authority opinions reached by international labor scholars, and ILO agreements ratified by Panama.[22] One aspect of the code that was specifically designed with Panama's service-oriented economy in mind was that of regulating *sociedades anónimas*, or "corporations that pierce the corporate veil." These measures were intended to protect workers who might be affected by the artificial manipulation of such companies.

The government pressured the commission to produce a new Labor Code quickly, and its members began consulting with the private sector and union leaders as soon as it was officially installed. It first met with representatives of both sectors in Panama City in early May,[23] and then traveled to key towns in the interior such as Chitré, Santiago, and Aguadulce.[24] The last stop of the commission was Chiriquí, where it met with banana workers and with members of that province's private sector.[25]

Organized labor joined forces in a "Comité Intersindical Pro Defensa del Nuevo Código de Trabajo" and spent time planning a strategy to have its wishes and expectations taken into account by the commission.[26] At the same time, the private sector presented a series of proposals to the commission regarding various aspects of labor. These proposals, published in the local newspapers, concerned strikes and work stoppages, collective agreements, maternity protection, and protection for sailors and marines.[27] The most comprehensive of these proposals pertained to the clauses regulating the work and rest periods (*jornadas de trabajo*) and included a comparison of wages as well as vacation time and the payment of Sundays in Panama and Central America. The private sector made a strong plea for being allowed to either pay for Sundays and reduce the amount of holiday and vacation time or to not pay for Sundays and leave the amount of vacation unchanged.[28]

---

[22] Interview with Lic. Jorge Fábrega.

[23] "Comisión revisora del Código Laboral invita a dos importantes reuniones," *Crítica*, April 30, 1971.

[24] "Discuten nuevo Código Laboral," *Matutino*, May 17, 1971.

[25] "Vienen a Chiriquí los comisionados del nuevo Código de Trabajo," *Estrella de Panamá*,

[26] Comisión Pro-defensa del nuevo Código de Trabajo," *Estrella de Panamá*, May 14, 1971.

[27] "Observaciones del Sector Privado al Anteproyecto del Código de Trabajo," *Estrella de Panamá*, May 13-14, 1971; "La empresa privada analiza jornada de trabajo y de descanso del nuevo código," *Estrella de Panamá*, June 10, 11, 13, 16, 1971; "Observaciones del CONEP al Artículo III," *Estrella de Panamá*, July 15, 1971.

[28] In the document published in the local press, the private sector called for paying Sundays and reducing the time of vacation and national holidays. "La empresa privada analiza, "

CONEP suggested that Labor Day (May 1) and Mother's Day (December 8) be among the national holidays to be eliminated if Sundays were to be paid. This and a paragraph insinuating that workers were lazy and preferred to receive their sustenance from Divine Providence were extremely insulting to labor groups.[29] Labor responded through the Committee for the Defense of the Labor Code[30] and presented its own demands, classified as basic aspirations of the working class.[31] These included payment of one-month bonus (*aguinaldo*, a bonus usually given at Christmas), one complete month of paid vacation, payment for the seventh day or Sunday, reduction of the workweek to 40 hours, union dues discounted by payroll, obligation to negotiate collective agreements, stability of employment, and the establishment of a family income and of unemployment insurance.[32]

From the time of its constitution in late April until the Labor Code was enacted into law at the end of December, the Labor Code Commission worked assiduously, meeting with all interested parties. The private sector had continual access to the commission, and labor groups met directly with Torrijos. The two main points constantly discussed by both groups were whether Sundays would be remunerated or, instead, a thirteenth-month salary would be paid to all workers and whether stability of employment would be instituted. In meetings held in August in Farallón[33] and in September in Panama City, labor leaders promised Torrijos to show their support to the government at the mass rally to be held in Panama City on

---

*Estrella de Panamá*, June 10, 1971. But other proposals and talks favored not paying for Sundays. Consejo Nacional de la Empresa Privada (CONEP), "Observaciones y Recomendaciones al Ante-Proyecto del Código de Trabajo, del 11 de enero de 1968, ante la Comisión Revisora." Mimeo; and interview with Dr. Rolando Murgas.

[29] "El descanso semanal representa un aumento de 16.7 % en el costo total de la mano de obra para todo el país. El volumen de producción y la calidad de la misma tiene que aumentar igualmente para poder mantener al presente nivel el costo por unidad de producto, por trabajo efectuado y por servicios prestados . . . Para producir más tenemos que trabajar más . . . y para poder trabajar más, se necesita de una paz y una armonía social que nutra las esperanzas y los anhelos de los que estudian todavía, de los que nacen día tras día y de los que todavía luchan por un sueño . . . Pero los sueños no se realizan descansando y pretendiendo vivir en terrenal paraíso donde quien se acueste a suspirar bajo la sombra de un árbol come y se nutre de la fruta que le viene a traer la Divina Providencia." "La empresa privada analiza jornada de trabajo y de descanso del nuevo código," *Estrella de Panamá* , June 13, 1971.

[30] Comité Nacional Sindical Pro Defensa del Nuevo Código Laboral comenta objeciones de CONEP," *Estrella de Panamá*, July 11, 12, 13, 1971.

[31] "Los obreros solicitan debate público entre el CONEP y la Comisión del Código de Trabajo," *Panamá América*, August 5, 1971.

[32] For the month of vacation only 26 days were paid, because Sundays were not remunerated.

[33] Farallón was the former U.S. base of Río Hato, where Torrijos established his headquarters. It is located in Coclé Province, on the Pacific side, about 120 kms. from Panama City.

October 11 to commemorate the third anniversary of the "revolution."[34] In return, Torrijos promised to make the Labor Code a key issue of his speech and assured labor that he was pushing for the remuneration for Sundays.

By September it was agreed by the government and the Labor Code Commission that the new labor code would include a system of job stability after two years of employment. To forestall the mass firing of workers with over two years of service once the contents of the Labor Code became known and before it was enacted into law, Cabinet Decree no. 191 was passed on September 2, 1971, prohibiting firings without just cause.[35] At that time, the government also decreed an educational tax to which all employers must contribute 1.25 percent of salaries paid and all workers 0.75 percent of salaries received.[36] Ninety-five percent of those funds were to be used for scholarships and other educational programs, and 5 percent were to be reserved for skills improvement and union education courses to be handled through MITRAB.

The government gave the Labor Code Commission a deadline of early October for the completion of the code so that the cabinet could look it over and incorporate some of its points in Torrijos's speech of October 11th.[37] During the mass rally, the Labor Code was used as a symbol of Torrijos and his "revolutionary process." The general actually held a copy of the Labor Code in his hand during part of his speech and said,

Panamanians, here is the Labor Code. Here it is. A Code that has been denied us (nos estaban negando) since 1947. Because the 1947 Labor Code was born a grandfather, was born old . . . This new Code contains your aspirations. This Code is the product of a tremendous effort, of a General Torrijos that has identified himself with you.[38]

He went on to speak of some of the substantive changes contained in the new code and mentioned that the issue of remuneration for the seventh day was still being studied. In his characteristic manner of appearing open but not committing himself one way or another, he said,

---

[34] "Respaldo masivo al General Torrijos – Creado Consejo Nacional de Trabajadores Panameños," *La Hora*, August 23, 1971.

[35] "Decreto de Gabinete no. 191 (2 de septiembre de 1971) por el cual se toman medidas sobre despidos injustificados de obreros," in *Código de Trabajo*, updated by Jorge Fábrega P., 6th ed. Panamá: Litho Impresora, 1981, Appendix 7, pp. 424-425.

[36] IFARHU, *Seguro educativo, significado y beneficios*. Panamá. 1972.

[37] According to Juan Materno Vásquez, presidential chief of staff at the time and later president of the Supreme Court, the two issues the government wanted to stress in that speech were the proposed reforms to the Constitution and the new Labor Code. Interview with Lic. Juan Materno Vásquez.

[38] "El que da cariño recibe cariño." Alocución del General Torrijos en la mas grande concentración humana realizada en Panamá, en conmemoración del tercer aniversario de la Revolución. PLaza 5 de Mayo, October 11, 1971, quoted in Omar Torrijos, *La batalla de Panamá*. Buenos Aires: Editora Universitaria de B. A., 1973, p. 85-86. Translated by author.

if [payment of] the 7th day benefits the worker without harming the economy of the people, then you will have your 7th day . . . I don't want, due to lack of consultation, to increase your cost of living. I prefer six days well paid than seven days paid with hunger rations.[39]

On November 1, a new minimum salary law was passed establishing 50 cents per hour as the minimum hourly wage in cities of over 50,000 inhabitants and a decreasing scale for smaller cities.[40] This was the first action that any government had taken regarding salaries since 1959, when the first minimum-wage law was passed. Meanwhile workers declared their disappointment with the new labor code because they had learned that it would not reduce the workweek to 40 hours and that the issue of the payment of the seventh-day versus the thirteenth-month salary was still being debated.[41] Workers also declared that they had expected a more complete system of job security.

While members of the Labor Code Commission were meeting with the public and appearing in televised programs to explain the new labor code, Torrijos continued to court labor groups.[42] It was during one of these meetings, at the anniversary celebration of the SITRACHILCO Union of Banana Workers of Puerto Armuelles, that he announced the passing of Cabinet Decree no. 221, which stipulated the payment of a thirteenth-month salary. He stated that he called it a thirteenth-month salary instead of a bonus month (aguinaldo, gift or bonus), because "an aguinaldo would appear to be a concession, and the thirteenth-month salary is a way of redistributing the riches that workers generate and reward to the great effort made by the working class."[43] Torrijos felt compelled to pass the decree regarding the thirteenth-month salary to assure workers of some tangible and immediate reward, because the private sector was so opposed to payment of Sundays and to the reduction of the workweek to 40 hours.[44]

While the government divulged the clauses regulating payment of the thirteenth-month salary, there were great debates through the media regarding its pros and cons.[45] This extra month of wages was to be paid in three installments, the first on April 15, in time for the purchase of school uniforms and supplies for the academic year beginning in late April. The

---

[39] Torrijos, La batalla, p. 87.

[40] "Nuevo decreto de salario mínimo," Crítica, November 17, 1971. This new salary raised wages 10 cents/hour for the largest cities.

[41] "Carta abierta de los trabajadores panameños," El Panamá América, November 8, 1971.

[42] "Exponen esta noche las proyecciones del Proyecto del Código de Trabajo," El Panamá América, November 17, 1971.

[43] "El General Torrijos en Puerto Armuelles," La Estrella de Panamá, November 18, 1971.

[44] Interview with Dr. Rolando Murgas.

[45] "30 millones al año aportará el 13 mes en beneficio a la masa trabajadora," La Estrella de Panamá, November 20, 1971; "Justicia al trabajador representa el 13o. mes," El Panamá América, November 19, 1971; "Editorial: El Decimotercer Mes," La Estrella de Panamá, November 24, 1971.

second installment was to be paid on August 15, and the last on December 15, in time for Christmas.[46] The employer could deduct the thirteenth-month salary as a production cost that would not be subject to any other taxes such as social security taxes or taxes for professional risks.[47]

The second installment of the thirteenth-month salary, or *segunda partida*, would not be paid to the worker but rather deposited in the Caja de Seguro Social (CSS). Subsequently, the government announced several plans regarding the use of the *segunda partida*. First it was to be used for construction of low-cost housing, then to increase the retirement pensions of the CSS beneficiaries. Originally, the plan was that after 10 years any worker could retrieve his portion of the *segunda partida*. But shortly before the 10 years were up, the government decreed that no money would be paid back.[48]

Once the Labor Code Project was completed, Torrijos named a cabinet commission to study it in depth and present it to the full Cabinet Council.[49] At that time, the Labor Code Commission met for two weeks with lawyers hired by CONEP and the Chamber of Commerce, who painstakingly discussed the project with them, article by article.[50] The Cabinet Labor Commission met at the Hotel Nacional of David, Chiriquí Province, for most of November and part of December. Once this commission made its recommendations, the full Cabinet Council met in permanent session from December 23, 1971, until the code was approved on December 30, 1971.[51] Panama's new labor code would become effective April 2, 1972.

## MAJOR CHANGES INTRODUCED BY THE 1972 LABOR CODE

Without doubt the most important change in the new labor code is the pro-labor tenor set forth in its first article, which reads:

> The present Code governs relations between capital and labor, establishing special state protection in favor of the workers, so that the state may intervene with the purpose of providing remunerative

---

[46] "Todo hombre que trabaja merece parte de los beneficios obtenidos por la empresa en el transcurso del año," *Crítica*, November 19, 1971.

[47] "Régimen legal del 13o. mes," *Crítica*, November 20, 1971.

[48] The use that has been given this money and the amount accrued remain a mystery, and a rallying cry for the working class demands repayment of the segunda partida. Comité Panameño por los Derechos Humanos, *La Caja de Seguro Social al borde de la quiebra*. Panama: 1981, pp. 8-9.

[49] The Cabinet Commission was integrated by Arturo Sucre, vice president of Panama, Jorge Fábrega and Arturo Hoyos, members of the Labor Code Commission, José de la Rosa Castillo, minister of labor, and Juan Materno Vásquez, minister of the presidency. Interview with Lic. Juan Materno Vásquez.

[50] Second interview with Dr. Rolando Murgas.

[51] "Sesión Permanente del Gabinete sobre el nuevo Código Laboral." *Matutino*, December 23, 1971.

employment to all those who lack it, ensuring every workman the necessary economic conditions for a decent standard of living.[52]

This article clearly set the stage for the role that the government perceived for itself in the relation between labor and capital. It provided for a complete break with the past and implicitly alluded to the progressive position of the state vis-à-vis the private sector and even to its future competitive role with private capital.

The basic changes introduced by the Labor Code can be separated into three groups: those regarding the individual, those of a collective nature, and those pertaining to procedural matters.[53]

Changes pertaining to the individual worker included:

1. Incorporation of all workers into the Labor Code, including those excluded previously such as sailors, *carretilleros* (sidewalk and cart vendors), etc.
2. Banning of private employment agencies.
3. Reduction of the number of foreign-born workers in any place of employment from 25 percent to 10 percent.
4. Stability of employment after two years.
5. Stricter regulation of overtime work.
6. Establishment of factory committees, or *comités de empresa*.
7. Restriction of the *jus variandi*, or the ability of the employer to change the working conditions unilaterally.
8. Regulation of special contracts.
9. Payment of a thirteenth-month salary.
10. Payment of a *prima de antigüedad*, or seniority bonus.
11. Protection of wages.
12. Increased maternity protection.

The most important measures of a collective nature introduced in the new labor code were:

1. Obligation to negotiate a collective agreement at the request of the workers.
2. Obligation of all workers to pay union dues when a collective agreement that benefits them has been negotiated.
3. Collection of union dues by direct payroll discount.

---

[52] Jorge Fábrega P., trans. *Labor Code of the Republic of Panama (Substantive Provisions)*. Panamá: Litho Impresora, 1974, p. 5. This was in direct contrast to Article 1 of the 1947 Labor Code, which stated that "the purpose of the Code is to regulate the relations between capital and labor, placing them on a structure of social justice . . . without harming either of the parts . . . [The Code should guarantee] the worker the necessary conditions for a normal life and capital a just return for its investments." Quoted in Ricord, "*El código*," p. 143.

[53] Jorge Fábrega P., "Historia del código de trabajo de 1972," *Lotería*, nos. 2-3(1972): 20-22.

4. Negotiations of strikes through the Ministry of Labor instead of through the labor courts.
5. Elimination of lockouts.
6. Reduction of the number needed to declare a strike to a simple majority instead of 60 percent.
7. Increased protection of unions and union leaders (*fuero sindical*).
8. In the case of a strike, obligatory arbitration when requested by the union or agreed on by both parties.
9. Norms regarding unfair labor practice.

Among the important changes regarding matters of judicial process, the following are the most important:

1. Power of the judge to insure a fair trial, avoid nullifications, and establish the truth among confusing facts.
2. Rule of *sana crítica* (sound judgment) in the probing stage.
3. Oral process and supression of formalities.
4. Special power to the judge regarding precautionary measures.
5. Preventive holding of property, without need of a bond.
6. Summary process for reintegration of a worker if he enjoys fuero sindical, and a very short process for all other workers.

As previously mentioned, the most controversial of these measures were stability of employment and the obligation to negotiate collective agreements at the request of the workers. Other measures that met with tremendous opposition from the employers included all those that translated into added labor costs, such as the prima de antigüedad and the stricter regulations of overtime, and all the measures that protected and fostered unionization and provided legal avenues to strike. The meaning and implications of these controversial aspects of the Labor Code are elaborated in the next section.

## Stability of Employment, or Job Security

The Labor Code provision for stability of employment essentially meant that after two years of employment a worker could not be fired unless the employer proved there was just cause for the dismissal. If an employer fired a worker and could not prove just cause, the worker had the choice either to ask for reinstatement or for indemnization. This choice given to the worker is what made the stability clause stand out. In the 1947 Labor Code, the employer had total freedom to fire any worker as long as he indemnized him according to an existing *preaviso* scale.[54] Apart from giving the worker the option to chose reinstatement or indemnization, the scale of indemnization introduced in the 1972 Labor Code doubled the *preaviso* one,

---

[54] The *preaviso* payment ranged from one week of salary for six months of employment, to six months salary for 25 years or more of employment.Ricord, "El código," p. 146.

so indemnization increased from roughly 4 percent of total salaries earned to as much as 8 percent.[55] Exceptions to this clause included high management employees (*empleados de confianza*) with less than five years in the company, temporary workers, domestic workers, sailors employed on international ships, and apprentices. All salaries due the worker (*salarios caídos*) from the time of the dismissal to the time of the judicial decision had to be paid to him if the case was ruled in his favor.

Although the members of the Labor Code Commission made a decision to publicly support the code in its entirety once it was approved, several declared in interviews that they had had difficulty with the stability clause and had tried to find alternatives to it.[56] According to Dr. Murgas, the commission approached the private sector with a proposal for an improved indemnization scale as an alternative to stability of employment but was totally rebuffed. In a meeting at the Sindicato de Industriales (SIP), members of the private sector declared that it was unaceptable to have the *preaviso* scale improved because the labor costs (*recargos*) were already unbearable. The most they could do would be to consider improving the scale for those employees with over 25 years of service.[57] During the Cabinet meetings of November and December a group of industrialists presented a more equitable indemnization scale through the Ministry of Commerce and Industry (MICI), again to be disavowed by the majority of the private sector. Faced with such an intractable situation, the Labor Code Commission saw no alternative but to recommend that a system of job security or stability of employment be adopted.

The causes acceptable for dimissal with just cause are described in Article 213 of the Labor Code and divided into three types. These include disciplinary reasons, reasons of a non-imputable nature, and economic reasons. Only the Ministry of Labor is competent to rule on reduction of the workforce due to economic reasons.

### Prima de Antigüedad or Seniority Bonus

The *prima de antigüedad* is a seniority bonus to be paid all workers with more than 10 years employment in the same company and over 40 years of age if male and 35 if female at the time they terminate their employment (Labor Code Article 224). This bonus is calculated at the rate of one weeks

---

[55] The new scale was as follows:
  1. If less than one year employment, one week for every three months.
  2. For one-two years, one week salary for every two months.
  3. For two-ten years, three additional weeks per year.
  4. For 10 or more years, one additional week per year. (Labor Code Article 225.)
[56] Interview with Lic. Jorge Fábrega.
[57] Interview with Dr. Rolando Murgas.

salary per year of service and represents roughly 2 percent of a worker's salary accrued over 20 years.[58]

## Regulation of Overtime

The main change from the 1947 Labor Code regarding overtime is that a worker cannot be forced to work extra hours if he does not want to, and no one can work more than three hours overtime per day and nine hours per week. Exceptions can be made at times of catastrophe, in which case workers can be asked to work as needed but must be paid with a 75 percent increase.

## Protection of Salaries

Article 161 of the Labor Code sets the conditions for salary retentions and deductions. A worker may not pay more than 30 percent of his wages for housing "when the lessor is an official institution or individual subject to establishment by the competent authorities of the maximum amount of lease." Nor can more than 20 percent of a worker's wages be deducted to pay debts incurred by buying on credit. The total deduction and retentions, in any event, cannot exceed 50 percent of the salary (Article 161).

## Added Maternity Protection or *Fuero de Maternidad*

The new code maintains the same provisions of the 1947 Labor Code regarding maternity benefits but has enhanced these with the proviso that a woman may not be fired from her job for one year from the date of her return to work after giving birth.

## Thirteenth-Month Salary

Prior to the enactment of the Labor Code, the controversy surrounding this issue stemmed from the debate on whether the payment of one extra month of salary was more acceptable to the employer than payment for Sundays. The Labor Code Commission favored paying the seventh day with certain conditions, one of which was that the worker had to work the previous six days without any absences.

The battle that ensued regarding the payment for the seventh day versus the thirteenth month had to do with costs: there are 52 Sundays in a year, but the thirteenth-month alternative represented the payment of only 26 days.[59] However, the payment of Sundays with the proviso that the worker be in attendance the previous six days should have had great appeal to the employers. It would have cut down on absenteeism and abuse of medical

---

[58] Programa Regional del Empleo para América Latina y el Caribe (PREALC), "Efectos del código de trabajo sobre el empleo, la productividad, los costos y la inversión en Panamá." Geneva: ILO/Documento de Trabajo PREALC/156, 1978, p. 12.

[59] In reality, the remuneration of Sundays meant paying eight more days than the thirteenth-month salary, if one adds to the last the 18 days of sick leave allowed by law.

leave, and the disbursement of money would have been made in small amounts instead of the three payments that the thirteenth-month salary entailed. This alternative would have been extremely helpful to small enterprises that operate with little or no capital and that probably bore the brunt of the thirteenth-month salary.

Frustrated by the campaign of the private sector against payment of Sundays and unsure of the reaction to be set in motion if it were passed above their protests, Torrijos went ahead and approved the thirteenth-month salary on November 18, 1971, by special decree and announced it at a meeting with the banana workers of Puerto Armuelles.[60] He stated, however, that the possibility of payment for the seventh day was still under consideration, and if it was ultimately included in the new labor code, then the thirteenth-month salary would be eliminated.

The debate continued through the Cabinet meetings prior to the enactment of the code. One of the members of the Labor Code Commission stated that "the Commission had opted for the 7th day," and if approved, it would have given the Labor Code a better image, because "one of the things said about the Code is that it didn't concern itself with productivity."[61] In the final analysis, the payment of the thirteenth month was a compromise between Torrijos and the private sector and an appeasement to labor, which had expectations of receiving something tangible upon the enaction of the Labor Code into law.

## Collective Bargaining

The 1972 Labor Code, in an unprecedented move, introduced a clause by which an employer is compelled to negotiate a collective agreement at the request of the union (Article 401). So strong was the government's commitment to promote collective bargaining that the refusal of the employer to negotiate an agreement was included as just cause for a strike (Article 480). The basic clauses governing collective bargaining are that the employer is obligated to enter into negotiations at the request of the union, that an agreement is binding for two to four years, that any benefits granted workers through approved laws cannot be reduced or nullified but can be improved, and that once an agreement is made, it applies to all workers whether members of the union or not.

Even though the private sector did not react strongly against this clause at first, it was the issue with the most far-reaching consequences for labor relations. The effects of collective bargaining and the reactions to it will be discussed in depth in Chapter 8.

---

[60] "El General Torrijos en Puerto Arumelles." *La Estrella de Panamá*, November 18, 1971.
[61] The implication was that payment of the Seventh day would have cut down on absenteeism and thus would have improved productivity. Second interview with Dr. Rolando Murgas.

## Strikes

The 1947 Labor Code had recognized the right to strike, but the regulations under which a strike could be declared legal were "deliberately anarchic and confusing, thus effectively nullifying this right."[62] The present code establishes precise rules for declaring a strike and specifies the steps that must be followed to set one in motion. The Ministry of Labor plays an important role in these matters, as it is the only entity with competence to arbitrate and conciliate in the event of a strike.

In order for a strike to be legal it has to follow the procedures established in the Labor Code. The union can be advised beforehand by MITRAB as to whether it meets the requirements for legality. A strike must have a clear motive, the backing of a majority of workers, and follow the channels set up for conciliation. Acceptable motives for a strike are the breakdown in negotiations for a collective agreement, management's lack of compliance with a collective agreement, attempts to achieve better working conditions, and general and reiterated violations by the employer of the legal dispositions protecting workers (Article 480).

To set a conciliation in motion, the union must present a list of demands, or *pliego de peticiones*, to the Ministry of Labor. The employer must respond to these demands within five days. If no agreement is reached, the union together with the employer and a conciliator can negotiate for seven days. After this, each party can ask for a two-week extension, but if this right is not exercised a strike can be declared within 12 days of presenting the demands.

A new concept regarding strikes introduced by the Labor Code is the imputability of the strike. If a strike is found to be imputable to the employer, it binds him to the payment of due salaries (*salarios caídos*) of the striking workers.

## Strengthening of Unions

The provisions of the 1972 Labor Code regarding collective labor relations were designed to strengthen the existing unions and to promote the growth of organized labor. The clause forcing employers to negotiate collective agreements and the one making workers that benefit from a collective agreement pay union dues whether they are union members or not are probably the strongest incentives to promote the growth of unions. The automatic deduction of union dues by payroll has had a considerable impact on the unions' financial situation, and the improvement and extension of union privileges (*fuero sindical*) has removed from union leaders the fear of summary dismissal and has forced the acceptance of union representatives in the place of employment.

---

[62] Ricord, "*El código,*" p. 152.

Union members are now able to attend training courses and seminars related to union activities, and employers are required by law to grant them leave for such activities. The 5 percent of the educational tax allotted to organized labor has made many of these courses and seminars possible. One section of the Dirección General del Trabajo of the MITRAB is devoted to trade union organizations and its role is to advise unions and monitor their activities.

### Changes in the Labor Judicial Process

The Labor Code Commission introduced methods that would make the judicial process related to labor as expedient as possible. The abbreviated process stressed in the 1972 Labor Code was not a new concept; it had been included in the 1947 Labor Code. However, it was seldom used. The criteria for using an abbreviated process was twofold: first, it would keep costs down, and second, it would avoid some of the tensions and traumas caused by a lengthy case, especially if the ruling went in favor of the worker and he asked for reinstatement. All procedural measures focused on the rapid flow of cases through the judicial system and their prompt resolution. Important in this regard were the extra powers given judges to insure the right to a fair trial, to request all proofs and witnesses present at the hearing, and to be able to visit the sites. For reasons of brevity, the oral trial was encouraged. This avoided the time and expense of having to prepare elaborate files. A final measure introduced was that the judge had to rule (*fallar*) at the hearing, and if for some reason he did not, the parties did not have to appear in person to hear the ruling at a later date. The verdict could be presented by edict and posted by the court secretary.

Had these measures been adhered to, some of the problems that arose due to the backlog of cases between 1972 and 1975 would have been avoided, and many of the faults wrongly imputed to the Labor Code would not have taken place.

### CONCLUSION

The 1972 Labor Code was a strong policy statement that provided the mechanism for the rapid changes the Torrijos regime sought for labor. This legislation would, through the incorporation and enhancement of the labor sector, change the balance of power of Panamanian society.

The capacity to enact legislation of such magnitude can only come about if the state enjoys a great degree of autonomy from the forces that would oppose such measures. This was the situation in Panama in 1972. The former ruling elite lost hegemony and control of the political machinery. The disorganization of the traditional rulers allowed the Torrijos regime enough autonomy to maneuver during its first years in power, which resulted in the enactment of progressive policy such as the 1972 Labor Code.

# 6

# THE AFTERMATH OF THE CODE

Before the enactment of the 1972 Labor Code the former ruling elite were diffuse in their attacks on the Torrijos regime and acted in a disorganized and unfocused manner. But the Labor Code provided the focus for the private sector to come together, to unite in their effort to unseat the "usurping" regime, and to do so by attacking the piece of legislation that they blamed for all the economic ills that affected the country in the 1970s. The 1972 Labor Code, then, acted as a catalyst for the former ruling class by providing the means for that class to coalesce and act as a united front against Torrijos.

The former ruling elite was aided in its pursuits by the fact that, although it had lost political power, it still held considerable economic power, which it manipulated to its advantage and to the detriment of the regime. The Torrijos regime lost its relative autonomy vis-à-vis the former ruling elite due to a series of factors that helped undermine the regime's position. The private sector organized to manipulate its considerable economic assets at the same time that it maintained a fierce anti-government campaign both in Panama and abroad. The private sector's efforts were aided by the economic recession of the mid-1970s brought about by the increase in oil prices--which had a lasting impact in Panama—and by the efforts of the regime to conclude treaty negotiations with the United States regarding the Panama Canal.

The external economic factors, completely outside the control of Panama, aided the private sector in its quest to undermine Torrijos's position. The other instrument at the private sector's disposal, U.S. public opinion regarding a new canal treaty, was used to its utmost by tapping all the important U.S. sources that opposed the treaty negotiations. The private sector played on the fact that the Torrijos regime had not been popularly elected, was military, and according to the former ruling elite had no legitimacy. Members of the elite also played on the fact that the internal economic situation was in a very precarious condition, which they attributed to the ineptitude and high level of corruption of the government as well as to policies such as the Labor Code.

The combination, then, of internal and external forces lost for the regime its relative autonomy with regard to the former ruling elite. And the drama of the power play between the actors can be discerned very clearly in the events that followed the enactment of the 1972 Labor Code.

## CHRONOLOGY, 1972-1976

After the Labor Code was enacted into law, the role of the Ministry of Labor was to set the guidelines for the new procedures to be followed and to oversee adherence to these procedures. This task was monumental given the fact that the ministry itself was of recent origin and that the role assigned to it by the Labor Code was quite demanding. The immediate problem faced by MITRAB was to rule on issues that for the private sector meant money outlays, such as how to pay the thirteenth-month salary, how to manage the *prima de antigüedad*, and how to settle labor disputes that involved indemnizations. Other issues requiring immediate attention included those that represented benefits or improvements for the workers, who began to press for the guidelines to become operational. The approval of internal regulations for the place of employment (*reglamento interno*) and the creation of *comités de empresa* were two issues the workers demanded immediate compliance with.

Perhaps most exacting of all for MITRAB was the management of collective agreement negotiations. Although the procedure for engaging in collective bargaining was described in the Labor Code, MITRAB had to arbitrate on specific issues and judge on whether the procedures were being followed or not. Another difficult task for the ministry was to arbitrate on requests for work-force reduction due to economic duress. MITRAB was the only agency that could judge in these cases, and the Labor Code spelled out in precise terms the time limits for such decisions. But when the Labor Code went into effect in 1972, the ministry lacked the trained personnel capable of passing judgment on these issues.[1] Furthermore, the conflictive role with which the Labor Code empowered MITRAB soon came under attack by the private sector. The private sector bitterly denounced the role assigned by the Labor Code to the Ministry of Labor, that is, the ministry was supposed to be a protector of labor as well as an arbiter in labor disputes.

Through most of 1972 and 1973, MITRAB enacted operational guidelines regarding these matters, such as how to pay for days off due to national holidays,[2] how to deal with dismissals of workers with *fuero sindical*,[3] whether the payment of the thirteenth-month salary superseded

---

[1] Interview with Dr. Rolando Murgas.
[2] "Sobre aplicación del Decreto 277 se pronuncia L. Shirley." *La Hora*, October 16, 1972.
[3] "Separación con sueldo también es violación del fuero sindical," *Matutino*, August 12, 1972.
[4] "Declaración a los trabajadores sobre el 13o. mes y bonificación de Navidad," *La Estrella de Panamá*, December 13, 1972.

a Christmas bonus,[4] the correct procedure for presenting demands, or *pliegos de peticiones*, for the negotiation of collective agreements,[5] and how to pay for overtime.[6]

At the same time, the main organizations representing the private sector, especially CONEP and the Cámara Panameña de Comercio e Industrias, kept up an unrelenting campaign against the Labor Code and tried to link all the economic problems faced by the country to that piece of legislation. The theme of the 1973 Conferencia Anual de Ejecutivos (CADE), sponsored by the Asociación Panameña de Ejecutivos de Empresa (APEDE) and held in April of that year, was "Employment: A Priority Factor for Development." The gist of the conference, however, was the negative effect of the Labor Code on employment.

Several prominent members of Torrijos's cabinet, among them Dr. Rolando Murgas, minister of labor, Lcdo. Fernando Manfredo, minister of commerce and industry, and Dr. Nicolás Ardito Barletta, minister of planning, were invited to the 1973 CADE to discuss the impact of the Labor Code on the employment situation.[7] This was one of the few public dialogues held between high government officials and important members of the private sector in four years. In the 1977 CADE, the government made overtures for a rapprochement with the private sector. This relationship continued into the 1978 CADE, at which Torrijos gave the closing speech.

Dr. Murgas' intervention at the 1973 CADE was an attempt to explain, once again, the goals that the codifiers had had in mind when they elaborated the Labor Code and to explain those aspects of the current socio-economic situation that could be attributed to the code and those that could not. He touched on the issue of productivity by saying that stability of employment was not designed to increase productivity. Instead, the incentive for increased productivity, he argued, should come from the employer through the selection and good training of his personnel. He also tried to divorce the code from the issue of employment. He pointed out, for instance, that based on 1970 census data, PREALC had anticipated an unemployment rate for Panama of 15 percent for 1980, and he mentioned some of the programs the government had planned to relieve that prob-

---

[5] "Importantes instrucciones de la Secretaría General de Trabajo," *Crítica*, December 21, 1972.

[6] "Señala Trabajo como deben pagarse las horas extras," *Matutino*, December 23, 1972.

[7] The Conferencia Anual de Ejecutivos (CADE) has been perhaps the most important forum held in Panama for the discussion of broad economic issues and goals from the perspective of the private sector. The themes selected are always very timely and the CADE was one of the few public avenues left open during the 1970s for an open communication between the private sector and the Torrijos regime.

[8] PREALC, *Situación y perspectivas del empleo en Panamá*, Geneva: ILO, 1974, p. 5, quoted by Rolando Murgas, "Política gubernamental en materia de empleo," p. 2, in Asociación Panameña de Ejecutivos de Empresa, *VIII Conferencia Anual de Ejecutivos de Empresa (CADE 1973)*, Panamá, 1973.

lem.[8] Murgas made an impassioned plea for the private sector to "lay down their prejudices and do away with the traumatized attitude adopted because of the social policies of the state."[9] Minister Manfredo, however, declared that what was needed was a rational salary policy and that the unions were irresponsibly pushing salaries to high levels with no regard for the economic situation of the sectors involved.[10]

Even though the industrialists and businessmen were very careful not to attack the government directly, several were highly critical of the labor laws and of the role of MITRAB. One businessman declared that MITRAB was prejudiced against the private sector and asked for an explanation of the difference between employer paternalism and state paternalism. He also criticized the government's lack of definition of its economic policies and its role in implementing them. After stating that productivity had gone down considerably, the expositor warned that "a Labor Code that does not consider the needs for development can become an unemployment code."[11] Another businessman warned that the Labor Code was prompting industrialists to invest in capital-intensive techniques in order to avoid labor conflicts, the primary cause of which was the stability clause.[12]

The controversy regarding the Labor Code did not die down. In September of 1973, another public debate took place at the University of Panama, and involved representatives of the government, the private sector, and the unions.[13] Regarding stability of employment, Murgas declared that "in no way did it constitute a guarantee for the inefficient or recalcitrant worker."[14] Many issues of public concern were raised during this debate. Government representatives presented the official view of the economic situation by emphasizing that the economic problems affecting the country were due to the reduced size of the internal market and to the fact that domestic production could not compete with foreign manufactured products. Labor representatives accused the *empresarios* of being bad managers, lacking in technical and administrative techniques. They also pointed out that although the new labor code was good, the labor codes of Mexico, Colombia, and Venezuela were far more progressive, and those countries were not experiencing the economic problems Panama was.[15]

---

[9] Murgas, "Política gubernamental," p. 11.

[10] Fernando Manfredo, "El empleo y la tecnología," p. 22 in *VIII Conferencia Anual*.

[11] J. J. Vallarino, "Proyectos generadores de empleo: quien los detiene?," pp. 2-5, in *VIII Conferencia Anual*.

[12] Guillermo E. Quijano, "Sector Construcción," p. 7, in *VIII Conferencia Anual*.

[13] The debators were: Dr. Rolando Murgas, minister of labor; Dr. Aristides Royo, member of the Legislative Commission at that time, and president of Panama between 1978 and 1981; Ing. O. Díaz, president of CAPAC; Dr. Morrice Maduro, consultant for CAPAC; and Axel Gonzáles and Julio César Pinzón, labor representatives. "Expectativa nacional por el debate sobre el código laboral," *El Panamá América*, September 13, 1973.

[14] "Editorial: Balance del Debate Laboral," *Crítica*, September 19, 1973.

[15] "Un forum que robusteció el Código de Trabajo." *Matutino*, September, 19, 1973.

Questions raised during this debate reflected the moods of the time as well as some of the inconsistencies that were felt by the parties involved and by the public at large.[16] A sample of those questions were:

1. Why aren't the labor laws applicable to public employees?[17]
2. When will workers receive the *segunda partida* of the thirteenth-month salary?[18]
3. Why do workers who are paying a mortgage have to forego the *segunda partida*?[19]
4. Why was the Christmas bonus abolished for public employees while the private sector was forced to pay it?[20]
5. Why do public employees not receive the thirteenth-month salary?
6. Why are there so many public employees who do not earn minimum salary?
7. Why is the worker forced to take his vacation?[21]
8. Are workers producing more or less after the passage of the Labor Code?
9. How much has unemployment increased after the passage of the Labor Code, and is this attributable to the code?

The questions raised during this debate pertained mainly to two areas that had created a lot of anxiety as well as speculation among the various groups and sectors affected. One was the obvious differences in the employer-employee relations and responsibilities for the private sector as opposed to the government. The other area of concern was the advantage that the government took from employers and workers through some labor measures, primarily the *segunda partida* of the thirteenth-month salary.

---

[16] "Preguntas al Ministro Murgas sobre el Código de Trabajo." *El Panamá América,* September 19 and 20, 1973.

[17] Although there had been a civil service previous to the Torrijos regime, it had not been continued after 1968, and public employees were not covered by the 1972 Labor Code.

[18] The special bonus called the thirteenth-month salary was supposed to be paid in three installments: in April *(primera partida)*, in August *(segunda partida)*, and in December *(tercera partida)*. However, the worker did not receive the *segunda partida*. Instead, that money was claimed by the government. The policy for its disbursement changed several times.

[19] The government had announced at first that it would create a housing fund with that money to provide loans for low-cost housing.

[20] MITRAB had ruled that if the Christmas bonus paid by employers prior to the Labor Code was greater than the *tercera partida* of the thirteenth-month salary, then they must continue paying the bonus instead of the *tercera partida*. Public employees, on the other hand, lost all Christmas bonuses.

[21] This was a decision made by the Labor Code codifiers not to allow employers to "buy the workers vacation time." A worker could accumulate vacation for two years, but after that he must take it. The codifiers felt that given the tropical climate of Panama, especially those laborers engaged in strenuous physical work needed a rest after a given period. Interview with Dr. Rolando Murgas.

Table 5    Private and Public Employment

| | 1971 | 1972 | 1973 | 1974 | 1975 | 1976 | 1977 | 1978 | 1979 | 1980 | 1981 |
|---|---|---|---|---|---|---|---|---|---|---|---|
| Total | 190647 | 201249 | 213127 | 226639 | 231634 | 229240 | 227258 | 215265 | 268268 | 269503 | 339842 |
| Private sector | 117198 | 119555 | 125300 | 129846 | 128857 | 124747 | 118995 | 99628 | 144037 | 166986 | 199929 |
| Private sector employees | 102330 | 107283 | 114171 | 119678 | 117658 | 112781 | 106146 | 85307 | 129578 | 152691 | 185235 |
| Banana workers | 4868 | 12272 | 11129 | 10168 | 11199 | 11966 | 12849 | 14321 | 14459 | 14259 | 14694 |
| Public sector | 60751 | 67735 | 73793 | 82160 | 88353 | 91875 | 95875 | 101359 | 109397 | 114598 | 125011 |
| Central government | 43932 | 48317 | 49250 | 53317 | 54823 | 55811 | 58680 | 61253 | 63714 | 63909 | 69122 |
| Autonomous agencies | 14066 | 16708 | 21573 | 25704 | 29969 | 31996 | 32309 | 35961 | 41648 | 46378 | 51305 |
| Municipalities | 2698 | 2710 | 2970 | 3139 | 3561 | 4068 | 4246 | 4145 | 4035 | 4311 | 4584 |
| Canal Zone | 12698 | 13959 | 14034 | 14633 | 14424 | 12618 | 13028 | 14278 | 14834 | 14919 | 14902 |

Sources: Figures for 1971-75: Panamá en cifras: Años 1971-1975, Panamá, 1976, p. 198; figures for 1976-1977, Panamá en cifras: Años 1976-1980, Panamá, 1981, p. 189; figures for 1978-1981: Panamá en cifras: Años 1978-1982, Panamá, 1982, pp. 224-225.

The question of public-sector versus private-sector employment was a serious one, because the public sector grew substantially during the Torrijos regime and the government was not about to apply to its own employees the labor measures it was defending so vehemently. Public-sector employment grew from 31.8 percent of total employment in 1971 to 38 percent in 1975 and to 47 percent in 1978. Subsequently it decreased, so that by 1981, employees in the public sector represented 36.7 percent of total employment (Table 5).

As the questions in the debate pointed out, many workers in the public sector did not earn minimum salary, nor did they get any of the new benefits such as the thirteenth-month salary. At the same time that they were not enjoying the new benefits, they lost some of the benefits they had previously had, such as the Christmas bonus. The government was not willing to play by the rules of its own game, a situation that provoked much antagonism both among private-sector employers and government employees.

The government's record as an employer was notoriously bad, and it got worse. Among the many grave misdeeds of the government, one was that it did not pay into the CSS but instead borrowed from that institution. Although the social security benefits of public employees were not immediately jeopardized by this ploy, the benefits of all workers were jeopardized by the threat of insolvency of the CSS.[22] Another instance in which the government as an employer failed to comply with its own laws was when it hired construction workers to build public housing. The government was not used to having its actions challenged by its employees because the

---

[22] Comité Panameño por los Derechos Humanos, La Caja de Seguro Social al borde de la quiebra. Panamá: 1981.

public sector was used as a sort of welfare solution to the increasing unemployment, so people who got jobs in the government were not about to complain publicly about mistreatment or lack of compliance with laws. But that was not the case with the Construction Union SUNTRACS.

The issue of the *segunda partida* was a very thorny one in which the government was able to increase its revenues substantially at the expense of both private sector employers and workers. The government decided arbitrarily to keep the *segunda partida* (one third of the thirteenth-month salary), instead of having it paid to the workers. The reasons given for this initially were that the government would create a housing fund with that money, to be used by workers who wanted to build a home. In 1975, with the economic situation deteriorating swiftly and this affecting drastically people on fixed incomes, the government decided to use the money of the *segunda partida* to increase the social security pensions of retired workers. At that point, the government still claimed that after 10 years any worker could withdraw his *segunda partida*. But shortly before the 10 years were up, the government declared that the *segunda partida* would not be returned.

The questions raised in this debate brought out very clearly the areas of concern and conflict between the private sector and the government and between workers of the two sectors and their respective employers. The conflictive role of the government as protector of labor, when it did not treat its labor force within the same parameters it tried to enforce for the private sector, was a very difficult one to accept. And the incredible sham of the *segunda partida* clearly cast the government in a suspicious position for all the actions it later claimed it took in favor of labor. It was arbitrary actions of this sort that gave the Torrijos regime a bad name and were difficult even for its staunchest supporters to defend in the light of rightful accusations. Although the idea of the housing bank that the government had first put forward for the *segunda partida* was a good one, it was very soon obvious that the money would be used for other things and would never benefit its rightful claimants. The questions regarding productivity and increased unemployment were the usual ones used by the private sector to attack the Labor Code. The issues involving those questions will be analyzed in depth in Chapter 8.

A month after the debate, Minister Manfredo declared during his presentation of the annual report to the National Assembly of Representatives that "industrial production has reached dangerous lows in the last few years in Panama." He argued that although the private sector blamed the Labor Code along with the price-control policy and the lack of fiscal incentives for lowered productivity, the real culprit was the private sector, who "are not producing for export, which is the only way to maintain the high growth level" of the previous decade.[23]

---

[23] "Señala Manfredo: No es el Código de Trabajo sino la falta de interés de industriales," *Crítica*, October 29, 1973.

Another constant complaint of members of the private sector was that they did not have access to Torrijos. Whether or not this claim is true, the private sector had their advocates within the government. President Lakas, himself the owner of a construction firm, met regularly with groups of businessmen and industrialists and conveyed their concerns to Torrijos.[24] And several prominent businessmen also held high positions in the government, as ministers and as heads of autonomous and semi-autonomous agencies. Fernando Manfredo, an industrialist who sits on the board of directors of several firms, is a good example of private-sector participation in government. Manfredo was minister of commerce and industry in the early 1970s, presidential chief of staff from 1976 to 1978, and since 1978 held the second-ranking position in the Panama Canal Commission. Rory Gonzáles, another member of the private sector, was minister of commerce and industry in the early 1970s. Another industrialist, José de la Ossa, was minister of finance during that same period. Edwin Fábrega headed the Instituto de Recursos Hidraúlicos y Electrificación (IRHE), and Juan José Amado, head of a large industrial complex, was minister of commerce and industry in 1979, following his term as president of CONEP. Amado later was named ambassador to the United States. Government agencies such as the Banco Nacional and the Caja de Ahorro have always been headed by members of the private sector.[25]

One of the most important government agencies between 1972-1978 was the Ministry of Planning (MIPPE), because it was responsible for the development programs promoted by the government. This ministry, under the leadership of Nicolás Ardito Barletta, was probably one of the most influential within the government. During this period, MIPPE was considered a "liberal, middle of the road Ministry," certainly responsive to the needs of the private sector.[26]

The many links between the private sector and the government outlined previously belie common assertions made by the private sector during this period. One of the most strident complaints of businessmen and industrialists was that the government did not listen to their plight. Instead, they maintained, the actions of the regime were dangerously skewed toward the working masses. However, the substantial involvement of businessmen in government undercuts the validity of these claims.

Alarmed by the turn the economic situation was taking, and undoubtedly influenced by the constant attacks of the private sector, some of the

---

[24] Lakas was appointed president in 1969 to give the regime a more democratic semblance and to ameliorate the effects of having a military man as head of state. In effect, Torrijos was in complete control of the government and used Lakas as an adviser and as a ceremonial figure.

[25] Ricardo de la Espriella was head of the Banco Nacional in the 1970s, became vice president in 1978, and president in 1981 when Royo resigned.

[26] Interview with Carlos Valencia.

highest-ranking members of the government met in November 1974 to discuss the policies and short-term goals the government should adopt to try and lift the country out of recession. This meeting produced the "Declaración de Boquete," issued on November 27, 1974. Its main points were that the government would subsidize interests on loans to the agricultural sector by 4 percent and to the industrial sector by 3 percent, that laws for new fiscal incentives would be enacted in order to foster the reinversion of profits and the export of non-traditional goods produced entirely or partially in Panama, that measures would be taken to protect consumers from exploitive credit rates, and that the government together with private banks would embark on a massive housing program with special emphasis on low-cost housing. A high-level economic commission was named by Torrijos to continue the search for solutions to the economic crisis.[27]

Shortly after the "Declaración de Boquete" was made public, CONEP and the board of directors of the Cámara de Comercio e Industrias de Chiriquí also held a meeting to review the economic situation and to try to align the members of the private sector in common action. Guillermo Chapman, a noted Panamanian economist, stressed the incongruity between government actions and the economic policies it was promoting.[28] One of CONEP's legal consultants declared that "what many of us in this country do not want to accept is state capitalism . . . we don't want to have a situation where there is only one position, and it becomes a sin and a crime to oppose it." And the president of CONEP ended the meeting by saying that "the cohesion of the private sector is imperative so that we can survive the monster we have in front of us."[29]

A summary report of the CONEP meeting in Chiriquí stressed that the private sector wanted redress in three areas: (1) a definition of its role within the economy; (2) a clear definition of the government's economic policies; and (3) a revision of the Labor Code. The report pointed out that while previously the private sector had asked for a revision of the Labor Code in its entirety, now they were only asking for the revision or abolition of some of its clauses, i.e. stability. The most progressive *empresarios* also asked for uniformity in the interpretation of the Labor Code.[30] Shortly afterward, in

---

[27] The commission was composed of Arturo Sucre, vice president; Fernando Manfredo, Nicolás Ardito Barletta, Gerardo Gonzáles, José A. de la Ossa, Rolando Murgas, all Cabinet ministers;and one member of the Legislative Commission. "Medidas para combatir la inflación adopta el gobierno," *La Estrella de Panamá*, January 14, 1975.
[28] Chapman is director of the firm Investigación y Desarrollo, S.A. (INDESA). Several economic reports produced by that firm are quoted in this study and were used widely by various actors but principally by the private sector to validate its position.
[29] CONEP. "Reunión del CONEP y la Junta Directiva de la Cámara de Comercio e Industrias de Chiriquí, Jueves 23 de enero de 1975," Mimeo. Panamá: 1975.
[30] "Hay diálogo en torno a la Declaración de Boquete," *Diálogo Social*, no. 65(1975): 40-41. "Brinda apoyo al Ministro de Trabajo," *La Estrella de Panamá*, March 16, 1975.

the most overt act of the regime against the private sector, 14 of the participants in the CONEP meeting were deported, the offices of the Asociación Panameña de Ejecutivos de Empresa (APEDE) were taken over by the government, and all activities of that organization became closely monitored.

Meanwhile, during the Thirteenth General Congress of the Confederación de Trabajadores de la República de Panamá (CTRP), Murgas declared that the Labor Code would not be changed, and he challenged the private sector to find the real causes for the economic ills experienced in Panama and for the drop in productivity.[31] Throughout February and March of 1975 there was a continuous exchange in the media between Minister Murgas and the private sector regarding the issue of productivity and the challenge he had made,[32] but no concrete facts emerged until much later.[33]

## THE ECONOMIC SITUATION

Panama's economic growth rate during the 1960s was high and sustained, averaging an 8 percent annual increase. Between 1970 and 1973 the growth rate remained high, averaging 7.2 percent per year due to sustained public and private investment. Public investment more than doubled from 1971 to 1972 and in that year reached 32 percent of GDP, the highest percentage attained since the Second World War.[34] Private investment also continued to grow, primarily because the construction industry experienced a boom in costly high-rise condominium construction during this period. In 1974, however, the level of growth entered a drastic downward spiral. That year the economy grew only 2.6 percent, in 1975 growth of the GDP did not reach 1 percent, and in 1976 GDP experienced a negative growth of -0.3 percent. Growth of the manufacturing sector dropped from 4.2 percent in 1973 to -4.4 percent in 1974 and -0.9 percent in 1975, and the construction industry experienced a yearly drop of -8.9 percent for the period between 1974-1978 (Tables 6, 7).

---

[31] "Dijo el Dr. Rolando Murgas: El Código de Trabajo permanecerá intacto," *La Estrella de Panamá*, February 24, 1975.

[32] "Aceptamos el reto dice empresa privada a Murgas," *La Estrella de Panamá*, February 28, 1975; "Respuesta de Murgas: El reto que proponemos no es choque o enfrentamiento," *La Estrella de Panamá*, March 4, 1975;"El CONEP solicita aclaración," *La Estrella de Panamá*, March 8, 1975;"El CONEP se dirige a Murgas," *La Estrella de Panamá*, March 11, 1975; "Brinda apoyo al Ministro de Trabajo," *La Estrella de Panamá*, March 16, 1975.

[33] In 1976, a study was commissioned by CONEP on this issue and that same year PREALC conducted one on various problems identified with the Labor Code, including productivity. INDESA, "Informe del estudio de productividad," Mimeo. Panamá: January, 1977; PREALC, "Efectos del código de trabajo sobre el empleo, la productividad, los costos, y la inversión en Panamá." Geneva: ILO/Documento de Trabajo PREALC/156, 1978.

[34] Guillermo O. Chapman, "Factores que afectan la demanda por mano de obra en Panamá," Informe preparado para el Ministerio de Planificación y Política Económica (MIPPE) y la Agencia para el Desarrollo Internacional (AID). Mimeo. Panamá: INDESA, 1979, p. 9.

Table 6   GDP by Sector at 1960 Prices (millions)

| | 1966 | 1967 | 1968 | 1969 | 1970 | 1971 | 1972 | 1973 | 1974 | 1975 | 1976 | 1977 | 1978 | 1979 | 1980 |
|---|---|---|---|---|---|---|---|---|---|---|---|---|---|---|---|
| GDP-1960 prices | 664.1 | 720.9 | 771.2 | 836.3 | 894.5 | 972.6 | 1033.8 | 1101.2 | 1130.1 | 1137.2 | 1133.6 | 1185.3 | 1262.2 | 1351.2 | 1417.6 |
| Percentage Increase | | 8.5 | 7.0 | 8.4 | 7.0 | 8.7 | 6.3 | 6.5 | 2.6 | 0.6 | -0.3 | 1.6 | 2.7 | 7.1 | 4.9 |
| Agriculture | 139.2 | 145.6 | 154.0 | 162.3 | 161.1 | 167.1 | 172.0 | 177.9 | 175.2 | 183.6 | 182.4 | 196.5 | 195.6 | 192.1 | 194.2 |
| Manufacture | 107.0 | 120.1 | 131.7 | 144.0 | 153.6 | 166.7 | 177.0 | 184.6 | 176.4 | 174.9 | 153.5 | 153.6 | 162.4 | 186.6 | 194.0 |
| Construction | 38.4 | 43.5 | 46.3 | 47.5 | 54.0 | 64.1 | 71.8 | 76.3 | 79.4 | 66.5 | 56.3 | 59.8 | 60.0 | 64.9 | 73.2 |
| Elec.,gas,water | 15.0 | 16.3 | 18.9 | 23.5 | 26.0 | 30.4 | 34.2 | 38.5 | 40.3 | 44.1 | 48.3 | 50.8 | 52.8 | 61.4 | 65.6 |
| Transp.,communication | 36.7 | 41.1 | 43.9 | 51.5 | 59.6 | 68.0 | 72.2 | 80.4 | 92.5 | 94.5 | 111.8 | 123.8 | 139.1 | 154 | 163.7 |
| Commerce | 92.0 | 99.9 | 106.9 | 115.7 | 126.6 | 135.9 | 144.4 | 153.7 | 161.7 | 153.7 | 148.0 | 141.1 | 160.6 | 183.4 | 198.9 |
| Banks, Insurance | 18.8 | 21.2 | 22.5 | 30.0 | 34.8 | 39.9 | 45.1 | 54.7 | 59.9 | 65.6 | 70.1 | 86.7 | 95.4 | 99.8 | 110.9 |
| Prop. Vivienda | 46.1 | 49.6 | 52.7 | 55.4 | 60.1 | 66.5 | 73.7 | 81.0 | 84.9 | 87.6 | 89.8 | 91.9 | 96.4 | 99.7 | 105.9 |
| Public Administration | 17.4 | 19.4 | 21.3 | 21.9 | 23.4 | 25.3 | 27.3 | 27.7 | 30.0 | 33.0 | 35.4 | 35.7 | 36.7 | 38.0 | 42.0 |
| Services, pub.& priv. | 95.6 | 101.5 | 105.3 | 110.8 | 122.7 | 132.8 | 142.0 | 147.9 | 157.4 | 158.5 | 163.1 | 170.5 | 180.6 | 187.5 | 194.7 |
| Service, Canal zone | 56.0 | 60.7 | 65.6 | 71.3 | 70.3 | 73.3 | 71.3 | 74.8 | 68.9 | 71.9 | 72.0 | 71.8 | 79.8 | 80.8 | 71.3 |
| Mines | 1.9 | 2.0 | 2.1 | 2.4 | 2.3 | 2.6 | 2.7 | 3.7 | 3.5 | 3.3 | 2.9 | 3.1 | 2.8 | 3.0 | 3.2 |

*Sources:* 1966-1975: Dirección de Estadística y Censo, *Panamá en cifras: Años 1971-1975*, Panamá, 1976, pp. 16-17. 1975-1980: *Panamá en cifras: Años 1976-1980*, Panamá, 1981, pp. 10-11.

Table 7   Public and Private Investment, 1966-1980 (millions)

| | 1966 | 1967 | 1968 | 1969 | 1970 | 1971 | 1972 | 1973 | 1974 | 1975 | 1976 | 1977 | 1978 | 1979 | 1980 |
|---|---|---|---|---|---|---|---|---|---|---|---|---|---|---|---|
| Public investment | 18.9 | 26.2 | 30.5 | 41.8 | 58.8 | 59.6 | 125.2 | 76.9 | 81.1 | 157.3 | 170.3 | 158 | 150.4 | 97 | 126.9 |
| Private investment | 131.3 | 132.3 | 149 | 63.7 | 183.4 | 216.4 | 208.1 | 238.9 | 200.6 | 152.7 | 152 | 82.6 | 170.7 | 204.1 | 192.9 |
| Total investment | 150.2 | 158.5 | 179.5 | 205.5 | 242.2 | 276 | 333.3 | 315.8 | 281.7 | 310.7 | 322.3 | 240.6 | 321.1 | 301.1 | 319.8 |

*Source:* Dirección de Estadística y Censo. *Panamá en Cifras: Años 1971-1975*, Panamá, 1976, pp.18-19. *Panamá en Cifras: Años 1976-1980*, Panamá, 1981, pp. 12-13.

Table 8 Central Government and State Enterprises Debt, 1966-1979 (millions)

| | 1966 | 1967 | 1968 | 1969 | 1970 | 1971 | 1972 | 1973 | 1974 | 1975 | 1976 | 1977 | 1978 | 1979 |
|---|---|---|---|---|---|---|---|---|---|---|---|---|---|---|
| Central government: | | | | | | | | | | | | | | |
| Internal | 7.4 | 83.5 | 97.8 | 133.9 | 144.9 | 155.0 | 190.3 | 179.9 | 231.4 | 294.6 | 344.9 | 342.0 | 387.2 | 416.4 |
| External | 68.3 | 71.2 | 70.8 | 104.8 | 140.5 | 173.4 | 214.8 | 296.8 | 358.8 | 427.3 | 510.2 | 614.0 | 1025.5 | 1344.0 |
| State enterprises: | | | | | | | | | | | | | | |
| External | | | | | | 136.7 | 138.2 | 156.6 | 285.2 | 433.7 | 898.8 | 1100.0 | 1540.5 | 1383.0 |
| Total external debt | 139.7 | 154.8 | 168.6 | 238.7 | 285.0 | 310.0 | 353.0 | 453.4 | 644.0 | 861.0 | 1409.0 | 1714.0 | 2566.0 | 2727.0 |

Sources: Dirección de Estadística y Censo. Panamá en cifras: Años 1971-1975, Panamá, 1976, pp. 18-19. Panamá en cifras: Años 1976-1980, Panamá, 1981, pp. 12-13. Total external debt 1971-1979: Socio-Economic Progress in Latin America, Washington, D.C., 1972-1980.

Panama's recession arose from concurrent effects of external and internal factors. The most crucial exogenous factor was the world recession brought about in 1974 by the drastic increase in oil prices and by the pernicious cycle of inflation and recession that it unleashed, which affected the world economic system for several years. Panama's economy is especially vulnerable to outside factors because it is a very open economy without a central bank or a currency of its own, thus negating the use of protective instruments such as monetary, fiscal, and exchange policies. The large percentage of Panama's GDP based on the import of goods and services illustrates the openness of its economy.[35]

By 1976, even though the world economic system experienced an upward trend and the economies of most Latin American countries began to recover, Panama's did not. The reasons for this continued stagnation are largely to be found in factors internal to the country. The construction industry began to collapse in 1973-1974. There was no private investment to take up the deficit left by the drop in construction, and the public sector was unable to fill the void left by reduced private investment. Although at the beginning of the 1970s public investment had been very high both proportionately and in real terms, by its middle, the government was overextended in external borrowing, which imposed severe limitations on its fiscal policies. (See Table 8.)

## Collapse of the Construction Industry

Private construction experienced an unprecedented growth during the 1970-1973 period due to speculation in real estate and the construction of expensive high-rise condominiums, especially on the waterfront area of Punta Paitilla in Panama City. In 1971, private construction increased by 25 percent and in 1972 by 38 percent.[36] Then in 1973, the government passed a series of laws regulating housing. The most notorious of these, Ley 93, froze rentals at their previous-year levels. The effect of these laws, known as *leyes de vivienda*, was that construction of rental units ceased completely.[37]

Because rental units were not being built and the expensive condominiums remained unsold, the financial sector panicked and tightened its credit supply to construction companies. Investment in this sector dropped from an annual volume of 73 million in 1972 and 1973 to 29 million in 1974. The percentage of GDP represented by the construction industry decreased from a high in 1971 of 18.7 percent to -16.2 percent in 1975 and -12.5 percent

---

[35] Inter-American Development Bank, *Economic and Social Progress Report in Latin America, Annual Report*. Washington, D.C.: 1981, p. 299.

[36] Chapman, "Factores," p. 11.

[37] Since that date only two such buildings were built by private firms and none by the public sector. Jaime Correa, "La problemática de la construcción de viviendas en Panamá," p. 45, in Asociación Panameña de Ejecutivos de Empresa, *XIV Conferencia Anual de Ejecutivos de Empresa (CADE 1979)*, Panamá, 1979.

in 1976. This industry experienced an average annual negative growth of -8.9 percent between 1974 and 1978 (Table 6), and credit provided by the banking system fell from 201.7 million dollars in 1974 to -15.9 million in 1975.[38] The public sector attempted to fill in the void left by the private construction sector. Public construction grew by 21 percent between 1970 and 1976 and by 37 percent between 1973-1976.[39] Private construction only began a modest upward swing in 1979.

## Drop in Private Investment

Along with the collapse of the construction industry, private investment also dropped in absolute terms. From a peak of 238.9 million (at 1960 dollars) in 1973, total private investment fell to 152.7 million in 1975 and reached its lowest level in 1977 with a total of only 82.6 million (See Table 7). The reasons for this drop are complicated and closely linked to the mood that prevailed in the country. There was a feeling of uncertainty during this time due to the ongoing negotiations of a new canal treaty. Investors held back in expectation of the outcome of the negotiations.

There was also a climate of distrust toward the regime due to what the private sector termed a lack of clear definition of governmental policies and goals. It is in this regard in particular that it becomes difficult to separate fact from fiction and to assess the behavior of the private sector in relation to its perception of the government. Members of the private sector had stressed often enough their concern over a lack of clear governmental economic policy and with the rapid encroachment of the government into areas that had previously been strictly in the domain of private enterprise. Several areas were of special concern, i.e., the price-regulation policy, the government's direct participation in the productive sector, the policy of fiscal incentives, and the labor policy.[40]

The price-control policy had been expanded in 1974 to include prices for almost all available goods, either imported or produced locally. Businessmen felt that this created a tremendous strain because it restricted their ability to adjust prices in keeping with increases in costs. Especially hard hit were those enterprises depending on oil imports and their derivatives, because the cost of this commodity continued to rise on an upward spiral.

A second reason for concern among private investors was the government's direct participation in profit-making ventures through the establishment of state and mixed capital enterprises. This inhibited private investment because investors were uncertain about which areas the government would chose to enter and were reluctant to compete with the state

---

[38] PREALC, "Panamá: instrumentos de incentivo al desarrollo industrial y su efecto en el empleo," Geneva: ILO/Documento de Trabajo PREALC/179, Cuadro I-2, p. 63.
[39] PREALC, "Panamá: estrategia de necesidades básicas y empleo," Geneva: ILO/ Documento de Trabajo PREALC/189, Cuadro 25.
[40] Chapman, "Factores," pp. 20-23.

in economic ventures. This concern could be explained by the regime's past history of starting and ending ventures abruptly or shifting directions in mid-course if it seemed convenient. Private investors saw the government as a powerful contender and competition with it as extremely unfair, and they hesitated to engage in ventures in which the rules of the game were in the hands of a contender whom they did not trust.

A third element in the drop in private investment had to do with fiscal incentives provided by the government to attract investment. A leading economist has classified these as "extremely generous,"[41] and a study by PREALC actually recommended that many of these incentives be phased out, as they did not accomplish their purpose and unnecessarily lost for the government large amounts of revenues.[42] Nevertheless, the private sector did not find these incentives adequate. Their complaints were loud and persistent enough for the government to approve a new Package of Fiscal Incentives at the end of 1976. The effects of the fiscal incentives seem to have been primarily to foster a greater use of capital intensive techniques to the detriment of those that would promote a fuller utilization of labor.

The fourth factor in the drop in private investment was related to labor policy and its effects as perceived by the private sector. While the economic effects of labor policy are the most difficult to assess, objectively the policy appears to have had minor, if any, adverse economic repercussions. Nevertheless, in the mind of the private sector the problems caused by labor policy, specifically the 1972 Labor Code, were the greatest detriment to business during the decade under study.

All of the above reasons prompted the drop in private investment, as members of the private sector took their money out of the country or simply chose not to invest. It is interesting to note the similarity of attitude and action between the private sector in Peru under Velasco Alvarado and in Panama under Torrijos. After the Comunidades Industriales (CI) were set up in Peru, the private sector in that country engaged in all sorts of subterfuges to bypass them. They maintained an unrelenting campaign against the Comunidades Industriales through the press and engaged in a massive investment strike.[43]

## Ley 95

Throughout 1975 and 1976, while the economy continued to deteriorate rapidly, debates regarding the Labor Code did not abate. The first serious indication that a revision of the code was indeed in the making was the replacement of Dr. Rolando Murgas as Minister of Labor by Lic. Adolfo Ahumada in November 1975. Earlier that year, when asked about a

---

[41] Chapman, "Factores," p. 22.
[42] PREALC, "Panamá: instrumentos," p. 56.
[43] Evelyne Huber Stephens, *The Politics of Workers Participation*. New York: Academic Press, 1980, pp. 147-150.

possible revision of the Labor Code in a meeting with the Sindicato de Periodistas, Torrijos declared in his usual noncommittal manner,

I am not saying that the Code will be changed. We'll see. What is true is that more than 300 small businesses have gone broke. I've seen too many little refreshment stands, small restaurants and little shops, where the owners have had to depart in an economic stampede, give up their dreams of being businessmen because they can't pay the *prestaciones* (labor costs).[44]

Torrijos was referring to a confidential study prepared by MITRAB that showed that 734 enterprises had closed down in the 20-month period between January 1975 and August 1976. The bulk of these (60 percent) were commercial concerns. The same report included data from the Ministry of Commerce and Industry (MICI), indicating that during the same period, authorization had been given for 4,549 new businesses. Neither ministry gave figures on loss of employment due to these business foreclosures.[45]

Organized labor responded to the attacks on the Labor Code by questioning the reliability of the studies. The CNTP posed several challenges to the validity of the private sector's claims. They asked if counted among the closed businesses were construction firms that had gone bankrupt after over-extending their credit in the building of luxury condominiums; if businesses located in condemned buildings slated to be demolished were included in the figures; if businesses that previously had barely provided a subsistence to their owners were being counted; and if small stores competing with supermarkets were counted.[46] They also asked what the ratio was between new and canceled business licenses since the Labor Code had been approved.[47] Labor speculated that the aim of the private sector was to undermine the unions and to lessen the merit of collective agreements and pointed out that although the code was being attacked due to the high labor costs (*prestaciones*), the only new item that had an immediate impact on labor costs was the thirteenth-month salary.

In October 1976, the government named a commission, Comisión Revisora del Código de Trabajo, to revise the Labor Code. Its members included Ahumada, the new labor minister; Murgas, the former labor minister; Manfredo, presidential chief of staff; and Darío González Pitti, a labor leader from the SITRACHILCO banana union of Puerto Armuelles and also an assemblyman and, at that time, president of the National

---

[44] "Posibles ajustes al Código de Trabajo," *El Panamá América*, September 29, 1976.

[45] "Cerradas 734 empresas en solo 20 meses," *El Panamá América*, November 21, 1976.

[46] Many buildings from the time of the French canal were being torn down in the densely populated areas of Chorrillo and Marañón.

[47] "En torno a reformas al Código de Trabajo," *Matutino*, October 25, 1976.

Assembly of Representatives.[48] Ahumada declared that the revision of the code was a complicated matter, not only in economic and juridical terms but also and especially in political terms, "because if it's not done properly, the revolutionary image of this 'Process' can be diminished."[49] At a meeting of the Federación Sindical de Trabajadores (FSTRP), he further asserted that no revisions would be made without ample consultation and input from labor groups.[50]

Prominent members of the private sector had already prepared a thorough revision of the Labor Code, which had reached Torrijos some months before.[51] The Comisión Revisora decided to forego its use because it implied a complete rewriting of the code and they had very little time in which to produce the changes. "We decided to put together something which would modify those things the businessmen [empresarios] had complained the most about. That is, come up with something about which we could say, this will ease the minds of the empresarios."[52]

Sensing that a change was really underway and that they would inevitably lose ground—above all because they would be bypassed in all consultations—the main labor organizations coalesced under the umbrella of CONATO. They unanimously agreed not to allow any modifications to the Labor Code that would undermine its bases or those of the labor movement in general.[53]

On December 22, a series of laws called the Paquete de Incentivos Fiscales were enacted, granting the added fiscal incentives promised in the Declaración de Boquete two years before. Among these, Ley 68 provided incentives to the construction industry, Ley 69 concerned special regulation for the depreciation of fixed debits, Ley 78 instituted a tax for real estate, and Ley 90, incentives for the increase of employment.[54]

Eight days later, on December 30, Panama's most important labor leaders were invited to meet with Torrijos in Farallón. They believed they were being consulted regarding the proposed labor changes and told Torrijos the reasons they felt the changes would not be beneficial to the working class.[55] Present at the meeting were the members of the Estado

---

[48] "Nombra Comisión Revisora del Código de Trabajo," El Panamá América, October 22, 1976.
[49] "Dijo el Lic. Ahumada en la Asamblea: El Código de Trabajo es un problema sensible y complicado," Matutino, October 23, 1976.
[50] "No habra revisión sin consulta obrera," La Estrella de Panamá, October 30, 1976.
[51] Interview with Carlos Valencia.
[52] Interview with Lic. Fernando Manfredo.
[53] This statement was signed by the secretary generals of the four labor centrals. "Manifiesto al pais del CONATO," Matutino, November 27, 1976.
[54] "Leyes de incentivos fiscales," La Estrella de Panamá, January 4, 1977. Although Ley 95, with which we are concerned in this study, was not passed together with this group of laws, it is considered part of the Paquete de Incentivos Fiscales.
[55] Interviews with Mr. Phillip Dean Butcher (CTRP) and Mr. José Meneses (CNTP).

Mayor of the National Guard, Vice President Gerardo González, and several cabinet ministers. During the meeting Torrijos declared that "if changes are made, the government will not allow the empresarios to abuse the labor sector." He also said he did not want the labor leadership to approve any changes but "just to give him a vote of confidence, so the government can try to solve the economic problems."[56] The labor leaders withheld this vote of confidence to Torrijos and his government, sensing that they were being made into sacrificial lambs for a situation with which they had little to do.[57]

The full impact of the cynicism of that meeting was brought home to labor leaders the next morning, when upon their return to Panama City, they read in the local media that Ley 95, which modified the most controversial aspects of the Labor Code, had been signed and published in the *Gaceta Oficial*, making it a *fait accompli* as they were meeting with Torrijos.

---

[56] "La patronal no podrá atropellar a obreros," *Crítica*, December 31, 1976.
[57] Interview with Mr. Phillip Dean Butcher.

# 7

# FROM MODIFICATION TO ACCOMMODATION: LEY 95 AND LEY 8A

Ley 95 signaled the loss of autonomy of the Torrijos regime with regard to the former ruling elite, which it had dispossessed of power in 1968. The factors that provided the leverage that led to this loss of autonomy were outside the control of the Torrijos regime and are representative of the effect of external forces on extremely dependent and weak economies. The private sector was able to use the economic vulnerability of the regime to regain some of the power it had lost with the National Guard takeover. As will be demonstrated in Chapter 8, the attacks made against the Labor Code based on economic arguments were not corroborated by the facts. The insistence of the private sector on revoking the Labor Code, then, was a political act of a group trying to regain power. Even though Ley 95 did not restore the previous position of the private sector regarding its workforce, it did curtail some of the benefits labor had attained through the 1972 Labor Code. Furthermore, Ley 95 represented the capitulation of the Torrijos regime and the starting point for the regaining of power by the former ruling elite.

The events that followed during the five years after Ley 95 was enacted are telling of the transformations undergone by the Torrijos regime. Through the enactment of Ley 95, the regime lost the relative autonomy it had enjoyed from the private sector. Although labor did not immediately engage in an anti-government campaign, the bond that had been established between Torrijos and labor was broken with the passage of Ley 95. Just as the Labor Code provided the catalyst that united the private sector, Ley 95 was the catalyst that ultimately united labor.

## LEY 95

Ley 95, one of the laws that formed the Paquete de Incentivos Fiscales, which was enacted into law in late 1976 ostensibly to bolster the economy, contained the revisions to the Labor Code, much awaited by the private labor during the Torrijos regime. As one labor leader stated, "it is the most anti-labor law [*ley más anti-obrera*] ever to be enacted in Panama."[1]

The main changes introduced by Ley 95 were related to stability of employment, collective agreements, and strikes. Regarding stability of employment, Article 13 of the law stipulated that if the employer was not able to prove just cause in dismissing a worker, he had the choice of reinstating him or paying the indemnization required in Article 225 of the Labor Code and dismissing him anyway. This reversed the tables and once again placed in the hands of the employer the unilateral option to keep or dismiss a worker. Ley 95 also stipulated that every worker with more than two years of employment who was dismissed for disciplinary or non-imputable reasons (as opposed to economic reasons) had to be replaced within 30 days (Article 15). This clause apparently was intended to protect employment, or maintain "numerical stability," as the drafters of Ley 95 called it, by preventing the firing of massive numbers of workers.

Collective agreements were frozen for two years, and Ley 95 provided new enterprises with a grace period of two years, during which they need not negotiate any agreement. Those firms that had collective agreements due to expire during the two-year freeze would increase salaries in proportion to the annual averages agreed upon in their current collective agreements.

Several clauses of the 1972 Labor Code regarding collective agreements were particularly disliked by the private sector and were modified in Ley 95. Article 403 of the Labor Code read as follows:

> The collective agreement, apart from the stipulations regarding working conditions, will include:
> 1. The names and addresses of the contracting parties;
> 2. The enterprises, establishments or businesses covered by it;
> 3. The rules and regulations of the factory committee (*comité de empresa*).
> 4. Procedures for grievances and for communication between the union and the enterprise.
> 5. Stipulations on wage rates and job classifications.
> 6. Duration.
> 7. Stipulations relative to the Internal Working Regulations, which if they already exist, shall be replaced by the collective labor agreement.
> 8. The stipulations of article 68 which apply to the nature of the collective agreement;

---

[1] Speech by José Meneses to the National Legislative Council on April 9, 1981, quoted in "Nueva Ley 95 perpetúa la injusticia." *Diálogo Social*, no. 134, May, 1981, p. 37-38.

9. The other stipulations that the parties agree on." (Labor Code, Article 403)

Ley 95 modified this article drastically. It eliminated the obligation to establish internal regulations and job classifications and limited the role of the factory committee to just hearing complaints from workers. It changed no. 9 to read "the other stipulations that the parties agree on as long as they do not interfere with the employer's right to determine the number of workers necessary for the normal functioning of the enterprise" (Ley 95, Article 9).[2]

The modifications to the collective agreement clauses removed any potential participation of workers in the management of the enterprise. This had originally been envisioned in the 1972 Labor Code as taking place through the workers' role in the *comités de empresa*. The modifications also eliminated any possibility for setting job standards and controlling the tasks demanded in any one job by not forcing the employer to provide job classifications and job descriptions. The clauses that were modified or deleted were those that provided the most tangible opportunities for workers to perform innovative roles in the enterprise. Why, one wonders, would such issues as job classifications and job descriptions pose such an affront to, and an infringement on, the rights of the employer? One could understand the reluctance of management in accepting the factory committees. But in the four years in which they were operational, these committees accomplished little or nothing. Workers complained that managers oftentimes found it beneath them to attend the meetings of such committees, or neglected to inform workers about impending management meetings, or withheld information regarding issues to be discussed.

Collective agreement negotiations as established in the 1972 Labor Code posed enormous practical problems and became a constant source of friction between management and labor. No basic guidelines regarding the substantive part of the negotiations were ever provided, and employers were extremely reticent to make available information regarding the economic situation of their enterprise and their capability or lack thereof, to grant salary increases, and so forth. Working in the dark, the unions opted to present inflated demands, or *pliegos de peticiones*, with the knowledge that they would be scaled down by the employers. Employers viewed this approach as an affront and as one more proof that the unions were trying to do them in. The negotiations took place under very tense and conflictual conditions. It is still true today that employers and labor view collective bargaining as a power confrontation instead of as a mechanism for the rational determination of the working conditions of the enterprise.[3]

---

[2] These changes were later retained in Ley 8a of 1981, which modified Ley 95.

[3] Jorge Fábrega, *Las convenciones colectivas en Panamá*. Panamá: n.p., 1981, p. 65.

According to Minister Manfredo, Ley 95 froze collective agreements "to restore the country, to give it a semblance of peace and tranquility by removing the anguish caused by the negotiations of such agreements."[4] It was believed that the negotiations of collective agreements "generated antagonisms which lead to strikes and disruptions," and in the midst of an economic recession, they became a "perturbing element."[5]

Article 480 of the Labor Code enumerated the reasons that could justify a strike. Number 1 of that article read that an acceptable motive for a strike was "to obtain better working conditions." This was changed in Ley 95 to read "to obtain better working conditions *which will not affect the income-yielding capacity* [rentabilidad] *of the enterprise*" (Article 12 of Ley 95). This change in effect manacled labor's most powerful tool for exerting pressure and seeking redress to grievances. By eliminating stability of employment and greatly curtailing the capacity for collective action, Ley 95 removed from the 1972 Labor Code the most important benefits it had granted to labor.

When the law was being drafted, more drastic measures were recommended by at least one of the drafters. Minister Manfredo wanted to introduce a clause by which MITRAB could place a 60-day moratorium on any strike. The reason for this is displayed in a question posed by Manfredo, who asked whether in a country as small as Panama, with such a reduced labor force, strikes are warranted at all.[6]

Manfredo also proposed other changes. The Labor Code stipulated that the decision to work overtime or not rested with the worker.[7] Manfredo wanted to increase the amount of overtime that an employee could work and to make it mandatory that an employee work two extra hours whenever this was requested by the employer. He also proposed changes regarding the Juntas de Conciliación y Decisión.[8] Among these were:

1. The ability to appeal the sentences of the juntas to a tripartite board composed exclusively of lawyers.
2. That in specific instances, the decisions of the tripartite board be susceptible to a *recurso de casación*, or appeal based on legal grounds, to be heard by the Supreme Court. A positive outcome

---

[4] Interview with Lic. Fernando Manfredo.

[5] Second interview with Dr. Rolando Murgas.

[6] Interview with Lic. Fernando Manfredo.

[7] Carta de Fernando Manfredo, Ministro de la Presidencia a Adolfo Ahumada, Ministro de Trabajo, 8 de octubre de 1976, p. 2.

[8] The Juntas de Conciliación y Decisión (JCD) were established in March 1975 as lay tripartite boards to hear all cases of dismissals, except those of persons with special privileges (*fueros*). The juntas also were expected to rule on all litigations that involved up to $1,500. They were set up in response to the complaints about the slowness of the labor courts, and their decisions were unappealable.

of this, in Manfredo's view, would be the unifying of labor decisions by the Supreme Court.

4. That the juntas hear all cases of dismissals of workers with special privileges (*fueros*), because the juntas reached decisions faster than the labor courts.[9] As the situation stood, when cases of this nature were pending, workers had to continue in their jobs, creating a great amount of tension in the place of employment.

None of the changes regarding the moratorium on strikes, increase in overtime, and those proposed regarding the Juntas de Conciliación y Decisión were ultimately adopted in Ley 95.

The effort to enact Ley 95 was led by the minister of planning, Ardito Barletta, and by Manfredo, who had been minister of commerce and industry and at the time was presidential chief of staff.[10]

Ley 95 was passed without any prior consultation with either labor or the private sector and was completely skewed toward the interests of the private sector.[11] It was designed to appease the private sector at a time when the lack of private investment was making the economic situation of the country extremely precarious. Ley 95 was also intended to curtail the labor movement and to bring a semblance of tranquility to the country at the height of the Canal Treaty negotiations. "There was a crisis in the country, and the government's hope was to achieve a truce during the period of the [Canal Treaty] negotiations."[12] One of the drafters of Ley 95 stated that "we tried to come up with something that would single out those issues more often mentioned as sources of conflict by the *empresarios*, and modify them. We came up with a package to appease the *empresarios*."[13]

The fact that Ley 95 was so skewed toward the private sector and that it was passed as an immediate solution to a crisis situation gave it a feeling of transitoriness.[14] According to Murgas, "the political compromise of the government with the workers was that Ley 95 was just a temporary measure."[15] Minister Manfredo says that he warned the government that the law was "too fragile and artificial . . . it cannot be maintained because it is not a balanced law."[16]

The reaction to Ley 95 was mixed. The private sector welcomed it with

---

[9] Carta de Fernando Manfredo, pp. 7-8.

[10] Second interview with Dr. Rolando Murgas. Manfredo claims that he introduced about 80 percent of the articles of Ley 95. Interview with Lic. Fernando Manfredo.

[11] Interviews with Dr. Rolando Murgas, Lic. Fernando Manfredo, and Lic. Carlos Valencia.

[12] Second interview with Dr. Rolando Murgas.

[13] Interview with Lic. Fernando Manfredo.

[14] This was enhanced by the fact that some of the provisions did have an expiration date. The moratorium on collective agreements, for instance, was to last two years.

[15] Second interview with Dr. Rolando Murgas.

[16] Interview with Lic. Fernando Manfredo.

relief, but many of its members were disappointed that it did not contain more sweeping reforms. Those *empresarios* would have been content with nothing short of the total revoking of the 1972 Labor Code. Businessmen who were satisfied with the changes interpreted Ley 95 as a thawing out of the government toward their interests and were determined to fight to make it a permanent law if they could not exert pressure for more thorough reforms.

Although labor leaders had foreseen for months that the Labor Code would be reformed, they were shocked at how the changes came about. First, they had expected to be consulted, at least symbolically, as had been the case in 1971 when the Labor Code was being drafted. Second, the reforms were presented to labor as a nationalistic gesture, so that their acceptance, or at least their acquiescence, was cast as a show of patriotism. This affected the various labor groups differently, in proportion to the degree of compromise they had attained with the government.

The CNTP, which was the organization most committed to and apparently most favored by the regime, was the most ambivalent in its reaction. It interpreted the changes as the conspiratorial outcome of the private sector and foreign interests and did not blame the government openly, as it saw the government as a pawn amidst those enemies. The CNTP was not immediately vocal against Ley 95 and kept a low profile during the first months after it was enacted. One of the CNTP leaders stated that "the timing was picked for those changes [Ley 95]. The issue of the moment was the great battle against the United States. It was not the time to protest, because it would have been said that Panama was in no condition to sign anything, with the country paralyzed and the political situation in chaos."[17]

The CTRP perceived the changes as a slap in the face by the government but also as a class issue in which the government was forced by the interests of the upper classes to sacrifice the labor movement. "The empresarios had a strong influence with the multinationals to put pressure on the government, to make it seem that the economy was going downhill on account of the Code, and that in order for Panama to receive certain international loans it was necessary to limit the Labor Code through Ley 95 ... It was a political move that the opposition used to create a conflict between the working class and the revolutionary government."[18]

Although the perception of Ley 95 by the two large centrals was not much different, their plans of action were at odds. The CTRP proposed an immediate massive protest against the new law. The smaller centrals, the CIT and CATI, approved of these plans. The CNTP did not go along, claiming it could not embarrass the government when the Canal Treaty

---

[17] Interview with José Meneses.
[18] Interview with Philip Dean Butcher.

negotiations were at stake. While the leadership of the CTRP spent the weeks following passage of Ley 95 organizing the demonstration, the CNTP leaders spent their time pressuring their SITRACHILCO Union of Puerto Armuelles to go back to work.[19] An added embarrassment for the CNTP was the comuniqué issued by the Sindicato de Tipógrafos, which stated that Ley 95 was unconstitutional in that it violated several articles of the constitution.[20]

The mass protest organized by the CTRP against Ley 95 was to be held on Sunday, January 16. Since the previous Thursday, MITRAB officials had begun calling meetings with CTRP leaders to "see what could be done." On Saturday, Labor Minister Ahumada invited Philip Dean Butcher, the secretary general of the CTRP, and the leaders of the other participating centrals to a meeting at the Ministry. Present at this meeting was Col. Araúz (head of Traffic of the National Guard), who told the labor leaders that they would be responsible for whatever happened the next day and that the government would not allow any rally to take place that might alter the internal order of the country. "In the manner in which Col. Araúz spoke to us, he made it clear that if we held the demonstration they would throw the *Guardia* [police] at us." After consulting with the leaders of the other centrals, "we agreed that it would not be prudent to hold the rally because we would be putting our people out as bait to be trampled down by the police."[21]

An item appeared in the local press explaining that the workers had suspended the demonstration because it could have been used by elements alien to the labor movement, opportunists "out to take advantage of these difficult moments and engage in activities against the Revolutionary Process."[22] The same article announced that five labor leaders would be named to the Comisión Laboral Nacional, which would shortly be formed to write the bylaws for Ley 95. The rank and file voiced harsh criticism against the leadership after the demonstration was suspended,[23] and members of the CNTP accused their leaders of selling out to the government.[24] An article in *Diálogo Social* intimated that the rally had been canceled in exchange for the positions in the Comisión Nacional Laboral and that

---

[19] The SITRACHILCO Union declared a strike on January 4 in protest of Ley 95. "Efectos de las reformas al Código de Trabajo," *Crítica*, January 5, 1977; "Diálogo entre líderes obreros y el Gobierno Nacional - Posible suspensión de la huelga de las bananeras," *El Panamá América*, January 6, 1977.

[20] The typographers claimed that Ley 95 violated articles 59, 64, 65, 66, and 69 of the Constitution. "Comunicado del Sindicato de Artes Gráficas," *El Panamá América*, January 7, 1977.

[21] Interview with Philip Dean Butcher.

[22] "Trabajadores acuerdan suspender manifiestación hoy," *Estrella de Panamá*, January 16, 1977.

[23] Interview with Philip Dean Butcher.

[24] Interview with José Meneses.

SITRACHILCO workers had been forced back to work because the CNTP did not think the timing was right to challenge the government.[25]

During the months following the enactment of Ley 95, the labor sector was quiet. High government officials made statements on the improvement of the economic situation, apparently for the benefit of the private sector. At the swearing in ceremony of the new board of directors of the Chamber of Commerce, President Lakas gave a speech in which he assured the private sector that the government would continue cooperating with them.[26] In March, barely two months after Ley 95 had been enacted, Minister Ahumada declared that some businesses had experienced increases in productivity of 15 percent and even 20 percent.[27] Later that same month, the Comisión Laboral Nacional was named, headed by the minister of labor, with five representatives from labor and five from the private sector.[28]

At the 1977 CADE held in May of that year, the private sector presented a set of propositions that they claimed were necessary to raise the low levels of private investment and to aid in the development process. These included "the consolidation of attitudes and expectations favorable to investment in the business community; the institutionalization of methods of communication between the private sector and the government at all levels, especially at the highest; and a [governmental] formula for setting up efficient channels of consultation with the private sector prior to approving legislative measures."[29] Other concessions demanded by the private sector included special labor laws to cover workers in the Colón Free Zone as well as hotel and bank workers. This new set of demands came less than five months after the package of fiscal incentives had been approved and the Labor Code had been modified according to the private sector's specifications. The private sector wanted nothing less than what they had lost in 1968, and finally they were finding ways of asserting their demands.

The Federación Sindical (FSTRP) of the CNTP declared that the private sector had "programmed the destabilization of the Revolutionary Process" and that their objective was to change the progressive course of the

---

[25] Aureliano Torres, "Cronología de una reforma," *Diálogo Social*, no. 86-87 (Feb.-Mar), 1977: 6-7.

[26] "Gobierno mantendra colaboración con la empresa privada," *Estrella de Panamá*, February 13, 1977.

[27] "Declara el Ministro Ahumada: Balance positivo arrojan interpretaciones laborales," *República*, March 9, 1977.

[28] "Instalada la Comisión Laboral Nacional entre CONEP y CONATO," *La Estrella de Panamá*, March 17, 1977.

[29] "Paquete de recomendaciones plantea sector privado a fin de propiciar el desarrollo," *La Estrella de Panamá*, May 15, 1977; "Conclusiones generales de CADE 1977," *La Estrella de Panamá*, May 18, 1977.

government, and to return to political power.[30] Even so, the government asserted that, thanks to Ley 95, labor conflicts had diminished greatly. The national director of labor, Julio César Acosta, declared that MITRAB did not look forward to the more than 300 collective agreements that would have to be negotiated in 1979, because those negotiations were nothing but a "headache."[31]

## LABOR JURISPRUDENCE

Once the Labor Code was enacted into law and its new provisions were set in motion, the common belief in Panama was that the number of labor litigations escalated to unmanageable proportions. This, together with the slowness of the labor courts, the skewed new provisions protecting the rights of workers, and the generous indemnizations granted to workers all conspired to have an immediate and negative effect of the Labor Code, felt in Panama's economy as deleterious to private enterprise in general and to small businesses in particular.

Among the issues raised in the anti-government campaign that ensued after the passage of the Labor Code, labor litigations were considered uppermost in their negative impact. Not only was the labor process attacked, but along with the increase in the number of cases taken to litigation, the slowness of the process was found wanting. If a worker won a case and had to be reinstated or indemnized, his due salaries (*salarios caídos*) also had to be paid. According to popular belief, many small and medium-sized enterprises folded after one lengthy case. Another common belief held was that workers were abusing the use of litigation, because they knew the labor process favored them. In Chapter 8, I will analyze the cost effects of the increase in labor litigations.

The labor court system in Panama consists of a series of lower labor courts (*juzgados sectoriales de trabajo*) that can hear non-appealable (*única instancia*) or appealable (*de primera instancia*) cases. Cases are appealed to the Tribunal Superior de Trabajo, located in Panama City, and further to the Third Chamber (Sala Tercera) of the Supreme Court. Plans had been made to establish either a labor court at the Supreme Court level (Corte de Casación Laboral) or a fourth chamber in the Supreme Court specifically for labor cases, but as this has not happened, labor cases continue to be heard in the Third Chamber, together with cases regarding administrative issues (*lo contencioso administrativo*).

To counteract some of the complaints regarding labor cases, the Juntas de Conciliación y Decisión were established in March 1975. Minister

---

[30] "Federación Sindical (FSTRP) se refiere a posición de la CADE," *Matutino*, June 6, 1977.
[31] "Disminuyen conflictos laborales," *República*, June 21, 1977.

Murgas was responsible for the law that established the juntas. The juntas were created to protect the Labor Code from the slanderous campaign of the private sector and to make the system for litigating labor cases more efficient.[32] The juntas were lay tribunals composed of a representative each from the labor sector, the private sector, and the Ministry of Labor. The juntas were to hear all cases of dismissals except those involving persons with special privileges (*fueros*) and all litigations involving amounts up to $1,500. Cases were made orally, with a summary presentation, and the judgment was given at the end of the hearing. Decisions made by the Juntas could not be appealed.

Before the juntas were established, the complaints of the private sector centered around the protracted legal process and the high amounts to be paid in indemnization and due salaries. Once the juntas were in operation, however, the complaints shifted to the sentences promulgated. The complaint was that the juntas favored workers and consequently no employer could expect justice from such tribunals.

Employers began appealing cases to the Supreme Court, even though the decisions of the juntas could not by law be appealed. The private sector found a loophole, and cases were appealed on the pretext that the constitutional rights of the employer had been violated by the decision of the junta. This meant that the case was not heard on the merit of the labor dispute, but at a more general level under the clause of *amparos de garantías constitucionales* (protection of constitutional rights).[33]

Just as the private sector believed that they could not get justice from the lower courts, workers believed that the Supreme Court was "owned" by private enterprise. And in this instance of the Supreme Court ruling on decisions made by the juntas, the legality of the Supreme Court hearing cases of this nature could be contested, which made the Supreme Court justices party to the charade by accepting those cases. This situation created inordinate tensions between the Ministry of Labor, the Supreme Court, the private sector, and organized labor.

---

[32] Interview with Dr. Rolando Murgas.

[33] "La casación no es simple alegato de lo que parece ser," *La Estrella de Panamá*, December 2, 1977; "La Corte concede amparo y revoca orden de Dirección de Trabajo," *La Estrella de Panamá*, December 17, 1977; "Manifiestan preocupación por algunos fallos de la Corte," *Matutino,* December 17, 1977; "Ahumada desafía a la Corte Suprema," *Crítica*, January 21, 1978; "Expresa Ahumada a La Estrella: No hay rebelión ni desacato entre la Corte y el MITRAB," *La Estrella de Panamá*, January 25, 1978; "Revocan orden de la Junta de Conciliación," *La Estrella de Panamá*, June 8, 1978; "Amparo constitucional contra paro de obreros," *Matutino*, January 27, 1979.

## THE ECONOMIC SITUATION

The Package of Fiscal Incentives and Ley 95 did not help raise the levels of private investment nor give the economy the quick boost the government had expected. Throughout 1977 and 1978 the economic situation continued to deteriorate. As time passed without recovery in sight, fear began to set in among all those concerned that the economic situation was out of control. The cost of living increased and the quality of life worsened. In the third quarter of 1977, credit available through private banks was practically paralized.[34]

Unemployment suddenly became a pressing issue. Although it had been high throughout the decade, and although three years before in the Declaración de Boquete, Torrijos had announced plans to cope with this problem, nothing had been done. In November, probably one of the most disorganized programs of the Torrijos government was made public. The Plan de Urgencia, or Plan de Emergencia as it became known, was proposed to help out the jobless. Minister Manfredo, who became its director, said that the "Plan de Urgencia only aspired to provide the minimum security to those people who could not even put something in the pot."[35]

The Plan de Urgencia was announced by Torrijos without much prior consultation with the Cabinet. Minister Manfredo said that he heard about it on his car radio as he was driving home. To his surprise, at the end of the speech Torrijos said, "Manfredo: take charge of all the administrative aspects of this plan."[36] The plan proposed to find positions in the state bureaucracy for the unemployed. Free buses would take the jobless to the stadiums in the cities of Panama and Colón, where a census would be taken. The jobs provided would pay $100 per month plus medical coverage through the social security system. Also, a different minister each week would hold court at the Legislative Palace as a "minister of ministers," to listen to complaints of the people who approached him and to try to find solutions to their problems.[37]

The Plan de Urgencia eventually found employment for 24,000 people, 30 percent males and 70 percent females. The jobs provided were extremely

---

[34] "Paralizado el crédito bancario," *República*, November 20, 1977.
[35] "Anunció Fernando Manfredo: Mil empleos se llenarán desde mañana," *República*, November 18, 1977.
[36] Interview with Lic. Fernando Manfredo.
[37] Torrijos also declared that needy children would be given two pairs of shoes each, one-and-a-half million school uniforms would be distributed free, and textbooks would be sold at cost. Also, Torrijos announced that the utility rates would be reduced once the canal treaties were ratified and that the housing problem was "seriously being looked at by the government." "Anuncia Torrijos al Pueblo: Ataque contra el desempleo y el hambre," *La Estrella de Panamá*, November 2, 1977.

menial, mostly as guards or in janitorial services in the various state agencies. Other than requests for employment, the "minister of ministers" received about 20,000 requests, with the bulk centering around needs for housing or for construction materials, for shoes and clothing, and for financial assistance to pursue studies.[38] The Plan de Urgencia cost the government $2.5 million per month and provided an enormous amount of amusement to the detractors of the regime. Fun was made of the haphazard way the program was presented, and blame for the economic situation was placed in part on the large number of government and state agency employees.[39] Even those benefiting from the Plan de Urgencia were uncomfortable about their position and felt they were pawns the government could use in anyway it saw fit.[40]

In a friendly gesture toward the government, the private sector proposed to create 5,000 jobs through construction projects[41] and to contribute five dollars to the salary of each person hired through the Plan de Urgencia. Torrijos suggested that the private sector use that money instead to increase the salary of its own workers.[42]

The passage of Ley 95 and the Paquete de Incentivos Fiscales provided no immediate respite for the economic ills of the country. As a matter of fact, the economic crisis became much more serious in 1977.

## GROSS DOMESTIC PRODUCT

The GDP experienced a slight improvement in 1977, since it grew from 0.03 percent to 1.7 percent. In 1978, growth of the GDP increased to 2.7 percent, still quite low by comparison to earlier years of the decade and to the 1960s. It was not until 1979 that the GDP showed signs of a healthy growth with a 7.1 percent increase, only to drop again in 1980 to 4.9 percent.

If we look at the investment figures, we observe some hard facts that need explaining. After peaking in 1972 at $333 million, total investment entered into a gentle downward slope in 1973, a real drop in 1974, and then

---

[38] Boris Chacón and Hugo Morgado, *Una política de empleo a través de un plan de urgencia: Implicaciones y perspectivas.* Panamá: Ministerio de Planificación y Política Económica, 1978.

[39] "Plan de Urgencia: ¿Por qué?" *República*, December 18, 1977.

[40] In interviews in 1979 during a nationwide teachers' strike, people in the Plan de Urgencia were concerned that if the government decided to stage demonstrations they would force all public employees to participate as was usually the case, and the Plan de Urgencia people would be made to march in front, as the most expendable. Sharon Phillipps, "The Changing Role of Working Class and Peasant Women," Paper presented at the Latin American Association Meetings, Bloomington, Indiana, October, 1980.

[41] "La CAPAC propone planes de construcción," *República*, December 16, 1977.

[42] "Sugieren al CONEP Torrijos y García: Aumento salarial para empleados de la empresa privada," *Matutino*, December 22, 1977.

fluctuated slightly for the rest of the decade, except for 1977, when it experienced a sharp drop. Public investment in 1972 experienced a 110 percent jump, only to drop again in 1973, although it remained 29 percent higher than in 1971. In 1975, public investment was equal to private investement. By 1976, public investment was 12 percent higher than its private counterpart, and in 1977, when private investment dropped to its lowest point since the early 1960s, public investment was 91 percent higher. Even though private investment appeared to recuperate in 1978, according to a study by the Colegio de Economistas de Panamá, a large percentage of that year's investment could be explained by the investment of CODEMIN-Texas Gulf, the group in charge of the Cerro Colorado Copper Mine Project. Because of the mixed nature of the enterprise, it appeared as private investment.[43] It is evident from these figures that the private sector was not investing at the rate it had before. Even though, according to members of the private sector, this was due to the worsening economic situation that affected them, there is a strong suspicion that this was caused by conscious withholding of investment or by capital flight.

In order to support its large development programs and, in a sense to hold up the economy, the government had to borrow heavily, up to a point where Panama's external per capita debt of $1,400 in 1978 was probably the highest in Latin America.

## THE BATTLE AGAINST LEY 95

After the Labor Code was amended, the private sector did not ease its pressure on the government for more concessions. Even though an apparent rapprochement had begun after Ley 95 and the Paquete de Incentivos Fiscales were passed and were strengthened by the 1977 CADE, the private sector was not satisfied. Businessmen still complained of not having access to Torrijos and intimated that they wanted direct access, and not through intermediaries.[44] Labor seemed to have lost the clout it had during the earlier years of the regime, and its campaign against Ley 95 was subdued and low-key. While labor leaders kept quiet, the rank and file founded a committee against Ley 95, which did not have the approval or cooperation of the leadership.[45]

The apparent rapprochement between Torrijos and the private sector finally took place during the 1978 CADE, at which Torrijos gave the final speech. He started by apologizing and taking the blame for the poor relations between the private sector and the government.

---

[43] Colegio de Economistas de Panamá, "Consideraciones en torno a la Ley 95," quoted in "Ley 95 se mantiene por razones políticas," *Diálogo Social*, no. 120 (1980): 23-26.
[44] Mario Augusto Rodríguez, "Los intermediarios," *República*, November 30, 1977.
[45] "Fúndase Comité contra Ley 95," *La Estrella de Panamá*, November 27, 1977.

On this occasion, I cannot initiate my talk, as I frequently do, by saying that we will renew our dialogue. Here we are not renewing but starting one. But the important thing is that I am conscious of the fact that we haven't talked in the past and that it is the government that has been to blame in this matter and has harmed economic growth by not doing so.[46]

On October 11, 1978, Torrijos gave up the title of chief of government, returned to the barracks, and left the visible day-to-day handling of the government to the civilian head of state. Lakas and Sucre were replaced by Aristides Royo a (former minister of education) as president, and Ricardo de la Espriella (former president of the Banco Nacional) as vice president. Although Royo was considered to have leftist leanings, he was apparently picked for the job to diffuse some of Torrijos's more critized programs and to give the government a more balanced appearance. All but two cabinet ministers were replaced or reshuffled. The labor minister, Adolfo Ahumada, was made presidential chief of staff, and Lic. Oydén Ortega, who until then had been personnel director of IRHE, was named the new labor minister.

As the temporary measures of Ley 95 were about to expire, Royo announced the formation of yet another Comisión Laboral Nacional to "find solutions integral to the labor question and worker-employer relations."[47] This marked the beginning of an active and forceful campaign on the part of labor to have Ley 95 revoked. Butcher, as secretary general of CTRP and president of CONATO, called for a massive demonstration to be held on December 20.[48] About 14,000 workers took part. The message delivered was that labor was determined to escalate the pressure until Ley 95 was revoked. The rank and file proposed to engage in a series of general strikes until they had accomplished their goal.[49]

Shortly afterward, the Colegio Nacional de Abogados made a public statement regarding the unconstitutionality of Ley 95[50] and held a round table discussion at the University of their position.[51] The Colegio Nacional de Abogados made the same points that the Sindicato de Tipógrafos had made two years before, when they charged Ley 95 with violating several articles of the Constitution, including Article 69. That article states that "no worker can be dismissed without just cause." Because the stability clause

---

[46] *El Ejecutivo*, no. 23 (January 1980), p. 9, quoted in Steve C. Ropp, *Panamanian Politics*, New York: Praeger, 1982, p. 65.
[47] "Plena vigencia a la Comisión Laboral Nacional," *La Estrella de Panamá*, November 23, 1978.
[48] "Trabajadores contra Ley 95," *Matutino*, December 13, 1978.
[49] Gilberto Vásquez, "Año nuevo: la misma vaina," *Diálogo Social*, no. 108 (January 1979): 15.
[50] "Consulta a Royo sobre Ley 95 hace Asociación de Juristas," *Matutino*, January 26, 1979.
[51] "A Mesa Redonda implicaciones de Ley 95," *Matutino*, January 31, 1979.

was removed through Article 13, Ley 95 violated the spirit of the Constitution. The attorney general in 1977 answered the Sindicato de Tipógrafos, by declaring that Ley 95 did not allow dismissals at will because the employer had to attempt to prove just cause before a dismissal. Because of this, he concluded that Ley 95 did not violate the Constitution, even though workers could still be dismissed whether or not just cause was found.[52] No one in the upper reaches of the governmental hierarchy bothered answering the lawyers' group, but the tide seemed to be turning against Ley 95. The Colegio Nacional de Abogados is one of the most serious and respected professional groups in Panama and includes the most highly regarded jurists in the country. Their statement was made after lengthy study and consultation, and their conclusions were presented not as a political statement but as a juridical one.

At about the same time, a study commissioned by the National Legislative Council regarding Ley 95 was made public. This study, undertaken by the Colegio de Economistas de Panamá, inferred that Ley 95 did not foster economic development and that the only purpose for keeping it in force (*vigente*) was to weaken the labor movement.[53] The study provided detailed observations regarding the most crucial economic aspects for which the Labor Code had been blamed and that Ley 95 was to correct, such as the performance of small businesses. It also touched upon the real causes of the inflationary-recessionary cycle and the worsening economic situation. The study concluded that Ley 95 was purely a political issue and that from an economic point of view there was nothing to justify it. The National Legislative Council, calling Ley 95 a "gag law," presented a bill to eliminate it and return the Labor Code to its original form.[54]

As the months passed in 1979, the issues that divided the advocates and the detractors of Ley 95 became sharper and more defined. So did the campaigns for and against the law. The private sector alluded to the unemployment issue, which became more acute by the day, and stressed that the Labor Code in its original form not only did not promote employment but fostered unemployment.[55] This was one of the most forceful arguments presented by the private sector in favor of Ley 95, which according to them fostered employment by ameliorating the effects of the Labor Code and by giving businessmen and industrialists an incentive to

---

[52] "Contestan a tipógrafos: Ley 95 no viola la Constitución Nacional," *La Estrella de Panamá*, May 4, 1977.
[53] Colegio de Economistas de Panamá, "Consideraciones en torno a la Ley 95," quoted in "Ley 95 se mantiene por razones políticas," *Diálogo Social*, no. 120 (February 1980): 23-26.
[54] "Consejo de Legislación estudia derogatoria de la Ley 95," *Crítica*, May 10, 1979.
[55] Walter Durling, "Empresa y sindicato frente a la creación de empleos," in Asociación Panameña de Ejecutivos de Empresa, *XV Conferencia Anual de Ejecutivos de Empresa (CADE 1980)*. Panama, 1980.

pursue labor-intensive techniques instead of capital-intensive ones. Another strong argument alluded to by the private sector in favor of Ley 95 was that it restored discipline in the place of work. Although this was never presented as a primary reason, it was the one that aroused the strongest feelings on the part of employers. Most businessmen interviewed mentioned this, usually in vehement terms, which would lead one to believe that the Labor Code had created a situation of insubordination and anarchy in the place of employment. Labor statistics, especially dismissals and voluntary resignations as well as the number of litigations stemming from these, would seem to negate this.[56]

The issue of discipline as presented by the private sector had more to do with the attitude of employers toward work incentives than with insubordination on the part of the workers. It appears that employers in Panama were most familiar with the use of negative incentives to motivate their workers. Thus, when the threat of dismissal was removed as an incentive, employers felt they had lost control. PREALC's study on the effects of the Labor Code concludes that the objection of businessmen to stability was based "not just on the need to fire workers, but in the wish to use this threat as a weapon to keep up output."[57]

According to the private sector, Ley 95 promoted peace and harmony in labor relations. There was less strife, lower numbers of strikes and dismissals, less labor litigation, and fewer small businesses going bankrupt. And, of course, productivity was up and the economy was on the mend. This was basically the tenor of a document presented by the then-president of CONEP, Ing. Dominador B. Bazán, to the National Legislative Council.[58] CONEP claimed that its document contained conclusive proof of the benefits brought about by Ley 95. As will be shown in Chapter 8, most of these assertions can be contested.

The private sector further reinforced its arguments by emphasizing that the economy was being shored up by Ley 95 and that any changes might lead to national disaster. "One must be very careful about touching this law because the total collapse of the national economy may depend on it."[59] Some private sector advocates even had the temerity to insinuate that Ley 95 was beneficial to the workers because it freed them from the holds of the unions.[60]

---

[56] The code "contained the necessary elements for the *empresarios* to do what they wanted," said Lic. Gustavo González, who succeded Ardito Barletta as minister of planning in 1978. Interview with Lic. Gustavo González.

[57] PREALC, "Efectos del código de trabajo sobre el empleo, la productividad, los costos y la inversión en Panamá." Geneva: ILO/Documento de Trabajo PREALC/156, 1978, p. 28.

[58] CONEP. "Efectos de la Ley 95 de 1976," Mimeo. Panamá, 1979.

[59] Jaime Correa, "Qué hacer para el empleo?" *Análisis*, 1:8(1978): 45-46.

[60] Antonio Ducruex, "Porque no se debe derogar la Ley 95," *Análisis*, 2:12(1980): 26-28.

In the midst of the furor over the Labor Code and Ley 95, other incidents that ultimately had an effect on labor issues were taking place in the country. In August 1979, the school teachers declared a nationwide strike. The motive for the strike was to demand salary increases, but the government's educational reform quickly became its main focus. After years of study and preparation, the government was about to institute an educational reform that it felt would bring education more in tune with the needs of the country and provide a uniform educational program. Many groups opposed the reform with a variety of allegations that boiled down to the concern that if the reform went through, it would provide the government with more centralized control of a huge human resource. The reform was portrayed by the opposition as a powerful stepping stone in the regime's plan to take the country toward communism.

By October, the doctors and paramedical personnel of the social security system had joined the teachers' strike. Then, on October 17, the teachers led a massive rally through the streets of Panama City. Estimates of the number of participants ranged from 50,000, according to the government, to 250,000 by foreign correspondents.[61] Along with the teachers, doctors, business, church, and civic groups, most of the labor groups joined the rally, as did most of the groups considered to the left, including most student and labor groups.[62] In a sense, the rally represented a generalized protest against the government and crystallized many discontents besides those having to do with education: the conflict over labor issues, the frustration due to the soaring cost of living, and widespread distrust of the regime.

The rally of October 17 was not easy for the government to dismiss. There had been much disruption from the teachers' strike, and the issues it raised had remained in the fore of the public's consciousness because the strikers and the children out of school had been highly visible. The rally also provided great contrast to the ceremony held on October 1 to celebrate the return to Panama of the Canal Zone. Those festivities were staged by the government. Although they were meant to reflect the country's joy and pride in finally regaining sovereignty over all of its national territory, they were devoid of much popular participation or enthusiasm. The crowd on the October 17 march, however, overflowed with enthusiasm and a feeling of camaraderie "in misfortune." The rally represented one of those true special moments when many dissonant voices coalesce into one common cause or objective. In this case, the common cause was an utter distrust of the government.

---

[61] Interview with Richard Koster, at that time a stringer for *Newsweek*.
[62] University of Panama student groups such as the Federación de Estudiantes Revolucionarios (FER), Federación de Estudiantes de Panamá (FEP), and Guaycucho-MIR were represented in the demonstration. All the centrals and important labor groups were also there.

Shortly after the October 17 rally, the CNTP took advantage of the prevailing mood and of the fact that there was a movement in the National Legislative Council to revoke Ley 95. On November 8, the CNTP held a demonstration in which approximately 25,000 workers participated.[63] The demonstration had begun the night before in Colón, from whence a group of workers walked to the capital city. They reached San Miguelito on the outskirts of the city by early morning, where another large contingent of workers joined them. The enlarged group then marched on to the Legislative Palace, where the secretary general of the CNTP, José Meneses, was given the floor (cortesía de sala). Afterward, the Plenum of the Assembly of Representatives approved the resolution against Ley 95. The demonstration, called massive by a Diálogo Social reporter, was branded as "communistic" by the private sector and boycotted by the CTRP and the CIT.[64]

In December, President Royo held a breakfast with labor leaders during which he declared that "he did not believe in the derogation of Ley 95 nor in stability of employment for the Panamanian worker."[65] The CTRP immediately called for a two-day general strike to be held in January in protest of the president's lack of respect for the working class. From Royo's statement, said Butcher, "we could see clearly that he was aligning himself with the private sector against the workers."[66] Butcher talked to all of the other labor leaders, and the strike was called by CONATO to be held January 28 and 29. As the time for the strike approached, various other organizations, including the government's party, the PRD, expressed their support for labor and asked for Ley 95 to be revoked.[67]

One labor group, the CPTT, had declared that it would support CONATO but not join the strike, to avoid paralyzing the country.[68] The rank and file of the CPTT, however, rebelled against their leaders and refused to work during those two days.[69]

La Estrella de Panamá, the most serious newspaper in Panama at the time, though not wholly independent from the government, came out against the strike, as did all of the TV stations.[70] Although the effects of the strike were

---

[63] "La Asamblea recomienda derogación de Ley 95," Matutino, November 11, 1979.

[64] Gilberto Vásquez, "Basta ya de conciliar: con el pueblo avanzar," Diálogo Social, no. 118 (1979): 15.

[65] "Huelga en enero de la CTRP," La Estrella de Panamá, December 22, 1979.

[66] Interview with Philip Dean Butcher.

[67] "PRD de Colón apoya a CONATO," Crítica, January 17, 1980; "Frente Sindical del PRD pide derogatoria inmediata de Ley 95," Matutino, January 21, 1980.

[68] "Transportistas no permitiran la subversión," Matutino, January 28, 1980.

[69] "Huelga nacional: un ensayo de lucha," Diálogo Social, no. 121 (1980): 12-13.

[70] "Paro Nacional de 48 horas inicia CONATO. Se espera poco respaldo público a la huelga," La Estrella de Panamá, January 28, 1980. A member of the Duque family (owners of the paper), Tomás G. Altamirano Duque, was minister of housing and had aspirations to become president.

not highly visible, mainly because the stores along Central Avenue in Panama City did not close, it was successful in paralyzing many of the larger enterprises, including the banana plantations, the ports, the refinery, and the large factories. Most of the milk production from the interior was lost, and 97 percent of public transportation was stopped.[71]

Not long after the general strike, in a speech delivered to an Extraordinary Session of the National Assembly of Representatives, President Royo announced the impending derogation of Ley 95 and the formation of a tripartite commission to find solutions to the labor problems. He also announced a salary increase of $25 per month for workers in the private sector.[72] Three months later CONEP and CONATO presented Law Proyects to the National Legislative Council for the establishment of the Tripartite Commission.[73] The president appointed the commission and empowered it to find solutions to Ley 95 and other labor problems.[74]

As soon as the Tripartite Commission was installed, CONEP's representatives again began working with other members of the private sector on a complete revision of the Labor Code, which they presented to the commission. CONEP's recommendations modified 65 articles of the Labor Code and added two new ones. Most of the changes proposed had to do with the cost of labor, collective bargaining, strikes, and discipline problems. Changes that would affect the cost of labor included overtime to be paid at a 40 percent increase in all cases instead of 50 percent for the first three hours and 75 percent thereafter (Article 33); days of national mourning that fell on regular working days would be paid as such instead of as holidays (Article 45); bonuses and monies earned from profit-sharing would not be considered part of the salary (Article 140); and indemnizations and the prima de antiguedad could be paid in installments (Article 225).

Changes proposed regarding issues of a collective nature set limits on the number of workers an enterprise must have in order to have to negotiate a collective agreement. If the enterprise did not have ten unionized workers, the employer would not be compelled to negotiate an agreement (Article 401). CONEP also proposed to maintain the change introduced in Ley 95 allowing new enterprises not to have to negotiate collective agreements for two years. CONEP also added that MITRAB and MICI could change that time limit to five years.

Regarding labor disputes, changes included the obligation of the worker to present his complaints to the employer before going to the MITRAB

---

[71] "Paro Nacional Obrero se fortaleció ayer," La Estrella de Panamá, January 30, 1980.

[72] "Reemplazarán la Ley 95," República, April 1, 1980.

[73] "Ley para beneficio mutuo acuerdan obreros y patrones," La Estrella de Panamá, July 8, 1980.

[74] The commission was established through Law 22 of July 14, 1980. "Fue sancionada por el Ejecutivo: Comisión que elaborará problemática laboral," Matutino, July 13, 1980.

(Article 423); the allowance to the employer to request arbitration and conciliation, whereas before this could only be done by the worker or by mutual consent (Article 425); reintroduction of the lockout (Article 475); and the stipulation that only a labor court could decide if a collective agreement had been violated instead of the MITRAB (Article 480). Regarding strikes, other enterprises were added to the list considered to be "public services," which could not shut down and which had to follow special strike procedures (Article 486). The new enterprises included agricultural, cattle, agro-industrial, and basic foodstuff producers.

The changes regarding disciplinary problems centered around Article 213, Acápite A, which specifies the grounds considered just cause for dismissal. The language of Article 213 was tightened and presented in a more substantive way to make a violation easier to prove. Also, four more grounds for just dismissal were added to the original sixteen. These included tardiness, proof of remunerated service to others during vacation or free time, and a general clause to the effect that verified violations of the collective agreement, work contract, or law, were also just cause for dismissal. The fourth cause had to do with the validity of medical certificates used to justify an absence. This stated that if an employer doubted the validity of a medical certificate he could ask the worker to be examined by a medical team of three doctors, one chosen by the employer, one by the worker, and one by the CSS. If the worker refused to subject himself to such an exam, this would be considered just cause for dismissal.[75]

Labor representatives expressed their complete disagreement with the changes proposed by CONEP and refused to consider them during the meetings of the Tripartite Commission. When it became obvious that revisions to Ley 95 were in the making, CONEP took its revisions directly to the minister of labor. Minister Ortega was cordial and promised to study the document, but members of the private sector bitterly declared that he did not even look at them.

The Tripartite Commission met for seven months and produced nothing. One labor representative of the commission said that labor felt cheated because the commission often met until late at night, and the newspapers the next day would carry items expressing only the view of the private sector. This same labor leader elaborated on the performance of the commission by saying that "we went to discuss the 20 articles of Ley 95 and had to take on the reform of 69 articles of the Labor Code. On this basis, no matter who was representing labor, no agreement could be reached."[76] He was alluding to the CONEP proposal that implied a thorough revision of

---

[75] CONEP, "Recomendaciones propuestas a la Comisión Nacional que fuera creada por la Ley 22 del 14 de julio de 1980," Mimeo. Panamá, 1980.
[76] "Nueva Ley 95 perpetua la injusticia—José Meneses sobre el Proyecto Ley 71," *Diálogo Social*, no. 134 (1981): 37.

major portions of the Labor Code and not a revision of Ley 95.

The National Legislative Council on February 25, 1981, approved Law 3 of 1981, suspending Ley 95 for three months and stipulating that if in that time an adequate substitute law was not presented, Ley 95 would be repealed for good and the Labor Code would revert to its original form. The MITRAB presented Law Proyect 71, which was discussed throughout April and voted into law on April 30, 1981. After three years of constant wrangling between labor, the government, and the private sector, Ley 95 was finally repealed, and Ley 8a took its place.

Although Ley 8a did not reinstate the original benefits of the 1972 Labor Code, specifically stability of employment, it did provide a compromise. Under Ley 8a, if an employer wants to dismiss a worker and cannot prove just cause, he has to pay a 50 percent penalty above the indemnization required in the Labor Code. Only 10 percent of the work force per year can be dismissed under these circumstances. This system of job security has been labeled "relative stability" by some labor jurists.[77] The other innovation of Ley 8a exempts small enterprises from the stability clause. These small enterprises have been defined as agricultural concerns with 10 or fewer workers, agro-industrial enterprises with 20 or fewer workers, manufacturing enterprises with 15 or fewer workers, and commercial and service enterprises with 5 or fewer employees, which in effect include a very large percentage of Panamanian establishments.

## CONCLUSION

Ley 95 had an effect on labor similar to that of the 1972 Labor Code on the private sector. Ley 95 was the catalyst that brought the labor movement together and that provided it with a rallying point around which to unite and fight for its rights. An important effect of the law and of the campaign to repeal it was that they provided an opportunity for labor to grow in strength and class consciousness. Consequently, the labor sector that emerged in the 1980s was much stronger and more cohesive than the one in evidence after the enactment of the 1972 Labor Code.

Even though by 1981 the Labor Code was amended and other progressive measures enacted at the outset of the Torrijos regime were past history, the one positive outcome of the regime's policies is that they permanently changed the socio-political landscape of the country. The process of incorporation could not be reversed completely, and those groups given a place and a voice in the power structure, once threatened of losing their newly acquired rights, found a way of uniting to protect their rights and their position. In sum, once

---

[77] Arturo Hoyos, *Derecho panameño del trabajo (Vol.1)*. San José, Costa Rica: Litografía Lil, 1982, p. 87.

incorporation had taken place, the act of excluding those newly incorporated sectors was much more difficult. The regime still considered itself populist and reformist and was not willing to take the drastic steps necessary to exclude or completely control the sectors it had incorporated.

The enactment of Ley 8a was a compromise by the Torrijos regime with both labor and the private sector. Ley 8a signaled the loss of autonomy of the regime vis-à-vis labor, just as five years before Ley 95 had signaled the loss of autonomy of the regime vis-à-vis the private sector. The regime was now vulnerable both to the former ruling elite and to the subordinate group it had chosen to incorporate for support and legitimacy. Ley 8a, then, marked the completion of a cycle for labor, from excluded sector to an actor with power to play in the political game of demand-making. It also marked the end of a phase for the Torrijos regime, from complete autonomy at the outset of its tenure to loss of autonomy to both the former dominant class and the subordinate labor sector.

# 8

# COSTS AND BENEFITS
# OF THE 1972 LABOR CODE

## COST INCREASE DUE TO THE LABOR CODE

Throughout the 1970s, the pros and cons of the Labor Code and subsequent labor laws were continuously and hotly debated by all parties concerned. The labor laws were an issue that could not be discussed with any sense of objectivity. On the one hand, the private sector publicly attributed to these laws most of the woes and ills it experienced during the period. Organized labor, on the other hand, fearful that the unremitting campaign maintained by the private sector might lead to changes in the laws and loss of benefits, zealously defended the Labor Code and tried to protect its rights. The government was divided between those with ties to the private sector, who were against the Labor Code, and those more concerned with social reforms, who were in favor of it.

Certain aspects of the labor situation that were affected by the laws in question were in the forefront of these debates. The private sector's argument against the Labor Code centered around the cost increase caused by the labor laws and by its perceived loss of control in the place of employment. The costs brought about by the Labor Code included wage increases and enhanced benefits (*prestaciones*). According to the private sector, the gains brought about by labor's improved capacity to bargain led to higher salaries and a loss in productivity, allegedly caused by the stability clause. Also included as factors leading to cost increases were the sanctioning of strikes, increases in labor litigations, the growth and expansion of organized labor, and absenteeism. The private sector also attributed to the Labor Code the deteriorated employment situation, which by the end of the decade was approaching chaos.

With the enactment of Ley 95, according to the private sector, productivity went up, the economy became stabilized, and revenue losses due to union activities such as strikes and labor litigations were considerably reduced. The frantic campaign engaged in by the private sector to try to stop the revoking of Ley 95 had as its main theme, underlying all other arguments, the idea that the economic well-being of the country rested on that law and that its removal or the return to the Labor Code would mean economic doom. These claims, however, exaggerate the effects of the labor laws under study.

The purpose of this chapter is threefold. The first is to analyze the arguments as carefully as possible in order to ascertain the validity of the claims regarding the Labor Code. A second objective is to find out what, if any, were the real gains to labor and the costs to employers brought about by the 1972 Labor Code. A third purpose is to ascertain the impact of the Labor Code as a distributive measure and to determine whether there were social costs (due to higher labor costs and lower labor productivity) stemming from the labor code. Although the data available are limited, particularly in the crucial area of absenteeism, analysis reveals general patterns that challenge the private sector's claims.

## Wages and Benefits

In this section we will consider the wage increases due to the Labor Code and other measures enacted in favor of workers. We will also consider the effect of collective agreements on wages and the cost increases to the employers due to the enhanced position of the working class after 1972.

Before the 1972 Labor Code was enacted but after Torrijos took power, an educational tax of 1.25 percent to the employer and .75 percent to the worker was levied on salaries. In addition, a law covering professional or work risks was also passed. The cost of the work-risk insurance was scaled according to the type of work performed, with a range from about .5 percent to 5.6 percent of salaries.[1] These costs were new to the employer, but not directly attributable to the Labor Code.[2]

The two new measures introduced in the Labor Code that implied added costs to the employer were a thirteenth- month salary and a *prima de antigüedad*. The thirteenth-month salary increased salaries by 8.33 percent. The *prima de antigüedad* is a bonus to be paid when employment is terminated if the worker has been employed for more than 10 years and is over 40 years of age if male and over 35 years of age if female. The *prima de antigüedad* represents approximately 2 percent of all the salaries received during the time of employment and is calculated as one week's salary per

---

[1] Prior to this, there had been a law that made accident insurance mandatory. However, workers were insured through private companies and there were no provisions to penalize employers who did not comply with the law. Consequently, very few workers were insured against work-related risks.

[2] The only extra cost related to wages that had been in effect since the 1940s was the social security tax. In 1972, the rate was 8.75 percent of wages to the employer and 6.25 percent to the worker.

Table 9 Cost of Hourly Wage

|  | Regular Worker | Construction Worker |
|---|---|---|
| Basic salary | 1.0000 | 1.0000 |
| 13th month | .0833 | .0833 |
| Prima de antigüedad | .0200 | |
| Social security | .0875 | .0875 |
| Educational tax | .0125 | .0125 |
| Work risk insurance* | .0259 | .0567 |
| Fondo de Garantía | | .0600 |
|  | 1.2292 | 1.3000 |
|  | $1.23/hour | $1.30/hour |

* For a regular worker the work-risk insurance given is an average of the lower ranges of the scale, while the construction worker must be covered at the highest level, thus the 5.6 percent.
Source: Interview with Eduardo Ríos, secretary general of SUNTRACS.

year of employment, using an average of the salary received during the previous five years.[3] Because construction workers are employed by project and would have no opportunity to accrue 10 years of employment and qualify for the *prima de antigüedad*, Law 72 of 1975 amended this aspect of the Labor Code in their behalf. Law 72 stipulates that at the end of a job, each construction worker will be paid 6 percent of the total wages earned during the job. This Fondo de Garantía provides some security until the worker is hired at another construction site. The Fondo de Garantía is not really an unemployment program but is considered as such by the parties concerned.

Table 9 reproduces the salary and benefits for one hour of labor of a worker earning $1.00 per hour after introduction of the 1972 Labor Code.

Because before the Labor Code wages carried an added cost of 8.75 percent to the employer, which represented the social security tax, the direct cost increase to the hourly wage after the Labor Code was 13 percent of basic salary for a regular worker and 19.6 percent for a construction worker.[4] Even though wage increases of 13 percent and 19.6 percent may seem high, they are nowhere close to the claims made by the private sector of 50 percent and 60 percent increases.

In order to ascertain the meaning of these wage increases in the overall economic picture, we must look at the growth of nominal and real wages and at the impact of the wage growth on the cost of labor as a percentage of output. How did wages fare after the enactment of the 1972 Labor Code and what were the effects of collective agreements and other pro-labor measures in protecting the wages of the laboring class? Table 10 presents

---

[3] PREALC, "Efectos del código de trabajo sobre el empleo, la productividad, los costos y la inversión en Panamá." Geneva: ILO/Documento de Trabajo PREALC/156, 1978, p. 37.
[4] Wages are somewhat higher because of the cost of vacation and holidays. However, those costs were in effect before the Labor Code and can in no way be attributed to it.

Table 10 Nominal and Real Wages and Annual Variation (monthly wages)

| | 1970 | 1971 | 1972 | 1973 | 1974 | 1975 | 1976 | 1977 | 1978 | 1979 |
|---|---|---|---|---|---|---|---|---|---|---|
| Private Sector | 183.3 | 187.99 | 182.85 | 191.52 | 231.87 | 246.34 | 269.73 | 285.56 | 294.03 | 309.29 |
| Annual growth | | 3% | -3% | 5% | 21% | 6% | 9% | 6% | 3% | 5% |
| Real wage | 183.3 | 184.376 | 170.6327 | 167.9731 | 177.6089 | 179.3657 | 189.2066 | 192.0526 | 190.1433 | 186.4042 |
| Annual growth | | 1% | -7% | -2% | 6% | 1% | 5% | 2% | -1% | -2% |
| Banana plantations | 144.31 | 140.36 | 149.9 | 156.28 | 202.47 | 187.99 | 197.75 | 207.77 | 223.53 | 257.06 |
| Annual growth | | -3% | 7% | 4% | 30% | -7% | 5% | 5% | 8% | 15% |
| Real wage | 144.31 | 137.6618 | 139.8843 | 137.0658 | 155.0890 | 136.8797 | 138.7151 | 139.7351 | 144.5524 | 154.9260 |
| Annual growth | | -5% | 2% | -2% | 13% | -012% | 1% | 1% | 3% | 7% |
| Central government | 177.14 | 185.22 | 185.62 | 195.72 | 231.16 | 239.33 | 242.31 | 247.25 | 251.98 | 290.15 |
| Annual growth | | 5% | 0% | 5% | 18% | 4% | 1% | 2% | 2% | 15% |
| Real wage | 177.14 | 181.6594 | 173.2176 | 171.6568 | 177.0651 | 174.2616 | 169.9724 | 166.2873 | 162.9504 | 174.8688 |
| Annual growth | | 3% | -5% | -1% | 3% | -2% | -2% | -2% | -2% | 7% |
| Autonomous agencies | 220.87 | 239.07 | 243.74 | 238.61 | 260.77 | 273.56 | 276.61 | 288.31 | 302.02 | 316.96 |
| Annual growth | | 8% | 2% | -2% | 9% | 5% | 1% | 4% | 5% | 5% |
| Real wage | 220.87 | 234.4743 | 227.4543 | 209.2736 | 199.7459 | 199.1852 | 194.0327 | 193.9021 | 195.31037 | 191.0268 |
| Annual growth | | 6% | -3% | -8% | -5% | -0% | -3% | -0% | 1% | -2% |
| Municipalities | 117.98 | 129.89 | 144.77 | 146.47 | 179.13 | 182.42 | 183.59 | 187.76 | 189.5 | 200.05 |
| Annual growth | | 10% | 11% | 1% | 22% | 2% | 1% | 2% | 1% | 6% |
| Real wage | 117.98 | 127.3930 | 135.0971 | 128.4619 | 137.2109 | 132.8241 | 128.7823 | 126.2775 | 122.5459 | 120.5669 |
| Annual growth | | 8% | 6% | -5% | 7% | -3% | -3% | -2% | -3% | -2% |
| Canal Zone | 399.47 | 420.12 | 444.97 | 466.45 | 498.2 | 590.5 | 607.75 | 661.4 | 788.39 | 821.65 |
| Annual growth | | 5% | 6% | 5% | 7% | 19% | 3% | 9% | 19% | 4% |
| Real wage | 399.47 | 412.0439 | 415.2390 | 409.1013 | 381.6137 | 429.9564 | 426.3165 | 444.8228 | 509.8362 | 495.1955 |
| Annual growth | | 3% | 1% | -1% | -7% | 13% | -1% | 4% | 15% | -3% |
| Annual growth | | 2% | 5% | 6% | 15% | 5% | 4% | 4% | 4% | 7% |
| Price level | 1 | 1.0196 | 1.071599 | 1.140181 | 1.305508 | 1.373394 | 1.425583 | 1.486883 | 1.546359 | 1.659243 |

*Sources:* Dirección General de Estadística. *Panamá en cifras: Años 1971-1975,* Panamá, 1976, p. 198; *Años 1976-1980,* Panamá, 1981; *Años 1978-1982,* Panamá, 1983, pp. 224-225.

## Figure 1: Real Wages in the Private Sector
### US dollars at 1970 prices

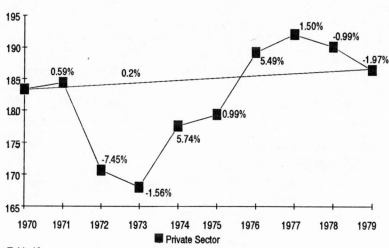

Private Sector

*Source:*Table 10.

nominal and real wages and their annual variation. Wages are given as monthly averages for workers in the various sectors. Taking 1970 as the base year, and looking at workers in the private sector, the figures show that it was only after 1976 that wages rose above the 1970 level, and by the end of the decade wages again were at the 1970 level. So, the wage increases and the enhanced position of labor thanks to collective negotiations were not enough to protect the wage level of the Panamanian work force during the 1970s. For most other sectors the same conditions held. As a matter of fact, the situation was so critical due to the inflationary situation, which Panama had no ability to control, that the government was forced to enact wage increases in 1974, 1979, 1980, and 1981. But even those increases were not successful in protecting the wage levels. Figure 1 presents a graphic representation of the wage fluctuations in the private sector.

From the time of the passage of the 1972 Labor Code, common belief among employers was that the clause compelling employers to negotiate collective agreements at the request of the unions increased the cost of labor disproportionately. The belief that collective negotiations could result in much higher salaries for the workers than individual negotiations was widely held. The private sector felt that this was an unfair situation, because labor was provided with too much leverage to negotiate on its own behalf.

According to a former minister of labor, in 1974 Nicolás Ardito Barletta, the minister of planning, "tried to prove that collective agreements were a factor contributing to inflation. He wanted to place a limit on the increases that could be negotiated through them."[5] A study was commissioned to back this move, but the results were opposite to what had been expected. For that year, salary increases attained through collective negotiations reached 8 percent, but inflation hovered between 14 and 20 percent. In view of this, instead of placing an upper limit on the amount of wage increases to be negotiated, the government was compelled to pass an emergency salary increase (Ley 33 del 29 de mayo de 1974).

So how did wages attained through collective negotiations really fare? Although it is known that about 45 percent of the collective agreements negotiated during the decade covered workers in the manufacturing sector and 39 percent those in commercial and service enterprises, we have no figures that show what proportion of workers in those sectors were covered by collective agreements.[6] But we do have salary increases achieved through collective negotiations for the manufacturing and commercial sectors as a whole. Table 11 compares wage increases achieved through collective negotiations in the manufacturing and commercial sectors as well as wage changes attained by the private sector as a whole. It also gives annual changes in consumer and wholesale prices. According to those figures, workers covered by collective agreements achieved slightly better wage increases (or smaller wage losses) than all other workers in the private sector in the years 1972, 1973, and 1975. In 1976 and 1979, wages through collective agreements were only slightly better, and in 1974 and 1980, wages for the sector as a whole fared better than those attained through collective negotiations. For the last two years mentioned, wage increases were decreed by law for all workers. The difference between wages for the private sector and wages attained through collective negotiations is not great, but it can be concluded that the sector as a whole fared slightly worse than workers covered by collective negotiations. So, even if collective agreements did not protect wages completely from inflation, those workers covered by a collective agreement had salaries slightly higher than the rest of the work force.

Even after ascertaining that salary increases reached through collective agreements were not even keeping up with inflation and publicly acknowledging this by passing an emergency measure to increase salaries, the government nevertheless gave the go-ahead for a freeze on collective agreements and the modification of the Labor Code.[7] Ley 95 stipulated that

---

[5] Second interview with Dr. Rolando Murgas.

[6] Jorge Fábrega, *Las convenciones colectivas en Panamá*. Panamá: n.p., 1981, p. 6.

[7] One could argue that in view of the failure of collective agreements to achieve adequate salary levels, the government acted wisely in this regard. But the motives of government officials behind the Labor Code modifications, namely Manfredo and Ardito Barletta, were not to protect the workers but to appease the private sector. In fact, both felt that the Labor Code was detrimental to the economy. Interviews with Lic. Fernando Manfredo and Dr. Nicolás Ardito Barletta.

Table 11    Annual Growth Rate of Wages and Cost of Living Indicators for Private Sector Workers

| Years | Nominal wages through collective negotiations Manufacture | Commerce | Nominal wage | Real wage | CPI | WPI |
|---|---|---|---|---|---|---|
| 1972 | 4.1 | 4.2 | -2.7 | -7.4 | 5.1 | 7.8 |
| 1973 | 6.1 | 5.9 | 4.7 | -1.6 | 6.4 | 10.5 |
| 1974* | 8.5 | 9.1 | 21.1 | 5.74 | 14.5 | 23.2 |
| 1975 | 8.8 | 7.0 | 6.2 | .9 | 5.2 | 12.3 |
| 1976 | 7.1 | 9.8 | .5 | .5 | 3.8 | 7.2 |
| 1977 | — | — | 5.9 | 1.5 | 4.3 | 6.7 |
| 1978 | — | — | 2.9 | -.9 | 4.0 | 5.1 |
| 1979* | 6.7 | 6.5 | 5.2 | -1.97 | 7.3 | 12.3 |
| 1980* | 4.2 | 3.7 | 8.8 | — | 12.1 | 13.3 |

*Increases in private sector wages decreed by law.
Sources: Figures for 1972-1976: PREALC, "Efectos del código de trabajo sobre el empleo, la productividad, los costos y la inversión en Panamá," Geneva: ILO/Documento de Trabajo PREALC/156, 1978, p. 17; figures for 1978-1980: Jorge Fábrega, Las convenciones colectivas en Panamá, Panamá: n.p., 1981, p. 34; nominal wage and real wage: Table 10; CPI and WPI: Dirección de Estadística y Censo, Panamá en Cifras, Años 1971-1975, pp. 20-21, and Dirección de Estadística y Censo, Panamá en Cifras, Años 1976-1980, pp. 16-17. Private sector workers include workers in manufacturing, construction, commerce, and services. Not included are workers in the banana plantations and the Canal Zone.

there would be no collective negotiations for two years and that new businesses did not have to enter into collective negotiations for the first two years of operation. An added proof that collective agreements have never been able to protect the real wage is the fact that in 1979, the year when such agreements could be negotiated again, the government passed another emergency law to increase salaries.

A study by PREALC for the years 1972-1976 showed that even including the thirteenth- month salary (and deflating by the Consumer Price Index), real salaries only increased 2 percent in four years (1972 to 1976), a period when the GNP grew by 10 percent and the economically active population by 3.4 percent. Considering that in the 1960s salaries had increased by 2 to 3 percent in real terms annually and that salaries negotiated through the new collective agreements should try to regain the buying power lost in previous years, PREALC concluded that collective agreements hardly presented a threat to employers due to large labor-cost increases or provided significant benefits to workers in terms of salary increments.[8]

The emergency measures regarding salaries, which were enacted into law in 1974, provided salary increases of between 5 percent and 15 percent plus a 10 percent increase in the minimum wage.[9] A companion law provided the same type of increases to public-sector workers.[10] In 1979 salaries were again increased between 5 percent and 17 percent.[11] Later that

---

[8] PREALC, "Efectos," pp. 16-17.
[9] Ley 33 del 29 de mayo de 1974, Gaceta Oficial, April 8, 1974.
[10] Ley 32 del 29 de marzo de 1974, Gaceta Oficial, April 4, 1974.
[11] Ley 10 del 30 de mayo de 1979, Gaceta Oficial, May 31, 1979.

year, the lowest minimum salary was increased from 40 cents/hour to 50 cents/hour, and the entire minimum wage scale was revised.[12]

During the period covered by this study there were two additional general wage increases ordered by law, in May 1980[13] and in May 1981.[14] Perhaps the most controversial of these laws was the last one, Ley 13 of 1981. It provided for a wage increase of $30/month for all workers in private enterprises, $15/month to workers in agricultural enterprises with 10 or fewer employees, and $7.50/month to domestic workers. Until then, laws for salary increases had only covered workers employed by their present employer by December 31 of the previous year. Ley 13 did not include this provision. Also, all previous salary increase laws had excluded agro-industrial enterprises with fewer than 25 employees. Ley 13 included all such workers and divided them into those working on farms with 10 or more employees, who would receive the same increase as all other private-sector employees, and those working on farms with fewer than 10 workers, who would receive half the increase.

Two other measures of Ley 13 were unprecedented and touched off a series of protests that were felt throughout the country. They regarded workers covered by collective agreements. Construction workers were granted a 15 cent/hour increase. This provision received strong opposition from the Cámara Panameña de la Construcción (CAPAC), who claimed its collective agreement with the Construction Union SUNTRACS took into account the inflationary situation and had a proviso for increasing salaries accordingly. The minister of labor was asked to interpret the law on this point and concluded that CAPAC must pay the hourly wage increase. CAPAC disregarded this decision and appealed to the Supreme Court, which reversed the MITRAB decision and ruled in favor of CAPAC. Before the Supreme Court's decision was made public, several SUNTRACS leaders, including Eduardo Ríos, the union's secretary general, took the Supreme Court justices hostage and held them at gunpoint for several hours.

The other controversial measure of this wage-increase law was a general provision contained in Article 4, which stipulated that all employers bound by collective agreements must increase their workers' salaries by 25 percent above the amounts agreed upon in those contracts. The private sector reacted strongly and claimed that the salaries agreed upon in the collective negotiations usually reached the upper limits of what they could afford.

---

[12] Ley 49 del 21 de agosto de 1979, *Gaceta Oficial*, August 22, 1979.
[13] Ley 12 del 16 de mayo de 1980, *Gaceta Oficial*, May 16, 1980. This law provided a raise of $25/month to all workers in private enterprises. An earlier law had provided a $20/month raise to public servants. Resolución del Gabinete no. 21 del 24 de marzo de 1980.
[14] Ley 13 del 15 de junio de 1981, *Gaceta Oficial*, June 15, 1981.

Other Collective Agreement Benefits

There is little doubt that one of the greatest impacts of the 1972 Labor Code was the clause regarding collective agreements. Before 1972 only 37 such agreements had ever been negotiated; by 1976 a total of 504 agreements had been successfully concluded, and after the 1976-1978 freeze, close to 300 agreements were made.[15]

Apart from salaries, other items generally negotiated in collective agreements are bonuses for attendance and punctuality, for vacation, Christmas, seniority, and sometimes bonuses increasing the amount of the thirteenth-month salary; financial assistance for marriages, birth of children, death of the worker or his immediate family; scholarships for the children of workers; sale of goods produced by the enterprise at reduced cost; and the provision of uniforms and security items such as boots, gloves, and hard hats.

More than 10 years after the passage of the Labor Code only two studies have been published about the collective agreements negotiated during this time, and neither does a cost analysis of such agreements.[16] The Sindicato de Industriales de Panamá (SIP) document analyzes 16 collective agreements representing 29 enterprises. It merely groups sample clauses from those agreements under specific headings. The Fábrega study is more elaborate but only lists the types of benefits generally included in agreements, without any indication of how many agreements may contain such benefits or how many workers benefit from them.

From these studies, a few generalizations can be drawn about such benefits. The larger and more solidly established enterprises are the more generous regarding added benefits. Logically, one can assume that no businessman is going to agree to benefits of such high costs as to jeopardize his enterprise. Thus, for instance, most agreements offer bonuses or incentives for attendance, but these are never higher than the 18 days a year allowed by law for sick leave. Many collective agreements offer some type of help for the educational costs of the workers' children. These are usually in the form of "scholarships" and are given to a range of between 2 and 3 percent of the enterprises' work force.[17]

One obvious conclusion is that collective agreements offer a number of very attractive inducements to the workers without exaggerated added costs to the employers.

---

[15] Many of these were previous agreements that had expired and were renegotiated.

[16] Jorge Fábrega, *Las convenciones colectivas en Panamá*. Panamá: n.p., 1981; Sindicato de Industriales de Panamá (SIP), *El Banco de Convenciones Colectivas del SIP*. Panamá: Imprenta Los Angeles, 1980.

[17] Fábrega, *Las convenciones*, p. 41.

Table 12    Cost of Labor as a Percentage of Value Added

| Years | Wages | Value Added (Thousands) | Percentage Cost of Labor |
|-------|-------|-------------------------|--------------------------|
| 1961 | 17,463 | 49,053 | 35.6 |
| 1962 | 19,718 | 50,549 | 39.0 |
| 1963 | 23,047 | 60,495 | 38.1 |
| 1964 | 24,493 | 71,914 | 34.0 |
| 1965 | 26,787 | 78,739 | 34.0 |
| 1966 | 30,906 | 89,482 | 34.5 |
| 1967 | 35,852 | 99,550 | 36.0 |
| 1968 | 39,256 | 109,067 | 35.9 |
| 1969 | 43,377 | 114,974 | 37.7 |
| 1970 | 48,492 | 146,741 | 33.0 |
| 1971 | 56,699 | 163,911 | 34.6 |
| 1972 | 64,191 | 173,915 | 36.9 |
| 1973 | 72,759 | 213,026 | 34.1 |
| 1974 | 80,651 | 257,620 | 31.3 |
| 1975 | 87,284 | 272,157 | 32.1 |
| 1976 | 90,391 | 267,891 | 33.7 |
| 1977 | 96,341 | 293,187 | 32.8 |
| 1978 | 101,929 | 300,224 | 33.9 |
| 1979 | 114,421 | 374,457 | 30.5 |
| 1981 | 156,040 | 528,376 | 29.5 |

Sources: Dirección de Estadística y Censo, Panamá en Cifras, Años 1976-1980, pp. 68-69. Percentage cost of labor was derived by dividing column 1 by column 2.

## LABOR COSTS AS PERCENTAGE OF TOTAL COSTS

Another strong complaint about the 1972 Labor Code is that the cost of labor as a percentage of total costs increased considerably, and as a result, profits were affected negatively by the increase in labor costs. This was always mentioned in interviews with businessmen, but only on one occasion were figures provided. I was told that in construction, after the passage of the 1972 Labor Code and the special laws covering construction workers, 35 to 40 percent of total construction costs were due to the labor factor.[18]

Table 12 gives the cost of labor in manufacturing (establishments of five or more workers) from 1961 to 1981. The cost of labor is shown to be rather stable over two decades, fluctuating between 30 percent and 40 percent. There is no indication of a sudden increase in cost after passage of the 1972 Labor Code, nor is there any jarring change in the figures that could be attributed to the labor laws under study. Furthermore, these figures are consonant with labor costs in other countries in the manufacturing sector as attested by the ILO labor statistics.

---

[18] Interview with Ing. Héctor Ortega, President of CAPAC.

## LABOR COSTS IN COMPARISON TO OTHER CENTRAL AMERICAN COUNTRIES

The private sector has been preoccupied with the relationship between labor costs in Panama compared to those of the rest of Central America. While the Labor Code was being debated in 1971, a large thrust of the anti-code campaign conducted by the private sector dwelt on this point. There is no denying that salaries in Panama are and have been higher than in the rest of Central America. This has been the case for several reasons. One is that the Canal Zone has always had a much higher pay scale and those wages are taken into account when averaging Panamanian wages. Second, due to the canal and to Panama's advantageous geographic position, the country has attracted a variety of service and commercial enterprises of an international nature that tend to pay high wages. According to figures for 1977 comparing wages for Panama and Central America, Costa Rica is reaching parity with Panama in salaries of industrial and agricultural workers, and wages in the other countries are from 30 percent to 60 percent lower than those in Panama.[19]

The private sector gives two reasons for concern about the discrepant wage situation between Panama and the rest of Central America. The first claim is that Panama would not be in a favorable position to trade with Central America. Second, the concern is expressed that Panama will become unable to attract foreign capital because the labor costs in the rest of Central America are much more appealing. Regarding these concerns, several observations are warranted. First, one cannot assume that because wages are higher, manufacturing costs will necessarily be higher. If a well-paid work force is producing at a high level of productivity, labor costs per unit of output may not be adversely affected by the high labor price. In a study of the Central American manufacturing sector, the average production per worker (*producto medio por ocupado*) for Panama was shown to be three times higher than that of Costa Rica, Salvador, Guatemala, and Honduras, and almost twice as high as Nicaragua's.[20] There is no doubt that that level of productivity would offset higher wages.

A second consideration has to do with the fact that traditionally Latin American countries have done very little trading among themselves, and Panama is no exception. Panama does not belong to any Latin American common market venture. Its trade with other Central American nations has not been significant. Throughout the 1970s, imports from Central America were never higher than 5 percent of all imports; exports to the area grew

---

[19] Allen Udell, "Determinación del costo de la mano de obra en Panamá." Panamá: MIPPE, 1980, p. 21.
[20] PREALC, "Instrumentos de incentivo al desarrollo industrial y su efecto en el empleo," Geneva: ILO/Documento de Trabajo PREALC/179, 1980, Cuadro I-25.

from 3 percent in 1971 to about 10 percent after 1977.[21] Because of the higher labor costs, among other factors, if Panama wanted to increase trade with Central America it would do so at a disadvantage, and it would have to maintain high tariffs against the products of these countries. But there is no reason to believe that in the mid-1970s the thrust of Panama's economic growth would be in terms of expanding its trade relations with Central America, when traditionally that trade relation has been rather insignificant.[22]

Regarding the attraction of foreign capital, according to Table 13 and Table 14, per capita U.S. direct investment in Panama is the highest in all of Latin America. U.S. direct investment in Panama increased considerably in the 1970s, and in 1978 was third highest for Latin America after Brazil and Mexico.

Table 13   U.S. Direct Investment in Latin America, 1929-1978
(millions of dollars)

| Years | 1929 | 1943 | 1950 | 1960 | 1970 | 1978 |
|---|---|---|---|---|---|---|
| Total Latin America | 3,519 | 2,798 | 4,576 | 9,249 | 14,760 | 32,509 |
| Brazil | 194 | 233 | 644 | 953 | 1,847 | 7,170 |
| Mexico | 682 | 286 | 415 | 795 | 1,786 | 3,712 |
| Panama | 29 | 110 | 58 | 405 | 1,251 | 2,385 |
| Venezuela | 233 | 373 | 933 | 2,569 | 2,704 | 2,015 |

Source: Multinational Corporations in Brazil and Mexico: Structural Sources of Economic and Noneconomic Power, Report to the Subcommittee on Multinational Corporations of the Committee on Foreign Relations, U.S. Senate (August 1975), p. 36. Survey of Current Business, Bureau of Economic Analysis, U.S.Department of Commerce (August 1979), p. 27, quoted in Steve C. Ropp, Panamanian Politics, New York: Praeger, 1982, p. 110.

Table 14   Leading Latin American Countries in Terms of Per Capita U.S. Direct Investment, 1978

| Country | Population (in Millions) | U.S. Direct Investment (in $ millions) | Per Capita Investment (in $ millions) |
|---|---|---|---|
| Panama | 1.8 | 2,385 | 1,325.0 |
| Venezuela | 13.2 | 2,015 | 152.7 |
| Peru | 16.8 | 1,429 | 85.1 |
| Argentina | 26.4 | 1,658 | 62.8 |
| Brazil | 116.4 | 7,170 | 61.6 |
| Mexico | 67.0 | 3,712 | 55.4 |

Source: Inter-American Development Bank, Economic and Social Progress in Latin America: 1978 Report, Washington, D.C., 1979, p. 415; U.S. Department of Commerce, Survey of Current Business, August, 1979, p. 27, quoted in Steve C. Ropp, Panamanian Politics, New York: Praeger, 1982, p. 110.

---

[21] Dirección de Estadística y Censo, Panamá en Cifras, Años 1971-1975, Panamá, 1976, pp. 106-107; and Panamá en Cifras, Años 1976-1980, Panamá, 1981, pp. 99-100.

[22] It may be that the industrialists considered Central America as a possible source for market expansion. But in realistic terms this would have hardly appeared enticing, because the rest of Central America is usually in worse economic conditions than Panama.

## PRODUCTIVITY

Perhaps the most damaging argument made by private enterprise against the 1972 Labor Code was the one regarding its negative effect on productivity. This claim was made for the economy as a whole, but the manufacturing sector was singled out as the most severely affected. Even though the sum total of factors that increased labor costs could affect the level of productivity, the principal culprit in this argument was felt to be the stability clause. According to employers, once a worker had been employed two years and achieved stability, his output went down noticeably, because the fear of losing the job was removed as an incentive to produce.

The attacks on the Labor Code regarding this issue began to appear in the media a few months after the Labor Code was enacted into law, and by 1973 the Conferencia Anual de Ejecutivos de Empresa treated this issue as serious and alarming. Although the pronouncements about the drop in productivity escalated during 1974 and 1975, it was not until 1976 that two studies were conducted that attempted to measure this factor. The first study was commissioned by CONEP from Investigación y Desarrollo, S.A. (INDESA), and the other study was conducted by PREALC.[23"]

The INDESA study compared the value of production, the man-hours worked, and the electrical consumption for the year 1971 (before the code) and 1974 (after the code), using a sample of manufacturing firms that represented 73 percent of total output.[24] Electrical consumption was included under the assumption that if a firm showed an increase both in productivity and electrical consumption, the change in productivity could be attributed to an increase in capital-intensive technology instead of on labor productivity. The study was done at the level of the enterprise, but the results were presented at the level of the total manufacturing sector.

The study concluded that productivity decreased by 5.46 percent between 1971 and 1974, or at a rate of 1.79 percent per year. It further claimed that in 76 percent of the enterprises there was a decrease in productivity and that although output increased in 11 sectors, only in two did it increase at a greater rate than the increase in electrical consumption. These two sectors represented only 3 percent of the man-hours worked in 1974.[25]

The INDESA report adds that the annual 2.94 percent increase in productivity from 1960 to 1970 established a valid historical trend, and the loss in productivity for the 1971-1974 period must take that into account. Had the trend continued, productivity for the period under study should have increased by 9.08 percent, and this, added to the actual loss in

[23] INDESA, "Informe del estudio de productividad," Mimeo. Panamá, 1977. INDESA is a consulting firm that does economic analysis;PREALC, "Efectos."
[24] INDESA, "Informe," p. 4.
[25] INDESA, "Informe," p. 6.

productivity of 5.48 percent, represents a total loss of 15.46 percent, and an annual loss of 4.91 percent for the 1971-1974 period.[26]

Several observations are warranted about this study and its conclusions. The 1960-1970 productivity rate was calculated using the total GDP for the manufacturing sector, but the 1971-1974 figures were taken from a sample of enterprises included in the industrial survey of those years. The data as such are not comparable. Second, in the calculations for 1960-1970, electrical consumption was not considered. For the comparison to be valid, the same assumption of electrical consumption used for the 1971-1974 period should have been applied to the 1960-1970 period, with the same assumption of capital versus labor intensity reflecting the level of production. Third, there are many inconsistencies in the figures presented for the two years under study. It is possible that at an aggregate level these inconsistencies balance each other out, but disaggregated they more than likely bias the results. Elsewhere, INDESA concluded that

> the enactment of the Labor Code coincided with a strong decline in labor productivity in the manufacturing sector. Even though it is not possible to establish a strict relation of cause and effect between one and the other phenomenon, it is unquestionable that the new labor policy has contributed in a significant manner to the drop in industrial productivity.[27]

This statement was a serious indictment of the Labor Code because the INDESA study was taken as gospel by the private sector and its conclusions were used constantly as proof of the damage caused by the Labor Code to the economy. Table 15 reproduces the figures used by INDESA to calculate productivity up to 1971 and extends these to 1979. These figures show that while output increased at a rate of 10.2 percent per year for the 1961-1970 period, it did so at only 1.9 percent per year for the 1971-1974 period. With such small increases in output, it is unreasonable to expect growth in productivity, and that was the case. Between 1971 and 1974 growth in productivity was zero. In the 1975-1979 period, output growth fell to 1.6 percent per year and productivity had a negative change of 1.5 percent per year. It is apparent by these figures that output and productivity trends were far more negative in the 1975-1979 period than in the 1971-1974 period. The latter is the period when the Panamanian economy came to a standstill and was heavily influenced by the wave of inflation and recession that affected the world economy. These figures also invalidate the pronouncements made by the private sector regarding the positive effects of

[26] INDESA, "Informe," p. 8.

[27] Guillermo Chapman, "Factores que afectan la demanda por mano de obra en Panamá," Informe preparado para el Ministerio de Planificación y Política Económica (MIPPE) y la Agencia para el Desarrollo Internacional (AID). Mimeo. Panamá: INDESA, 1979, p. 114.

Table 15   Productivity, 1961-1979

| Years | GDP Manufacturing sector (millions) | Man-hours worked (1,000) | Productivity $/hour |
|-------|------------------------------------|--------------------------|---------------------|
| 1961 | 63.0 | 22,290 | 2.8254 |
| 1962 | 75.3 | 24,498 | 3.0737 |
| 1963 | 85.6 | 25,145 | 3.4043 |
| 1964 | 90.5 | 26,213 | 3.4525 |
| 1965 | 98.1 | 26,833 | 3.6559 |
| 1966 | 107.0 | 29,458 | 3.6323 |
| 1967 | 120.1 | 31,938 | 3.7604 |
| 1968 | 131.7 | 34,433 | 3.8237 |
| 1969 | 146.1 | 36,743 | 3.9763 |
| 1970 | 153.7 | 38,552 | 3.9842 |
| 1971 | 166.7 | 44,172 | 3.7730 |
| 1972 | 177.1 | 45,362 | 3.9041 |
| 1973 | 184.6 | 47,240 | 3.9077 |
| 1974 | 176.4 | 46,790 | 3.7700 |
| 1975 | 174.9 | 46,154 | 3.7894 |
| 1976 | 153.5 | 45,193 | 3.3965 |
| 1977 | 153.6 | 46,503 | 3.2973 |
| 1978 | 162.4 | 48,360 | 3.3581 |
| 1979 | 186.6 | 52,363 | 3.5635 |

| Annual Output | Growth | Annual Productivity |
|---------------|--------|---------------------|
| 1961-1970 | 10.2 | 3.89 |
| 1971-1979 | 1.4 | -2.11 |
| 1971-1974 | 1.9 | 0 |
| 1975-1979 | 1.6 | -1.5 |

Sources: Figures to 1971: INDESA, "Informe del estudio de productividad," Mimeo. Panamá, 1977, Cuadro 5, n.p.; GDP 1972-1979: Dirección de Estadística y Censos, Panamá en Cifras: Años 1971-1975, 1976-1980, Cuadro 011-01; man-hours 1972-1976: Dirección de Estadística y Censos, "Encuestas Industriales," 1976; man-hours 1977-1979: Dirección de Estadística y Censos, "Encuestas Industriales," (unpublished).

Ley 95. After that law was enacted and businessmen were attesting to its beneficial impact on the economy, both output and productivity were at their lowest, with no indication of recovery.

The other study dealing with productivity was conducted by PREALC in 1976, and it included a sample of 84 manufacturing firms producing the same item over a period of time.[28] The study compares the productivity of these firms in 1971 (pre-Labor Code) with 1973 and 1974 (post-Labor Code), using 1970 as the base year. Regression analysis was used to measure the effects of man-hours worked, salaries paid, and differences in subsectoral output within those years on an index of real value added for the manufacturing sector. The results show that the effects of man-hours worked was very significant in explaining the variations in the levels of production.[29]

---

[28] PREALC, "Efectos," pp. 109-114.
[29] At the 1 percent level.

There was no significant change in the worker-product relation before (1971) and after (1973, 1974) the Labor Code was enacted into law. Therefore, the study concludes that no significant effect of the Labor Code on productivity could be established.[30]

The results of the PREALC study are congruent with those of Table 15. That is, no effects of the Labor Code can be readily detected in the changes in growth of output or productivity. The explanation for those changes has to be found in macro-economic variables affecting the entire economic system. The added claim made by the private sector that after the passage of Ley 95 the economic situation was on the mend, proof of the deleterious effect of the code on productivity, is also not substantiated. After passage of Ley 95, the economy continued to deteriorate and both output and production decreased substantially.

In conclusion, no direct correlation can be detected between the level of productivity and the labor laws in question. Because the level of productivity was lower in the 1975-1979 period, this invalidates the arguments made by the private sector of the positive effect of Ley 95 on the economy. If labor legislation was one of the principal factors influencing productivity, one would have to conclude that Ley 95 had a negative and not a positive effect on the economy. But this is a fallacious argument, because the level of productivity hinges on the overall health of the economy and on the growth of output, neither of which fared very well during the years in question.

### INCREASED UNION ACTIVITIES

According to Article 160 of the 1972 Labor Code, any worker asked to represent his union or the country (in the case of sports competition, for instance) has a right to three weeks paid leave if the event is in the country and up to two months paid leave if traveling to a foreign country. PREALC analyzed the requests for paid leaves for the first six months of 1976 and found that approximately 1,000 union leaders participated in seminars authorized by MITRAB. Their participation averaged two weeks and cost the enterprises about $150,000 per year (using a figure of $2,000 per man year).[31]

I have calculated these costs somewhat differently. If we assume that there were about 192 unions in the country between 1972 and 1980 (the number of unions grew from 137 in 1972 to 192 in 1979) and that each union can have 11 officers, if each of these officers took the maximum three weeks leave allowed by law, the amount of worktime to be paid would be 120 man-years. Since the average salary in private enterprises increased from $2,196

---

[30] PREALC, "Efectos," pp. 23, 109-114.
[31] PREALC, "Efectos," p. 18.

per year in 1972 to $3,708 in 1979, the approximate cost for leaves for union seminars increased from $263,000 in 1972 to $445,000 in 1979.

The previous costs were the absolute highest limits that could be reached, and the actual costs to the enterprises probably were much less between the years 1972 and 1979. But assuming that these figures represent actual costs to the enterprises and calculating them as a percentage of total wages paid in the manufacturing sector, they represent 0.4 percent of total wages.[32] These costs would be much lower if we could calculate them for the total amount of wages to all sectors in private enterprise, and as stated previously they are based on the highest possible participation of all union officers. Apart from the fact that much of this cost could and probably was passed on to the workers or to the consumers, the figures appear to be too small to represent a significant added cost to the enterprises.

There are many other educational activities that the unions provide for the rank and file but these usually do not entail extra costs to the employers. There is only one educational program that includes skills training and improvement, in which the employer and the union participate. This is carried out under the auspices of CAPAC-SUNTRACS, and the cost of the courses is paid jointly by the union and CAPAC. However, this is a very unique situation, which unfortunately has not had any spillover effect to other unions and employers.

## COSTS DUE TO STRIKES AND LITIGATIONS

In this section I will consider those complaints made by the private sector regarding increased cost of labor due to the sanctioning of strikes, the increase in labor litigations, and the sums awarded through them.

### Strikes

The 1972 Labor Code made it possible for strikes to be declared legal in Panama. Furthermore, it provided for strikes to be imputable to the employer, in which case, the employer had to pay workers' wages for the duration of the strike. The imputability of a strike had to be ruled by the labor courts, which could treat this matter as an abbreviated labor process. Table 16 shows the figures for strike activities between 1968 and 1980. The figures for the number of strikes are from the ILO, and according to them, a total of 70 strikes took place between 1973 and 1980. The private sector places the number of strikes during this time at 67, but the official figures provided by MITRAB place the number at 60.[33]

---

[32] This is the only sector for which we have a wage bill.

[33] CONEP, "Efectos de la Ley 95 de 1976," Mimeo. Panamá, 1979, p. 13; Ministerio de Trabajo y Bienestar Social, Asesoría de Programación Sectorial, *Estadísticas laborales 1978-1980*, p. 20.

Table 16    Strikes and Strike Activities, 1968-1980

| Years | Petitions to strike | Strikes declared | Strikes effected | Workers involved | Work-days lost |
|---|---|---|---|---|---|
| 1968 | * | * | 3 | 1075 | 609 |
| 1969 | * | * | 9 | 1835 | 968 |
| 1970 | * | * | 6 | 17510 | 13148 |
| 1971 | * | * | 280 | 15606 | * |
| 1972 | * | * | * | * | * |
| 1973 | 173 | 22 | 11 | 1414 | * |
| 1974 | 159 | 29 | 3 | 232 | 1063 |
| 1975 | 130 | 15 | 6 | * | * |
| 1976 | 192 | 54 | 15 | 2080 | 18939 |
| 1977 | 57 | 17 | 4 | 205 | 915 |
| 1978 | 46 | 30 | 3 | 867 | 3003 |
| 1979 | 117 | 39 | 10 | 1161 | 44292 |
| 1980 | 201 | 28 | 18 | 2438 | 158740 |

*Data not available.

Sources: Strikes, number of workers, and workdays lost: Yearbook of Labour Statistics, 1973, Geneva: ILO, 1973, and Yearbook of Labour Statistics, 1981, Geneva: ILO, 1981; number of petitions to strike and strikes declared: Ministerio de Trabajo y Bienestar Social, Asesoría de Programación Sectorial, Estadísticas laborales 1978-1980, Panamá, 1981, p. 20.

In comparison with other Latin American countries, the number of strikes in Panama is quite low. The increase in strikes in 1976 may have been due to the talks of reforming the Labor Code and the wish of workers to protect their rights. The activity in 1979 and 1980 reflected workers' frustrations regarding their lack of success in having Ley 95 revoked as well as with the cost of living increases and the erosion of the purchasing power of their wages.

These figures, however, do not represent the real situation regarding labor unrest in Panama. Because MITRAB is the agency that officially recognizes a strike, and it chose not to recognize the general strikes at the end of the decade, those figures are not included in these statistics. Also, because MITRAB does not recognize wildcat strikes, those strikes are also left out. According to several observers, wildcat strikes increased considerably between 1979 and 1981, especially after the temporary provisions of Ley 95 expired and labor pressed for the law to be revoked.

According to Table 16, from 1972 on, 8.7 strikes took place each year, and between 1968 and 1970, 6 strikes had occurred per year.[34] Although figures for the number of establishments are not available, 2,000 is a rough and probably low estimate.[35] Eight or nine strikes in a universe of 2,000 establishments hardly appears as anything but insignificant.[36]

---

[34] We have disregarded 1971 because that number is so discrepant that it appears to be a mistake in reporting.

[35] The most recent figures give the following numbers for enterprises with five or more employees: 628 in industry (1979), 558 in commerce (1971), and 751 in services (1971). Figures provided by the Ministerio de Comercio e Industrias (MICI).

[36] The reaction of an economist well versed in these matters is that the number is ludicrously low. Interview with Peter Gregory.

Lack of better data prevent further analysis on the total cost of strikes. That cost would have to be assessed as the cost of wages if the strike was imputable to the employer and as loss of productivity in the affected enterprise or sector. In the worse year for which we have figures for workdays lost on account of strikes, the cost of wages as a percentage of value added for the manufacturing sector was 1.9 percent, with the figures being much lower for all the other years. Even though this figure is a very rough estimate of the actual cost of strike activity, taken together with the number of strikes, it can give an idea of the impact of strikes on the country's economy. In my estimation that impact was low.

The sectoral breakdown for strikes between 1976 and 1980 show that 41 percent took place in the commercial sector, which includes wholesale and retail establishments as well as hotels and restaurants. The construction sector is the next most heavily afflicted, with 27 percent of the strikes. Much lower are the manufacturing and service sectors with 9 percent each of the strikes called in this period.[37]

Table 17   Strikes by Centrals and Unions, 1976-1980

| Labor Organizations | 1976 | 1977 | 1978 | 1979 | 1980 | Total |
|---|---|---|---|---|---|---|
| CNTP | 3 | 1 | 2 | 1 | 6 | 13 |
| CTRP | 3 | 1 | 1 | - | 8 | 13 |
| CIT | - | - | - | 1 | 2 | 3 |
| SIELAS* | 1 | - | - | 1 | 1 | 3 |
| SUNTRACS | 2 | 2 | - | 7 | 1 | 12 |
| TOTAL | 9 | 4 | 3 | 10 | 18 | 44 |

*Sindicato Industrial de Empleados de Líneas Aéreas y Similares.
Source: Ministerio de Trabajo y Bienestar Social, Asesoría de Programación Sectorial, Estadísticas laborales 1978-1980, Panamá, 1981, p. 23.

As for the unions and centrals that foster strikes, there are many misbeliefs held in Panama. Table 17 has the number of strikes by affiliation. Of the two large centrals, the CNTP is the most feared and vilified. This is so because it is communist, because it is said to be against private enterprise, and because it harbors some of the oldest and most bellicose unions.[38] The CTRP, however, is seen with benevolent eyes, because it is tied to U.S. labor—through the AFL-CIO American and the Institute for Free Labor Enterprise (AIFELD)—and because some of its largest unions are the locals that operate in the Canal Zone, as well as in firms tied to U.S. capital. In the five years of strike statistics provided by MITRAB with sectoral breakdown and labor affiliation, the CTRP and the CNTP had the

---

[37] Ministerio de Trabajo, Asesoría de Programación Sectorial, Estadísticas laborales 1978-1980, Panamá, 1981, p. 17.
[38] The CNTP's slogan "Empresa cerrada - empresa tomada" is often quoted as definite proof that its leaders want nothing less than the destruction of private enterprise and the socialization of capital.

same number of strikes. This would lead one to believe that in Panama ideology does not weigh heavily in fostering strikes but rather that they are motivated by the more pressing issues of better wages and more decent working conditions. As a point of fact, in 1979, 1980, and 1981 there were mass protests and general strikes, something new in the history of organized labor in Panama. These movements were led in two instances by the CTRP and in one by the CNTP.

Since early 1979, the CTRP pushed for a general strike to demand the revoking of Ley 95. The CNTP, which was deeply compromised with the government, did not want to go along on the pretext that any such movement would be interpreted as an internal weakness on the part of the government at a time when it was important to maintain a front of national unity. For the first mass demonstration, the CTRP went at it alone and the movement was not very successful. As dissatisfaction continued regarding Ley 95, in November 1979, the CNTP held a mass demonstration. After this, all the centrals planned and carried out the general strike of January 1980. The CTRP was the guiding force behind that effort.

## Labor Litigations

Many of the negative commentaries made about the Labor Code and other labor laws had a conditioning clause. It was often said that it was not so much the Labor Code as such that was to be blamed for all the problems as the way it was applied. This statement implied that there was partiality in the application of the laws by the MITRAB and the labor courts, both of which were considered to rule in favor of the workers. These arguments were often heard regarding labor litigations.

According to members of the private sector, the application of the Labor Code gave way to a myriad of abuses by workers.[39] In some cases a worker would stage a situation in order to be fired, and then he would proceed to the labor courts knowing that the chances of obtaining a ruling in his favor were very good. Another complaint was that the labor courts were so backlogged that by the time a case was ruled upon, usually many months had passed since the time of the complaint. If the case was decided in favor of the worker, the employer had to pay all those months of due salary plus the indemnization and the court costs. One or two labor litigations could break almost any enterprise, except the very large and well-endowed ones. This was and still is the common belief held by the private sector regarding labor litigations.

---

[39] Businessmen had all sorts of anecdotes about ruses by workers to take advantage of the system. I heard a story several times about a secretary who financed her vacation to Disneyland with her sick-leave payment and many stories of workers who claimed some type of disability or managed to get fired and with the indemnization money built a house or bought a taxi and set themselves up in business.

Table 18   Labor Litigations — Panama and Panama Province, 1970-1978

|  | 1970 | 1971 | 1972 | 1973 | 1974 | 1875 | 1976 | 1977 | 1978 |
|---|---|---|---|---|---|---|---|---|---|
| **Panama (Country):** | | | | | | | | | |
| No. of cases | 2958.0 | 3403.0 | 4066.0 | 4965.0 | 5676.0 | 5971.0 | 4750.0 | 5522.0 | 4783.0 |
| Annual variation | | 15.0 | 19.4 | 22.1 | 14.3 | 5.1 | -20.4 | 16.2 | -13.3 |
| Total amount awarded | | | | | | | | | |
| (thousands) | 377.8 | 512.8 | 512.9 | 876.1 | 995.1 | 1063.9 | 1062.3 | 1132.2 | 1059.0 |
| Annual variation | | 35.7 | 0.0 | 70.8 | 13.5 | 6.9 | -0.2 | 6.6 | -6.4 |
| Average settlement ($) | 128.0 | 151.0 | 126.0 | 176.0 | 175.0 | 178.0 | 224.0 | 205.0 | 221.0 |
| **Panama Province:** | | | | | | | | | |
| No. of cases | 2617-0 | 2105.0 | 2628.0 | 3779.0 | 3882.0 | 3672.0 | 3772.0 | 3763.0 | 3164.0 |
| Annual variation | | -19.5 | 24.8 | 43.7 | 4.6 | -3.1 | 2.5 | -15.9 | |
| Total amount awarded | | | | | | | | | |
| (thousands) | 217.0 | 215.0 | 214.0 | 371.0 | 518.0 | 476.0 | 578.0 | 739.0 | 561.0 |
| Annual variation | | -0.9 | -0.5 | 73.3 | 39.6 | -8.1 | 21.4 | 27.9 | -24.0 |
| Average settlement ($) | 83.0 | 102.0 | 81.0 | 98.0 | 131.0 | 124.0 | 157.0 | 196.0 | 179.0 |
| Annual variation | | 23.0 | -21.0 | 21.0 | 34.0 | -5.3 | 27.0 | 25.0 | -8.7 |

*Source*: Ministerio de Trabajo y Bienestar Social, *Estadísticas Laborales, 1970-1973*, Panamá, 1974, Cuadro 4. *1975-1978*, Panamá, 1979, Cuadro 6. *1978-1980*, Panamá, 1981, n.p.

Table 18 provides figures on litigations. It includes the number of cases and total amount paid due to labor litigations for the entire country, as well as for the Province of Panama between 1970 and 1980. The average settlement increased from $83 in 1970 to $179 in 1978 and there was a 13 percent annual variation during that period. An interesting fact is that after an increase of about 1,000 cases brought to litigation immediately after the enactment of the 1972 Labor Code, the number of cases remained almost the same for the rest of the decade.

After the Juntas de Conciliación y Decisión (JCD) were established in 1975, they had sole jurisdiction in cases of dismissals, because the backlog in the labor courts and the alleged payment of large amounts of due salaries was what brought the JCD into being in the first place. The juntas also had sole jurisdiction in cases involving litigations of up to $1,500. Table 19 presents the number of cases heard by the juntas, the number ruled in favor of the worker, the total amount awarded, and the average settlement. The increase in the amount of the settlements awarded by the juntas as opposed to the labor courts may be explained by the fact that dismissal cases involved payment of indemnization as well as due salaries and that after 1976, the indemnization in unjustified dismissals increased considerably.

An important fact to note about the awards granted by the juntas is that between 50 and 75 percent of the cases under litigation were ruled in favor of the employer. This is stressed because most businessmen interviewed claimed that the juntas were completely skewed in favor of the workers and that employers had no chance of having cases ruled in their favor. This belief is what led members of the private sector to appeal decisions made by the juntas to the Supreme Court, claiming violation of their constitutional rights by the juntas (*amparos de garantías constitucionales*).

Table 19    Labor Litigations - Juntas de Conciliación y Decisión, 1975-1980

|                          | 1975  | 1976  | 1977  | 1978  | 1979  | 1980  |
|--------------------------|-------|-------|-------|-------|-------|-------|
| No. cases                | 416   | 492   | 389   | 333   | 338   | 388   |
| In favor of worker       | 182   | 187   | 181   | 174   | 112   | 123   |
| Total amount awarded     |       |       |       |       |       |       |
| ($ 1,000)                | 83.4  | 131.0 | 85.1  | 57.8  | 73.3  | 80.2  |
| Average settlement ($)   | 458   | 700   | 470   | 332   | 642   | 652   |
| (Annual Increase=7.1%)   |       |       |       |       |       |       |

Source: Ministerio de Trabajo y Bienestar Social, Asesoría de Programación Sectorial, *Estadísticas laborales, 1978-1980*, Panamá, 1981, p. 18; and figures provided by the Ministerio de Trabajo.

In an effort to find out the real costs of labor litigations and place them within a framework of total labor costs, we have calculated the total amounts awarded in labor settlements as a percentage of total wages. It must be pointed out that labor litigations did not arise subsequent to the enactment of the 1972 Labor Code, but as the figures show, there was not much of a radical increase in the number of labor litigations or in the amounts awarded before and after the Labor Code.[40]

The total amount awarded through labor litigations increased from $337.8 thousand in 1970 to $1.05 million in 1978, with an average annual increase of 10.1 percent. The amount disbursed grew from 0.7 percent of total labor costs (using the figure of total wages paid in the manufacturing sector) to 1 percent in 1978.

## SUMMARY OF COST INCREASES

In the preceding sections we have tried to assess a dollar value to the increase in the cost of labor directly or indirectly related to the 1972 Labor Code. The increase has been calculated as a percentage of value added for the manufacturing sector, which is the only figure we have that can be used as a measure of production for the private sector. The figures we have used, then, represent a much higher percentage of cost because they are assessed against only one sector. Had we been able to use value added for all income producing sectors, the assessed costs of labor would have decreased considerably.

With the above considerations in mind, and using the highest possible figure for each category, we offer the following summary. Wages as a percentage of value added did not increase with the enactment of the 1972 Labor Code; cost of union activities such as participation in seminars, increased the cost of labor by 0.4 percent; strikes increased the cost of labor by 1.9 percent; and labor litigations by 1 percent. As already mentioned,

---

[40] I would have liked to show the figures on amounts disbursed due to labor litigations for the 1960 decade, but those figures were unavailable at the MITRAB.

these percentages represent the cost increase as a percentage of value added for the manufacturing sector and would probably be much lower, if not negligible, if value added for the whole economy was available. Nevertheless, the total increase in costs as represented by these figures is 3.3 percent, hardly an increase that could break a firm or cause the downfall of an economy, as the 1972 Labor Code was made out to have done.

## PROBLEMS OF SMALL ENTERPRISES

In the dispute regarding the effects of the Labor Code, small enterprises became what one codifier called the "Achilles heel" of the Labor Code.[41] Among the most alarming results imputed to the Labor Code was the massive foreclosure of small businesses due to the increase in labor costs, which they could not meet. The first time Torrijos spoke openly about the possible reform of the code, he mentioned a study regarding this problem and said he was concerned that owners of over 300 small enterprises "had had to leave in an economic stampede."[42] Although Ley 95 did not directly benefit small enterprises, it was felt that their situation improved when the labor demands eased up.

The campaign launched by the private sector to forestall the removal of Ley 95 constantly alluded to the improved economic climate brought about by that law, which the private sector claimed greatly improved the situation of the small enterprise. The CONEP document presented to the Assembly of Representatives contained a chart showing that between 1973 and 1976 an average of 209 small enterprises had closed per year, with an average loss of 4.7 jobs per enterprise, but that after Ley 95 was passed and up to the date of the CONEP study in 1977, only 69 enterprises had closed down, with a loss of 721 jobs.[43] One theory brought forth during the unyielding campaign against the Labor Code was that the role of the code was not to protect workers but to destroy the small national industry, which did not fit Ardito Barletta's development program.[44]

Table 20 presents figures provided by the Ministry of Commerce and Industry (MICI) on the number of requests for licenses to establish and to close enterprises. It also shows the figures provided by CONEP.[45] The figures conform to the macro-economic trends affecting the country, so that

---

[41] Interview with Arturo Hoyos.

[42] "Posibles ajustes al código de trabajo," El Panamá América, August 29, 1976.

[43] However, these figures would indicate a loss of 10.4 jobs per establishment, or the closure of much larger establishments. CONEP, "Efectos de la Ley 95 de 1976," Mimeo. Panamá, 1979, p. 20.

[44] José E. Torres Abrego, "Panamá: efectos del régimen de Torrijos en la estructura económica," Comercio Exterior, 32(1): 66.

[45] A survey carried out at MICI with 1976 figures showed that industrial and wholesale commercial enterprises on average represent five jobs, and retail commercial enterprises represent six jobs.

Table 20    Licenses to Operate Businesses, Granted and Cancelled

|                           | 1972 | 1973 | 1974 | 1975 | 1976 | 1977 | 1978 | 1979 | 1980 |
|---------------------------|------|------|------|------|------|------|------|------|------|
| Licenses granted          |      |      |      |      |      |      |      |      |      |
| Commerce—wholesale        | 143  | 206  | 269  | 215  | 191  | 239  | 286  | 309  | 312  |
| Commerce—retail           | 1177 | 1579 | 1862 | 1733 | 1810 | 1728 | 1955 | 2109 | 2241 |
| Industrial establishments | 174  | 195  | 255  | 219  | 197  | 284  | 329  | 285  | 338  |
| Total                     | 1494 | 1980 | 2386 | 2167 | 2198 | 2251 | 2470 | 2703 | 2891 |
| Licenses cancelled        |      |      |      |      |      |      |      |      |      |
| Commerce—wholesale        | 19   | 50   | 57   | 54   | 55   | 62   | 61   | 76   | 96   |
| Commerce—retail           | 479  | 510  | 613  | 583  | 635  | 640  | 608  | 573  | 697  |
| Industrial establishments | 16   | 34   | 38   | 43   | 36   | 44   | 40   | 32   | 36   |
| Total                     | 514  | 594  | 708  | 680  | 728  | 746  | 709  | 681  | 829  |

Source: Figures provided by the Ministerio de Comercio e Industria, Sección de Planificación, Panamá, 1981.

between 1975 and 1977 when the rate of increase in GDP reached its lowest, there is a coincidence with the decrease in requests for new licenses. Closures also coincide with the trend in GDP. The figures do not establish, however, any correlation between the effects of Ley 95 and the set-up of new businesses or closure of established ones.

Very little is known about small enterprises in Panama. None of the ministries have pertinent information, nor do the commercial and industrial sectors representing them.[46] The 1976 survey by MICI and the census material classifying enterprises by number of employees seem to be the only material available regarding small enterprises.

The Agency for International Development contracted INDESA in 1980 to do a study on small enterprises as a preliminary step in a program to help small business[47] The researchers investigated 22 enterprises, of which only 6 had fewer than 8 employees. Some of the results presented by INDESA are as follows: of the credit available to small enterprises through the four existing programs, most of the credit was given to medium-sized and large enterprises; the greatest problem for industrial enterprises was shortage of working capital,[48] and for commercial enterprises, the drop in profitability due to rapidly increasing costs and to the price-control system.[49] Businessmen reported that to keep unions out and to get around the constraints placed by the Labor Code on working overtime, they did not hire workers in Panama City, and much less in Colón, but hired their labor from the interior. They also felt that small enterprises should be exonerated from the

---

[46] Prof. Félix Pardos Rubio, the moving force behind the Unión Nacional de Pequeñas Industrias had no reliable figures on members of the organization, number of employees, amount of capital invested, and other such pertinent data. Interview with Prof. Pardos Rubio.
[47] INDESA, "Situación de la pequeña empresa en Panamá," Estudio preparado para la Agencia de Desarrollo Internacional (AID), Mimeo. Panamá, 1980.
[48] INDESA, "Situación," p. 46.
[49] INDESA, "Situación," pp. 42, 46.

high indemnization costs incurred in cases of dismissals as well as from having to negotiate collective agreements.

The campaign in favor of the small enterprise was heeded by the government, and Ley 8a, which modified Ley 95, contained provisions exempting small businesses from the stability clause.[50]

## EMPLOYMENT

During the 1960s, with a sustained economic growth of 8 percent per year, Panama was able to decrease unemployment from slightly over 9 percent at the beginning of the decade to 7 percent at the end of it. Employment increased at a rate of 3.7 percent yearly, with the largest increase taking place between 1960 and 1963, when unemployment dropped to 5.8 percent. During the rest of the 1960s, the unemployment rate fluctuated between 6 and 7 percent. However, the employment situation was heavily influenced by several factors. Employment in agriculture decreased from 50 percent of the total economically active population (EAP) in 1960 to 36.5 percent in 1970.[51] Manufacture, construction, commerce, and finance, however, registered annual increases of 7.1 percent, 8.9 percent, and 7.1 percent, respectively.[52] The decade also experienced an increasing rate of female participation in the work force. This reached almost 25 percent, which meant that in order to register the total drop in unemployment mentioned above, women were incorporated into the active work force at a rate of almost 6 percent per year.[53]

Most experts on employment agree that sustained economic growth is one of the most important conditions for maintaining high levels of employment. There seems to be a direct correlation between growth of GDP and growth of employment. In order for the unemployment rate to decrease from 7 percent to 4.7 percent, PREALC estimated that economic growth in the 1970s would have to be sustained at 8 percent per year. In the event that economic growth could only be sustained at a yearly rate of 6.5 percent, not a mean achievement by any standard, open unemployment would reach 11 percent by the end of the decade, which was the unemployment rate (11 percent) that PREALC predicted for Panama. One reason for this was that the work force experienced a very high growth rate—3.4 percent per year. Other contributing factors were the expansion of the work force in non-agricultural activities and the unresponsiveness of the rate of

---

[50] Ley 8a defined small enterprises as agricultural enterprises with 10 or fewer workers, agro-industrial enterprises with 20 or fewer workers, manufacturing enterprises with 15 or fewer workers, and retail commercial and service enterprises with five or fewer workers. (Article 1 of Ley 8a).

[51] PREALC, *Situación y perspectiva del empleo en Panamá*. Geneva: ILO, 1974, p. 216.

[52] PREALC, *Situación*, p. 217.

[53] PREALC, *Situación*, p. 3.

employement to variations in the capacity of the agricultural sector to absorb or retain labor.[54]

For the unemployment rate to drop when the EAP is growing at a rapid rate, two conditions are required in addition to sustained economic growth: (1) an increase in the rhythm of demand for labor, and (2) an improvement in the skill levels of the labor force. The first will be influenced by the sectoral structure and the geographic distribution of the increase in production. The second condition implies adequate educational and training programs to improve the skills of the work force to levels suitable to the needs for economic expansion.[55]

Panama owed its sustained growth of the 1960s to the increase in import substitution industrialization as well as to the increase in construction and commerce. But although the industrial sector reached very high levels of growth in the early 1960s, by the end of the decade this had tapered off substantially.

During the 1970s, even though the economy did not stagnate until 1974, it was only in 1979 that it registered a growth rate of over 8 percent. For the 1970-1978 period, GDP in manufacture and construction grew at 0.2 percent per year, and in commerce at 2.2 percent yearly. The construction industry continued to grow until mid-1974 but it subsequently crashed and did not recover until late 1979. And the commercial sector also experienced a considerable slowdown during the 1970s.[56] As could be expected, along with the drop in GDP, the rate of increase in employment also declined. Thus in manufacture, employment grew at a rate of only 1.9 percent per year during the nine-year period, while construction grew by 1.7 percent and commerce by less than 1 percent. What seems remarkable is that with economic growth so low, these sectors did register some, albeit low, growth in employment.

Although experts in employment were aware that employment growth had not reached an optimum level, even with the high and sustained economic growth of the 1960s, and that the trends in the economy since the early 1970s gave few indications for comfort, no effective steps were taken to alleviate the problem. Public investment in the early 1970s was geared to highly technical and capital-intensive infrastructural projects and to the nationalization and reorganization of the utilities, all of which offered little potential for new employment. The private sector was afflicted by the woes of a recession. After the passage of the Labor Code, its efforts were geared to enhancing enterprises in terms of fewer labor demands. By mid-decade

---

[54] PREALC, *Situación*, pp. 172-177.

[55] PREALC, *Situación*, p. 174.

[56] Transportation, finances and utilities all experienced a healthy growth of 10.4 percent, 10.8 percent, and 9.3 percent respectively, but those are sectors with low employment ratios.

Table 21  Employment by Sector. 1960-1978 (percentages)

| | 1960 | 1963 | 1964 | 1965 | 1966 | 1967 | 1968 | 1969 | 1970 | 1971 | 1972 | 1973 | 1974 | 1975 | 1976 | 1977 | 1978 |
|---|---|---|---|---|---|---|---|---|---|---|---|---|---|---|---|---|---|
| Agriculture | 50.0 | 48.4 | 47.6 | 47.1 | 45.3 | 40.4 | 39.1 | 37.4 | 36.5 | 34.6 | 33.8 | 33.2 | 30.7 | 30.2 | 31.4 | 31.4 | 30.2 |
| Mines | 0.0 | 0.0 | 0.0 | 0.0 | 0.0 | 0.0 | 0.2 | 0.0 | 0.1 | 0.1 | 0.0 | 0.0 | 0.0 | 0.2 | 0.0 | 0.0 | 0.1 |
| Manufacture | 8.0 | 8.3 | 8.8 | 8.6 | 10.2 | 9.9 | 12.6 | 11.2 | 11.0 | 9.7 | 9.6 | 9.6 | 10.5 | 10.6 | 9.9 | 10.2 | 10.0 |
| Construction | 3.3 | 3.5 | 3.8 | 4.3 | 4.3 | 5.2 | 4.7 | 4.8 | 5.4 | 6.0 | 6.8 | 6.9 | 6.3 | 6.3 | 6.3 | 5.1 | 5.5 |
| Electricity, gas, water | 0.3 | 0.6 | 0.6 | 0.9 | 0.8 | 0.8 | 0.8 | 0.7 | 1.0 | 1.0 | 1.2 | 1.2 | 1.0 | 1.1 | 1.5 | 1.2 | 1.3 |
| Commerce and finance | 9.4 | 10.0 | 10.1 | 9.7 | 10.2 | 12.0 | 11.4 | 12.6 | 12.9 | 15.7 | 16.4 | 16.5 | 16.7 | 17.4 | 16.9 | 16.9 | 17.4 |
| Transportation and communication | 3.0 | 2.7 | 2.7 | 3.1 | 3.2 | 3.4 | 3.7 | 3.8 | 3.8 | 4.1 | 3.9 | 4.0 | 5.2 | 5.3 | 5.2 | 5.4 | 5.3 |
| Services | 20.0 | 20.1 | 20.1 | 20.6 | 20.2 | 22.9 | 21.8 | 24.1 | 24.1 | | | | | | | | |
| Canal Zone | 6.0 | 5.9 | 5.9 | 5.7 | 5.9 | 5.2 | 5.7 | 5.2 | 5.2 | | | | | | | | |

*Sources:* 1960-1970: *Situación y perspectiva del empleo en Panamá.* Geneva: ILO. 1974. p. 216. 1970-1975: calculated from figures in Cuadro 441-02. *Panamá en cifras: Años* 1971-1975. and *Años 1976-1980.*

Table 22  Growth Rate of the Economically Active Population, 1970-1978 (percentages)

| | 1970 | 1971 | 1972 | 1973 | 1974 | 1975 | 1976 | 1977 | 1978 |
|---|---|---|---|---|---|---|---|---|---|
| Total | 3.3 | 1.6 | 3.0 | 2.1 | 5.0 | -2.5 | -0.8 | -0.2 | 4.7 |
| Agriculture | 0.8 | -3.7 | 0.5 | 0.5 | -2.8 | -4.4 | 3.6 | -0.3 | 0.7 |
| Mines | 25.0 | 20.0 | -33.3 | 0.0 | -25.0 | 200.0 | -66.7 | 33.3 | 25.0 |
| Manufacturing | -9.0 | 0.0 | 2.3 | 2.1 | 15.1 | -1.2 | -7.3 | 2.3 | 2.9 |
| Electricity | 11.8 | 23.7 | 12.8 | 5.7 | -16.1 | 10.6 | 32.7 | -18.8 | 16.1 |
| Construction | 16.3 | 11.4 | 18.2 | 3.9 | -4.6 | -2.9 | -0.7 | -19.2 | 12.9 |
| Commerce | 15.4 | -2.3 | 7.2 | 2.2 | 0.5 | -1.5 | -1.5 | 0.3 | 2.5 |
| Transportation | 3.1 | 11.0 | -1.6 | 4.5 | 35.3 | 0.0 | -3.2 | 4.1 | 2.7 |
| Finances | -4.5 | 6.5 | 9.2 | 5.6 | 40.7 | 11.9 | -11.8 | -1.9 | 27.9 |
| Services | 0.4 | 7.0 | 2.3 | 3.2 | 13.1 | -4.6 | 1.5 | 2.0 | 7.3 |
| Canal Zone | | 6.7 | -4.6 | 1.3 | -10.0 | -1.9 | -18.6 | 10.8 | 1.1 |

Source: Guillermo Chapman. "Factores que afectan la demanda por mano de obra en Panamá."Panamá. 1979. p. 60.

the government had enacted some employment-incentive measures in the private sector, but these produced no tangible effects.[57]

Apart from the PREALC study on employment, which was published in 1974, several other studies dealing with the problem were produced from the mid-1970s on. The Plan Nacional de Desarrollo 1976-1980 recognized the need to create 100,000 jobs by 1980 in order to reduce open unemployment to 5.8 percent. However, the projects proposed would create a total of 33,142 jobs at a cost of approximately $33,000 per job. This plan also assumed that the GDP would increase at a rate of 7.4 percent per year. The developmental thrust was in services and infrastructure, and it was expected that the spillover from that would be used to develop the agricultural sector.[58] A study done by ICASE-IFARHU used a more realistic GDP growth of 4.3 percent to 1980 and 3 percent to 1985 and forecast an open unemployment of 11.7 percent for 1980 and 17.8 percent for 1985.[59] Another report completed by the World Bank in 1978 forecast an unemployment rate of 12 percent for 1980, and concluded that the method for measuring unemployment in Panama was not accurate and that unemployment at that time was probably around 16 percent.[60] These studies, in contrast with the Plan Nacional de Desarrollo, emphasized incentives for industrial output for export as well as a revision of the price-control policy

---

[57] Ley 90, in the Paquete de Incentivos Fiscales, offered temporary tax deductions for each new job created within a given period. This measure had no impact. "Leyes de incentivos fiscales," *La Estrella de Panamá*, January 4, 1977.

[58] Ministerio de Planificación y Política Económica, *Plan Nacional de Desarrollo 1976-1980*. Panamá: MIPPE, 1981.

[59] This study is mentioned in Chapman, "Factores," p. 73.

[60] Quoted in Chapman, "Factores," pp. 75-77.

and the tax incentives laws. It may be that the drafters of the Plan Nacional de Desarrollo engaged in an exercise in wishful thinking, because the economy not only did not recover but took a turn for the worse in 1976, and only in 1979 did it experience a healthy growth of 7.1 percent. However, in 1980 this decreased to 4.9 percent. The public sector only created 17,522 new jobs between 1976 and 1979 and the private sector 15,517 during the same period. Open unemployment in Panama, according to official figures was 8 percent in 1980. Unofficially, the figures ranged between 12 percent (World Bank) and 16 percent (IMF). Unemployment in the City of Panama was close to 20 percent and in Colón, near 40 percent.[61] The government declared that these statements were part of an anti-government campaign and that those figures should be completely disregarded.[62]

Even though it was expedient to use the Labor Code as a scapegoat for employment problems, it is obvious from the above that the reasons for the high level of unemployment lie elsewhere. One important factor seems to have been the lack of coherence in government policies proposed for economic growth. It seems that some government sectors, in particular the Ministry of Planning, were promoting the continued improvement of the infrastructure and the increase of the service sector, with scant regard to the effect this would have on employment. Another group, centering around the MICI and backed by the private sector, pushed for the growth of manufacturing but with emphasis on fiscal incentives, which traditionally lead to capital-intensive improvements.

Another problem is apparent when considering the studies dealing with employment. That is, even though the magnitude of the problem was acknowledged, no real solutions were proposed. The Plan Nacional de Desarrollo saw the need for 100,000 jobs and came up with projects to create 30,000. Added to this was the fact that the assumption about the improvement of the employment situation was directly linked to the sustained high growth of GDP, which was unrealistic given the fact that the economic situation offered no signs of improvement.

In conclusion, while one cannot overlook the fact that the Labor Code had a bearing on the employment situation, there were other much more serious factors affecting it, such as the slow growth of the GDP, the lack of coherence of government policy regarding economic development, and the international economic situation that had strong repercussions on Panama's internal situation.

---

[61] Declarations to this effect by Guillermo Chapman to the press and related to an austerity plan proposed by the International Monetary Fund prompted the rebuttal by the government.
[62] *La Prensa*, October 21, 1981.

CONCLUSION

The effects of the Labor Code on the Panamanian economy and society are difficult to assess. Although a strong case has been made for many of the arguments presented against the Labor Code, lack of appropriate data prevents an assessment of others.

As has been demonstrated, the increase in wages due to the Labor Code was not that steep, and it does not appear to have had a negative impact on the wage cost as percentage of value added. Still, the fact that wages could not keep up with inflation and that mechanisms totally outside the control of the labor sector and of entrepreneurs (the wage increases decreed by law) had to be used often to remedy that situation demonstrate that the Labor Code was in no way a guarantor of adequate wages for the work force. Nor does the increase in wages show any correlation with the level of productivity. Moreover, the other complaint voiced by the private sector regarding productivity, that the stability clause prevented them from running their businesses efficiently, didn't prove to be true when there was a need to reduce the work force, as was the case during the 1974-1976 period, in which employment was reduced by 8 percent.

Many of the other complaints just seem petty and appear to have been used as an excuse to keep alive the campaign against the Labor Code. In this category I would place the level of organized disruption, especially strikes and labor litigations. Regarding the last, because there are no figures to compare the level of litigations prior to the code, it is difficult to assess the real impact of the code in this regard. Nevertheless, the increase of 1 percent in the cost of labor (the total cost of litigations reflected by the manufacturing sector) due to labor litigations does not seem high enough to have caused the damage imputed to it.

Other issues considered very important by the private sector could not be analyzed at all for lack of data. Absenteeism is a good example. The level of complaint regarding this issue was so high and the accusations so strong that one wonders why more effort was not made to provide adequate documentation.[63] Yet private-sector employers had all sorts of strategies to catch doctors who they suspected of writing false medical excuses and even made the proposal that a worker subject himself to three medical exams or lose his job if his medical excuse was suspect to the employer.[64]

The enterprises most affected by the Labor Code were primarily those that employed large numbers of workers and that had complex organiza-

---

[63] In the only two instances when figures were discussed, these did not point to any blatant abuses. In one case, the employer mentioned that one worker had 14 days of absence and several other workers had 6 or 8 absences in a year's time. When I pointed out that the law allows for 18 days, I was not permitted to copy the figures.

[64] CONEP. "Recomendaciones propuestas a la Comisión Nacional que fuera creada por la Ley 22 del 14 de julio de 1980," Mimeo. Panamá, 1980.

tional structures. The ones that more easily fell into those categories were industrial manufacturing enterprises (including agro-industries), as well as some service enterprises with large labor components, such as hotels. Of those, the enterprises that seem to have had less trouble with the application of the Labor Code were those run by foreign companies or with large foreign segments. This is the case because probably foreign companies had a less paternalistic and more institutionalized approach toward their labor force and followed management practices that more easily conformed to those espoused in the 1972 Labor Code. Many foreign companies already provided some of the benefits included in the Labor Code or had less trouble accepting them as adequate and just.

The complaints of Panamanian businessmen were that the benefits were exhorbitant and beyond their means. What they were really complaining about was not just that they had to pay higher benefits but that they were being told when and how to pay them. The effect was to remove from their control the ability to act as they pleased and instead make them conform to the structural constraints set up by law for the provision of those benefits. As PREALC concluded in its study of the Labor Code, the main problem was that the Labor Code forced employers to treat their workers in an institutionalized and rational manner, and Panamanian employers were used to dealing with their personnel in a paternalistic, non-systematic way.[65]

However, the Labor Code was not the marvel it was made out to be. Among its drawbacks was the fact that it only covered a reduced number of workers, about 40 percent of the work force. Excluded from the code were workers in the public sector, self-employed persons, Canal Zone workers, and family workers. Another drawback was the ease with which the government was prone to make exceptions to the Labor Code. Bank employees have not been allowed to unionize, and exempted from the labor laws are the *maquilas*, or off-shore companies, and the workers in the Colon Free Zone enterprises. As Torrijos's obvious control of the day-to-day running of the government seemed to get weaker, the government appeared to be more positively inclined to grant exemptions to the Labor Code.

A worse situation yet was the one that arose when the government, as employer, would not honor the labor laws. The case of the Ministry of Housing, which contracted members of SUNTRACS for the construction of low-cost housing and paid well below union wages, was scandalous. Even more so was the fact that that ministry tried to disregard safety measures and to get away without paying into the Fondo de Garantía.

All of the above point to the fact that while the Labor Code was progressive and provided immediate and visible benefits to some seg-

---

[65] PREALC, "Efectos," pp. 26-27.

ments of labor, not the least being labor's improvement in status and recognition as a societal force, it also had its problems and was not the complete panacea it has been portrayed to be. In general, perhaps the most detrimental aspect of the code was the role it gave the MITRAB as protector and controller of labor and the position it placed organized labor in, that of dependent minion of the government. In this respect, the role of the MITRAB was and continues to be pervasive. The ministry can control almost every aspect of organized labor. This situation is not only not salubrious but raises the question of what would happen if the government, instead of being pro-labor, became anti-labor.

The 1972 Labor Code became a symbol of the Torrijos regime. It represented a break with the past and was a tool in the making of the new forces the regime fostered. The inability of the private sector to accept this policy was indicative of its inability to accept its loss of power and redefined role. On those grounds, attacks on the code would have been acceptable and understandable. What became ludicrous was the whole performance of the national economy attributed to a piece of legislation, which at most affected the internal economic development of the country only tangentially.

# 9

# IMPLICATIONS AND LEGACY
# OF THE TORRIJOS REGIME

## DEPENDENCY, CLASS STRUCTURE, AND POLITICAL ALLIANCES

Several factors that had long been present in Panamanian society can explain the National Guard takeover and the rise to power of Omar Torrijos. By 1968, these factors had coalesced and presented the right conditions for the rise of an entirely different political form represented by a populist authoritarian leader whose purpose in ruling was to bring about reforms and to restructure society. The situation in the country came about as the outcome of an articulation of conditions that are present in extremely dependent peripheral countries in which the dominant class is allied with and responsive to external interests at the expense of internal ones. The dominant class can maintain power as long as it has consensus among its factions and as long as the demands of groups outside the power structure are not strong enough to threaten the status quo. If consensus is lost or the status quo altered, the situation may become unmanageable for the dominant class. That was the situation that crystallized in Panama in 1968: the ruling elite lost hegemony, precipitating a representational crisis. The loss of hegemony of the ruling elite facilitated the emergence of a new type of regime in which an outsider had the opportunity to rise to power unencumbered by political constraints or previous liaisons and to enact reforms, challenge the position of the former rulers, and overturn the status quo.

In underdeveloped countries such as Panama, the dominant ruling elite's involvement with foreign capital and foreign interests makes it highly responsive to the exigencies and demands of external factors. This dependency on external forces makes the national bourgeoisie unresponsive to the internal needs of society, except as society specifically relates to the bourgeoisie's private interests. In this situation, political control is maintained as long as the ruling elite can maintain the status quo. This is only possible when a certain degree of consensus exists among the factions of the ruling elite, when the demands of the social system are not severe enough to threaten the status quo, or when those groups making the demands are weak and ineffectual. The ruling elite's interest in maintaining political control rests on the need to cater to its own interests, and it accomplishes this through the exertion of naked and unopposed power.

The above description reflects the situation that existed in Panama in the early 1960s. The ruling elite did not respond to the social needs of a country with an increasingly complex social situation and with a large segment of its population dispossessed. From the mid-1950s, Panama experienced an economic boom, the increase of its service sector, the growth of its manufacturing sector through import substitution industrialization, a rapid population growth, and the swift increase of an urban, educated class that found no entry into the productive sector or a voice in the power structure. Panamanian society was increasingly divided between the haves and the have-nots.

Seemingly oblivious to these changing internal conditions, the ruling elite continued playing its power games of staging elections and jousting for power without trying to address some of the more pressing social problems. Even if the elite did not win elections, it was assured continuance in power by the National Guard, who was there to back the faction of the elite that offered them the best deal or that promised to respect their integrity. The only real threat to this panorama was Arnulfo Arias, a populist leader of the 1940s, who during two previous presidential tries had disavowed the authority of the National Guard. Arias was the only political figure in Panama who had enough popular support to win elections, but because he did not play by the rules, he was not acceptable either to the ruling elite or to the National Guard.

Consensus among the factions of the elite was lost in the 1960s because of divergent interests among them. The elections and subsequent administrations of that decade became mocking circuses in which all of the contenders either attacked each other or made alliances with each other, mainly for the sake of winning. This led to a political stalemate and subsequently to a representational crisis in which the contending powers canceled each other out, with a consequent loss of hegemony.

The political game had never been played very differently in Panama, but the social conditions of the previous decades had been much simpler and manageable. The political crisis peaked during the Robles administration (1964-1968). That administration, which came into power by electoral fraud, tried to address some of the more pressing social needs by bringing into the government several reform-minded technicians, but was completely ineffectual in carrying out any of its programs (See Chapter 2).[1] The ruling elite, perceiving that its fragmentation and lack of consensus would

---

[1] Arnulfo Arias won the elections but Robles was declared president by an alliance of the National Guard and the Partido Liberal Nacional.

lead to a loss of representation of its interests, established an organization to act as a ministry without portfolio in the government. The role of that agency, the Consejo Nacional de la Empresa Privada (CONEP), was pervasive during the Robles administration, when it acted as a stumbling block to any progressive or reformist measures. Subsequently, CONEP has continued to play a formidable role in the Panamanian political arena.

The loss of hegemony of the traditional ruling elite provided the propitious conditions for an independent regime to arise, which for a period of several years achieved sufficient autonomy to enact progressive policies. This regime was not completely independent and was still tied to international capital, but its independence from the internal societal forces was sufficient to allow it some leeway, or "limited structural autonomy," to institute changes that would have a lasting impact on society. Furthermore, as Stallings demonstrates in the case of Velasco in Peru, the access to and availability of foreign resources enhances the state's capacity to achieve relative autonomy.[2] The conditions that prevailed in Panama were similar to those in Peru under Velasco because foreign capital was forthcoming until the mid-1970s and allowed the Torrijos regime the leeway to maintain a course of reformist action quite contrary to the interests and wishes of the private sector.

The Torrijos regime adopted a populist authoritarian approach with the enactment of policies that led to the incorporation of popular sectors previously outside the political spectrum. The incorporation of these sectors by mandate, or "from above," provided the regime with popular support, which lent it legitimacy and at the same time assured it the necessary backing to keep the former ruling elite at bay. As a consequence of the incorporating policies enacted during this period, the country's political landscape was radically changed.

The other contemporary example of an inclusionary authoritarian state is the one of Velasco Alvarado in Peru, in power from 1968 to 1975. As described by O'Donnell, inclusionary authoritarian regimes arise in societies with low levels of social differentiation and political activation, incipient industrialization, and a prevalence of foreign capital in their export sector. Peru during the Velasco period was the prototype of this type of regime. The Torrijos regime shared with Peru these characteristics. The country's level of social and political development was very low, with hardly defined political institutions and scant citizen participation. Panama also depended on foreign capital, but differed from Peru in that its economic thrust was not on expanding its domestic markets or on fostering the growth of its manufacturing sector. Panama's economy is based on the infrastructure and services it provides through the canal and the transit

---

[2] Barbara Stallings, "International Lending and the Relative Autonomy of the State: A Case Study of Twentieth-Century Peru," *Politics & Society*, 14:3 (1985).

area. One of the findings of this study, then, is that inclusionary authoritarian regimes need not be based on the expansion of the industrial base and internal markets as long as there is availability of resources to sustain them and allow them the freedom to engage in autonomous actions while keeping the former ruling bloc in abeyance. In both Peru and Panama, the resources were forthcoming from foreign sources, which provided the state the capacity to act with relative autonomy.

Probably the most important characteristic of inclusionary authoritarian regimes is the incorporation "from above" of sectors previously excluded from society. These sectors tend to be the popular ones, that up to then have been dispossessed, with no power or impact in the evolution of their society. Among these sectors, labor is singled out as the most important, because it usually has some degree of organizational capacity and includes a considerable mass of people who will lend both support and a semblance of legitimacy to the incorporating regime. Through the use of inducements and constraints, labor is easy to control, and usually the measures that favor it imply a low cost in proportion to the political benefits accrued to the state.

The one unexpected outcome of labor's enhanced position is the changes suffered by labor organizations—i.e., their growth in strength, in political savvy, in organizational tactics and strategy—which may, in the long run, permanently alter the political landscape of the country. In the case of Peru, Stephens argues convincingly that Velasco's inclusionary approach to labor in effect stimulated labor militancy and increased the strike rate.[3] In Panama also, the structure of the labor sector was altered considerably. In 1980 and 1981, the country experienced the first general strikes in its history, which resulted in the enactment of Ley 8a and labor's regain of some of the benefits lost in 1976. After Torrijos's death in 1981, labor was constantly threatened and in fear of losing the gains achieved during the 1970s. But the unions stayed on the warpath; not only did they protect their rights but in 1983 they regained the portion of the thirteenth-month salary (the *segunda partida*), that up to then had been appropriated by the government.

Even though none of those who controlled power after Torrijos' death have championed labor as he did, the sector has been able to maintain its enhanced position. After many threats from the government during the Noriega years of an impending reform to the 1972 Labor Code, a new labor law was enacted in 1986, which primarily dealt with issues pertaining to small enterprises. The new law also modified the pay scale for overtime work.[4] On the whole, labor has stood its ground and has been able to safeguard its interests. Organized labor could probably have done more

---

[3] Evelyne Huber Stephens, *The Politics of Workers Participation*. New York: Academic Press, 1980.

[4] Arturo Hoyos, *La reforma laboral, Estudio sobre la Ley 1a. de 17 de marzo de 1986*. Panamá: Arias, Fábrega y Fábrega, 1986.

had its leadership been less co-opted by the government. But one cannot chastise labor for what is an outcome of the lack of strong institutional structures, which permeates the entire society and which has prompted many to act out-of-bounds and in an opportunistic fashion.

The findings of this study suggest that inclusionary authoritarian regimes need not be constrained to countries with economies based on manufacture but can arise in countries with other types of economies, such as those based on services, as long as they can sustain the incorporation of a large mass of the popular sector. What is important for inclusionary authoritarian regimes is that the availability of resources be sufficient to absorb a large sector previously not incorporated, which will provide the regime with the support to allow it the leeway to enact independent policy.

Another point corroborated by this study is that foreign resources can facilitate state autonomy, even in cases of exceptional states. In the case of Panama under Torrijos, the fact that foreign investments and foreign loans continued to be available greatly enhanced the state's capacity to act independently of the former ruling groups.

Lastly, the analysis of the enactment and implementation of labor policy and of its amendments allows for a clear view of how inclusionary authoritarian regimes function and of the shifting of balance among sectors in favor of or against such policies. In the case under study, the analysis of labor policy is a key to discerning the regime dynamics and furthers our understanding both of the long-run failure of inclusionary authoritarian regimes and the long-term impact they have on the political landscapes of their societies.

## DOMESTIC-INTERNATIONAL REASONS FOR LABOR POLICY REFORM

The period of relative autonomy that afforded Torrijos the leeway to enact reformist measures was short-lived, for a series of internal and external factors colluded and essentially curtailed the regime's autonomy. Internally, the 1972 Labor Code provided the catalyst that united the various factions of the elite. This regrouping of the former ruling bloc, which came about for the purpose of opposing and eventually toppling the regime, focused on the Labor Code as the symbol of all that was unacceptable about the Torrijos regime. The elite presented the Labor Code as a mechanism established by Torrijos to destroy private enterprise and consequently as a clear indication of the regime's "communistic" tendencies. While internal opposition to the regime grew among the elite, certain external factors also coalesced and affected the regime in a negative manner. External factors that affected the regime's relative autonomy were the rapidly deteriorating economic situation experienced by Panama during the mid-1970s and the pressure brought to bear on Torrijos by U.S. public opinion regarding Panama during the Canal Treaty negotiations.

Hamilton has singled out three principal factors that limit state autonomy. First, any effort of the state to challenge existing structures will confront increasing opposition by the dominant class. A second and very important constraining element that limits the autonomy of the state is the relationship of certain state factions with dominant class interests. And third, state autonomy based on alliances with subordinate groups is limited by the contradictions that such alliances entail.[5]

By the very manner in which they come to power, inclusionary authoritarian regimes are likely to be unstable and will only have autonomy to maneuver while they are riding the crest of initial popularity and before the former ruling groups have time to realign their forces. Given the proper conditions, for a period just after their rise to power, these state forms can attain a high degree of structural autonomy in which they can act without constraints and institute measures that will affect the social structure. These measures may be of such magnitude that they will threaten the very existence of the former dominant class by radically altering the social structure. Under those circumstances, if the former dominant class has any power left, it will react violently to the structural changes and fight to regain control.

Whereas before the 1972 Labor Code there had been no specific measure to unite the private sector in a common front, the Labor Code became the catalyst for such a measure. The private sector, as a band of the "wronged," united in a quest to get rid of the code, and hopefully of Torrijos, at the same time. By doing so, it hoped to put the laboring class back in its place and return the country to the "normalcy" of the pre-1968 years.

The Labor Code ended the fragmentation of the ruling elite and brought unity to that sector in a way it had not been able to achieve before. It was unity against a very specific issue, which in turn symbolized the complete rejection of the Torrijos regime. Once the former dominant class felt its very nature threatened by the state, it reacted in a cohesive manner and in full force. The very fact of having its existence threatened united it. And even if the ruling elite had lost political control, it still had economic power and resources, which it used as leverage against the regime.

A second condition that presents a limit to state autonomy is the relation of certain state factions with the dominant class. In Panama's case, even though very strong pro-Torrijos factions controlled the government apparatus, the state had to rely on the services of any bureaucrats and technicians who had strong ties to the former ruling elite. Notwithstanding the reformist nature of the regime, several ministries and agencies, such as the Ministry of Finance, the Ministry of Industry and Commerce, and the Banco General, were considered advocates of private-sector interests. During the

---

[5] Nora Hamilton, *The Limits of State Autonomy*. Princeton: Princeton University Press, 1982, pp. 282-285.

initial years of the regime, those ties with the dominant class did not present a problem because the Torrijos factions were in complete control. But as the economic situation deteriorated in the mid-1970s and Torrijos became vulnerable, the pro-private-sector faction entered into ascendancy, so much so that by 1976, the Torrijos regime lost hegemony and had to accede to their demands.

The national bourgeoisie was aided in its quest to regain political control by two external factors. First, the world recession caused by OPEC's oil price increase in the mid-1970s had a strong and lasting effect on Panama's economy. The Labor Code was made the scapegoat of the worsening economy, and the only appeasement acceptable to the private sector was the revoking of the code. The other external factor that weighed heavily on the country's internal situation and also contributed to the reversal of labor policy was U.S. public opinion about Panama, increasingly fueled by Panama's private interests as the negotiations for the Canal Treaty approached a resolution. The combination of the economic recession and the anti-government campaign launched by the private sector, at a time when Torrijos desperately sought the positive resolution of a new Canal Treaty with the United States, brought to an end the period of relative autonomy for the regime and produced the amendment to the Labor Code as an act of appeasement to the national bourgeoisie.

## CONDITIONS FOR REVERSAL AND RECOVERY OF LABOR GAINS

With the amendment of the Labor Code, the Torrijos regime acknowledged its loss of autonomy from the former ruling elite, and while it did not quite enter an exclusionary phase, it tried to use constraint and demobilizing mechanisms to keep labor under control after withdrawing the benefits it had granted that sector through the 1972 Labor Code. In presenting the labor law reforms to labor leaders, Torrijos alluded to the need to show "national unity" during the difficult period of the Canal Treaty negotiations and to the worsening economic conditions. The country, according to the government, could not withstand strains such as those caused by the strikes that labor threatened to engage in to try to regain its lost benefits. The regime also invoked severe constraint mechanisms such as the threat of using the full force of the police in the case of strikes to keep the labor sector in check.

After the enactment of Ley 95, the labor sector did not begin immediately to fight for its rights, as the private sector had done after passage of the Labor Code, because of its lack of cohesion and because its incorporation "from above" had rendered it dependent on the government for its enhanced position. Both of these reasons had prevented labor from acquiring a solid class consciousness that would allow it cohesive action. However, the loss of benefits caused by the reforms to the Labor Code presented labor with an opportunity for common action, which it took once the obstacles to class unity were overcome. It took three years of unrelenting labor activity for the partial recovery of labor's lost benefits through the enactment of Ley 8a of 1981.

The growing activity of the labor sector exacerbated an intrinsic conflict within the inclusionary authoritarian nature of the Torrijos regime. In Hamilton's analysis, the alliance of the state with subordinate groups may limit state autonomy. Such an alliance becomes a limitation due to the internal contradictions that it poses.[6] This type of relationship between a state and subordinate classes will ultimately lead to a form of class conflict, which if not checked will threaten the stability of the state. Thus, a crucial element in limiting state autonomy is the level of class consciousness of the subordinate groups.

The greater the consciousness of these groups, the more efficient they will be in defending their interests and advocating their rights. This in turn will lead to a greater threat to the state's relative autonomy. Following this line of argument, it is in the interest of the state to maintain the subordinate groups in a condition in which they lack cohesion and class consciousness and do not recognize the differences between their interests and those of the state. But as demonstrated by Stephens in the case of Peru, the enhanced position attained by these sectors—through the process of incorporation and through the prominence given to them by the state—will strengthen them and may lead to an increased class consciousness, with eventual recognition of the existing discrepancy between their interests and those of the state.[7]

In the case of Panama, labor at first failed to recognize the differences it had with the state and placed its complete trust in the Torrijos regime. Following passage of the Labor Code, the labor sector followed Torrijos's lead and relied on him for protection of its rights. The fact that the Labor Code was enacted on the labor sector's behalf and not because of pressure brought to bear on the state by labor made that sector's position rather precarious and dependent on the regime. Other factors such as the lack of unity among labor groups exacerbated labor's weakness. Because of the internal cleavages within the labor sector and because its incorporation from above placed constraints on its actions and forced it to turn to the state for benefits, labor remained complaisant, divided, and dependent on the state.

The cleavages within the labor sector had different causes. Perhaps the most important one was ideological, with each central following a different ideological line. Further cleavages among the labor groups were the result of the varying degrees of commitment of those groups to the government. Right after the 1976 reform to the Labor Code, the greatest obstacle to labor

---

[6] Hamilton, *The Limits*, pp. 284-285.
[7] Stephens, *The Politics*.

unity was the loyalty of the communist central (CNTP) to the government and their acceptance of Torrijos's appeal for national unity. Later on, when the two largest centrals (CNTP and CTRP) united in a common front, some important labor groups such as the CPTT still held back because of the co-optation of their leaders by the government. But once the two principal centrals agreed to join forces, the rank and file of the co-opted groups disavowed their leaders and joined the rest of the labor sector in the fight to regain their rights.

What were the political and economic conditions that allowed for the revoking of the 1972 Labor Code in 1976? And how did these conditions change in the five years between the time when the labor policy was reversed through Ley 95 and 1981 when labor gains were partially recovered through Ley 8a? Again, the factors that need to be taken into account regarding these two policy changes are of an internal and external nature. One of the important factors that acted upon the government at the time of the first policy reversal was the worsening economic situation caused by external factors over which Panamanian national forces had very little control. A second factor, also tied to external conditions, had to do with the Canal Treaty negotiations and with the media campaign unleashed in the United States regarding this issue. The private sector was able to use both to its advantage, to press for reforms to the Labor Code, and ultimately to bring Torrijos to his knees. With the worsening economic situation, the former ruling elite engaged in tactics of capital flight and a non-investment campaign that exacerbated the economic situation and made the government's position extremely precarious. The year before the Labor Code was amended, private investment dipped to pre-1960s levels and the government had to make up the deficit, with the level of public investment reaching 51 percent of total investment.

In addition to the worsening economic situation, the principal preoccupation of the Torrijos regime was the ongoing Canal Treaty negotiations with the United States. A campaign in that country, unleashed by politicians and groups opposed to a treaty more favorable to Panama, presented Panama in a bad light and the Torrijos government as corrupt and unstable. The Panamanian private sector helped fuel this campaign through its many contacts with U.S. groups lobbying against a new canal treaty. Ley 95 was Torrijos's response to this pressure: he hoped that the appeasement of the private sector on the labor issue would mellow its members and reduce their interference with the treaty negotiations. At that point Torrijos gambled that he would be able to keep labor under control and buy peace with the private sector by reforming the Labor Code. As a matter of fact, Torrijos presented Ley 95 to labor as a necessary measure for national unity and appealed to labor's sense of nationalism for acceptance of the law.

In the years between the enactment of the reform to the Labor Code (1976) and the partial recovery of labor gains (1981), the negotiations for the new canal treaty were concluded and ratified. The economic situation did not improve, invalidating the arguments presented earlier by the private sector of the positive impact of Ley 95 on the economy.

By 1978, when the temporary measures of Ley 95 expired and collective agreements could be negotiated again, the Canal Treaty had also been approved, removing the main obstacle for the consolidation of the labor sector. Labor came together in spurts and aborted tries and finally coalesced in late 1979. In 1980 and 1981, Panama experienced the first general strikes in its history, which led to the partial regain of labor's lost benefits.

In coming together, the labor sector realized that its interests were different from those of the regime, but its break with Torrijos was not complete. By revoking Ley 95 and enacting Ley 8a at the same time that it announced considerable increases in the minimum wage, the regime made a conciliatory move toward labor and signaled that it still held the ideals of an inclusionary regime and wanted labor as an ally. However, Ley 8a did not restore stability of employment, which was a strong indicator to the private sector that the regime was in a conciliatory mood toward them. Ley 8a was an appeasement measure with different messages for each sector affected but signaled the partial loss of hegemony of the regime both to private capital and labor.

Whereas before the enactment of the 1972 Labor Code, the labor sector had been weak and divided, with little or no impact on its fate, by 1981 it had acquired some degree of class consciousness and was successful in having its demands recognized by the state. The growth and maturation of the labor sector is an important and lasting legacy of the Torrijos regime, as the changes brought about for labor would insure that the socio-political landscape of Panama would not easily revert to its pre-1968 form once the regime was no longer in power.

The regime, which began in a situation of relative structural autonomy regarding the former dominant class, eventually lost its autonomy from both the former ruling elite and labor. Whereas in its early days it had enjoyed complete freedom of action, by 1981 it was somewhat constrained by both the dominant and the subordinate sectors.

# 10

# THE AFTERMATH OF THE TORRIJOS YEARS

The Torrijos regime came to an end in 1981 with the death of Omar Torrijos, but as early as 1976, pressured by external and internal forces, the state had partially lost its autonomy. It had toned down its actions and had become more conciliatory toward the business community and the former ruling elite. This was in part due to Torrijos's effort to institutionalize his "revolutionary process" through a party in the image of the PRI in Mexico, which would ensure the regime's continuity through more acceptable means of apparent political participation. These efforts ended with the death of Torrijos, because those who followed him had neither enough foresight nor his interest in changing Panama's social structures in ways that would lead to a more just and equitable society.

Since Torrijos's death and until Noriega's ouster in 1989, those in control of Panama have been primarily interested in enhancing their personal power and riches. The two commanders in chief who held power during this period, Rubén Darío Paredes and Manuel Antonio Noriega, were vain and superficial men whose main concern was with increasing their wealth as quickly as possible and spending it in lavish and extravagant ways.[1] Another preoccupation of these two men, but especially of Noriega, was how to prove the extent of their power, which they usually tested through petty, mean, and oftentimes incredibly cruel methods.

The outcome of this state of affairs is that between 1981 and 1989 Panama was governed through sheer force by a small coterie of civilians and Defense Forces members close to the commander.[2] There was hardly any formal planning, and measures were usually instituted as reactions to situations rather than as a result of well-thought-out, rational plans. Without a shred of remorse, they reversed most of the progressive measures of the Torrijos years.

---

[1] Florencio Flores became commander in chief immediately after Torrijos's death but retired a few months later when he reached the mandatory retiring age.

[2] After Noriega took power he changed the name of the National Guard to Defense Forces.

From 1985, members of the former ruling elite who were not in collusion with Noriega and the Defense Forces carried on an opposition campaign, which gained momentum in 1987. The campaign against Noriega began in earnest after the decapitated and heavily tortured body of Dr. Hugo Spadafora was found near the Costa Rican border. Spadafora had been vice-minister of health in the 1970s and had headed a Panamanian brigade that fought with the Sandinistas in Nicaragua. He was sort of a folk hero and was immensely popular. At the time of his death, he was traveling from Costa Rica, where he then lived, to Panama City to denounce Noriega's activities with drug dealers and with the CIA. He also claimed to have proof of Noriega's responsibility for Torrijos's death.

The popular outcry and relentless campaign by his family and friends to investigate Spadafora's death cost Nicolás Ardito Barletta the presidency when he agreed to the investigation. The ousting of Ardito Barletta proved once and for all how ruthless Noriega could be. From then on, most people who were not with the government joined the campaign against it. This effort was led by the Cruzada Civilista, or Civic Crusade—which represented civic and business groups—and by guilds and unions, all under the directorship of the Chamber of Commerce and the business community.

The first real break for the Civic Crusade came in 1987 when a rupture in the highest echelons of the Defense Forces became apparent. A fight between Noriega and Díaz Herrera for the leadership of the Defense Forces became public.[3] Apparently Díaz Herrera lost, and he was forced to resign from the force. After this, Díaz Herrera gave interviews in which he accused Noriega of being responsible for Spadafora's death and also made allegations regarding a series of other involvements of Noriega's, including in Torrijos's death. Díaz Herrera became a virtual prisoner in his home, which Noriega machine-gunned and bombed until Díaz Herrera gave himself up. He was jailed for some months and after his release, he was allowed to leave the country and join his wife and children in Venezuela.

The Civic Crusade continued its efforts to oust Noriega and showed its opposition to the government through acts of peaceful civil disobedience. Between 1987 and 1989, there were constant civil disruptions in the entire country. In the cities there were daily marches, silent vigils, and masses with huge numbers attending, as well as caravans of cars honking their horns and flying white banners at noon and late afternoon. Those at home joined by banging pots and blowing whistles. White became the color of the Crusade, and for marches and demonstrations people dressed in white. The Defense Forces responded by attacking marchers with tear gas, water, and buckshot, and by arresting anyone wearing white.

---

[3] Roberto Díaz Herrera was a cousin of Torrijos, had been executive secretary of the National Guard during the Torrijos regime, and at the time was chief of staff.

In May 1989 elections were held, with an official candidate hand picked by Noriega and an opposition slate. The opposition slate of a candidate for president and a candidate for each of the two vice-presidental posts was a compromise among all the groups involved in the civil disobedience and some of the old political parties that still had a following. When it was apparent that the opposition was winning three to one, the government stopped the vote counting and annulled the elections.

In December 1989, when Noriega was ousted by U.S. invading forces, the winning candidates of the May elections were sworn into power. These individuals, President Endara and vice presidents Arias Calderón and Ford, and the people they called on to help them form a government basically represent the interests of the ruling bloc that was in power until 1968. The only new element is the Christian Democratic party represented by Arias Calderón, who is so authoritarian and inflexible that it is hard to find anything different or progressive in his style of governing.

A deplorable corollary to this story is that the ruling elite of Panama learned little or nothing during the years they were out of power. What we can discern about those in control of the government since Noriega's ouster is that they are a very weak group, and are mired in petty in-fighting, without a program or a vision of what they want for the future of the country and without much concern for the society they set forth to lead. This group is beset by the same problems of the pre-1968 years, i.e., extreme factionalism and an exaggerated interest in power without a clear idea of why it wants the power or what it will do with it.

Another real problem is that this group perceives the United States as the solution to all of Panama's problems, an attitude that curtails the encouragement of innovative and independent action on the part of those who govern. Even if the reality is that many of Panama's problems can only be solved with U.S. help, it is also a fact that this approach, which was the traditional one followed before 1968, precludes the seeking of internal solutions and the growth and strengthening of political institutions.

Regarding the labor laws, the present government has recently named a commission to study and make recommendations for a thorough reform to the 1972 Labor Code. Knowing the interests that the present heads of government represent, there is no doubt as to the line such reform will follow. The findings of this study clearly demonstrate that the benefits of the Labor Code were substantial in relation to their costs. A very large segment of the population was incorporated into society and given a voice and a role to play. It would seem that the positive effects of that action and objective considerations of the facts would prompt government leaders to retain the Labor Code and enhance some of its progressive aspects. Given their actions since they came into power, this hardly seems the way they will go.

Even though this study only dealt with the Labor Code and labor laws, there were many other progressive measures instituted by the Torrijos regime, such as much of the social legislation enacted during the period that produced benefits probably outweighing costs. But because those are measures not likely to be supported by the business sector, they will probably also be rescinded.

A regrettable aspect of the way the history of Panama has unfolded in this decade is that now that Noriega is no longer in power, analysts are looking at the period of "military," or "National Guard," rule without making a distinction between the Torrijos regime and the period that followed. This is unfortunate because neither Paredes nor Noriega had a shred of concern for the polity they controlled, and their time in power can only be characterized as one of excess and plunder. This is distressing because so many of Torrijos's programs and policies will be overlooked in this generalization of the "military period" and ultimately rescinded, prompting the clock to turn back more than 20 years for the majority of the population.

# APPENDIX 1

# LABOR ORGANIZATIONS*

## CATI—CENTRAL AUTENTICA DE TRABAJADORES INDEPENDIENTES

CATI was organized in 1974 after its main federations split from CIT. The government officially recognized it in 1981. It has three federations: Federación Auténtica de Trabajadores (FAT), Federación de Trabajadores de la Industria de la Construcción, Materiales, Madera y Similares (FETICOMMS), and Federación Sindical de Trabajadores de la Provincia de Chiriquí (FESITRACHI). The first two federations were previously members of CIT, and the third one had been independent.

Presently, these federations have 19 unions and approximately 4,000 members. CATI does not have outside affiliations nor does it follow a particular party line.

## CIT—CENTRAL ISTMEÑA DE TRABAJADORES

CIT began in 1959, as the Asociación Sindical Panameña, and was considered the Christian contingent of organized labor. In 1960, it changed its name to Federación Istmeña de Trabajadores Cristianos, and in 1971 it took its present name.

CIT is affiliated to the Central Lationamericana de Trabajadores (CLAT) based in Caracas, Venezuela; and to the Confederación Mundial del Trabajo (CMT) based in Brussels, Belgium. This central follows a Christian Democratic line.

CIT has 6 federations, 25 unions, and about 4,000 members. Most of its unions are in services and commerce. It lost an entire federation to the CPTT when the government organized that central. CIT officials estimate they

---

*Previously published in Sharon Phillipps, "Panama," in *Latin American Labor Organizations*. Edited by Gerald M. Greenfield and Sheldon L. Maram. New York: Greenwood Press, 1987.

lost about 8,000 members, because there was a large number of bus and taxi drivers among the membership.

## CNTP—CENTRAL NACIONAL DE TRABAJADORES DE PANAMA

The CNTP received official recognition as a new labor central in 1970; its core unions had all been part of the Federación Sindical de Trabajadores de la República de Panamá (FSTRP). It is affiliated with the Comité Sindical de los Trabajadores de Centro América (CUSCA) based in San José, Costa Rica; with the Congreso Permanente de Unidad Sindical de los Trabajadores de América Latina (CPUSTAL), founded in 1968, and based in Mexico City; and with the Federación Sindical Mundial (FSM) based in Moscow, U.S.S.R.

The CNTP has 7 federations, 36 unions, and approximately 18,000 members. Among its important unions are the tailors' and seamstresses' union, the typographers' union, the shoemakers' union, and all the unions of the banana workers except for SITRACHILCO of Bocas. It also represents the light and telephone workers' unions. Historically, the CNTP—and formerly the Federación Sindical—has without doubt played the most important role in Panama regarding organized labor. Very few labor-related events have taken place in which it, or one of its member unions, was not directly involved. Some of its leaders, such as Angel Gómez, Marta Matamoros, and Domingo Barría, are synonymous with organized labor in the minds of Panamanians.

## CPTT—CENTRAL PANAMEÑA DE TRABAJADORES DEL TRANSPORTE

Organized in 1974 at the prompting of the government, CPTT brings together many of the existing federations and unions of public transportation drivers. The latest official figures (1978) sets its membership at 5,000, and CPTT officials claim to have about 23,000 members.

CPTT is not affiliated to any outside labor organizations. This central is not a member of CONATO, as some of its members are not considered workers but employers because they own their vehicles and rent them out part time. The leadership of the CPTT was prominent in the government's official party, the Partido Revolucionario Democrático (PRD).

## CTRP—CONFEDERACION DE TRABAJADORES DE LA REPUBLICA DE PANAMA

Founded in 1956 by members of the Federación de Sindicatos Independientes, Federación de Agricultores de Panamá, and the Federación de Trabajadores Marítimos, the CTRP is backed by the AFL-CIO and receives support from the AIFELD. Its goals, as stated in its statutes, are to defend the socio-economic rights of its members and to prepare labor leaders through union education.

The CTRP is affiliated with the Confederación de Trabajadores Centroamericanos (CTCA) based in San José, Costa Rica; to the Organización Regional Interamericana de Trabajadores (ORIT) based in Mexico City; and with the Confederación Internacional de Organizaciones Sindicales Libres (CIOSL) based in Brussels, Belgium.

The CTRP has 11 federations and 65 unions with approximately 25,000 members. The most important federations at present are the Federación Nacional de Trabajadores Democráticos, which includes Local 907, (the Panamanian workers in the U.S. army installations - 1,400 members); the Federación de Sindicatos de Trabajadores de las Provincias Centrales, which includes the sugarcane workers union (2,400 members); and the Federación Industrial de Trabajadores de Alimentos, Bebidas, Hoteles y Afines (FITAHBA), which claims most of the hotel and supermarket workers, as well as laborers in the food-processing industries.

The CTRP has three unions not affiliated to any federations, two of which warrant special mention. One is the Sindicato Nacional de Empleados Bancarios (SINABAN, about 7,000 members). The government refuses to give official recognition to this union, because there is said to be a tacit agreement with the foreign banks against unionization of bank employees, in order to avoid potential disruptions from strikes and labor unrest.

The other independent union is the Sindicato de Trabajadores de la Chiriquí Land Company de Bocas del Toro. This union was originally a CTRP affiliate, then in the early 1970s it changed its affiliation to the CNTP, and in 1979 returned to the CTRP.

In 1981 the CTRP celebrated its twenty-fifth anniversary by announcing that it would abandon its apolitical stance and would follow a social democratic line.

The unions representing the construction and banana workers deserve special mention because of their size and the role they have played within the labor movement and in the political life of the country.

## SUNTRACS—SINDICATO UNICO NACIONAL DE TRABAJADORES DE LA CONSTRUCCION Y SIMILARES

SUNTRACS evolved from one of several unions representing construction workers to the largest union at present, with a membership of 17,000 and offices in Panama, Colón, Veraguas, and Chiriquí. In 1974 SUNTRACS negotiated its first collective agreement with the Cámara Panameña de la Construcción (CAPAC), and in 1979, its second one. CAPAC encompasses about 90 percent of construction companies, and all workers hired by these companies are covered by the agreement with SUNTRACS. SUNTRACS was also responsible for two new laws that modify the Labor Code in favor of the construction workers. One of these laws is for the payment of production bonuses and the other sets an unemployment fund to be handed to the workers when the construction project is over. The fund, called Fondo de Garantía, represents 6 percent of the total earnings during the construction project.

At present, if not the most bellicose labor group, (the banana workers are in competition for this title), it is certainly the most visible. Between 1978 and the first trimester of 1979, SUNTRACS had about 15 wildcat strikes. Although labor law in Panama does not allow wildcat strikes, SUNTRACS can engage in them because it controls most of the workers in the sector. Eduardo Ríos, the secretary general of SUNTRACS, claims this to be the only way the Union can attempt to redress some of the most blatant abuses by the construction companies, such as sending workers to work sites without boots or protective helmets and not paying into the Fondo de Garantía.

## SITRACHILCO—SINDICATO DE TRABAJADORES DE LA CHIRIQUI LAND COMPANY
### (and other unions representing banana workers)

From the mid-1930s, the banana workers strove to organize with every effort made by the United Fruit Company to prevent it. Finally by 1950, the company agreed to allow two company unions (sindicatos amarillos) to form, one to represent workers in Puerto Armuelles and the other to represent the laborers of Bocas del Toro. In 1960, both unions went on strike and after that conflict was resolved, two independent unions emerged to replace them. These unions became very well organized and militant. They have had an extremely competent and dedicated leadership, and during the 1960s, the legal advice of two of the most prominent labor lawyers. The Puerto Armuelles union had been independent until 1973 when it affiliated with the CNTP. The Bocas union was affiliated with the CTRP in the 1960s, then became a CNTP affiliate from 1973-1979 and that year returned to the CTRP. Several SITRACHILCO leaders have been elected to public office and have served in various official capacities.

The SITRACHILCO unions became politically prominent in the early years of the Torrijos regime, because they were used to fill the void left by the traditional parties and to provide the mass support needed by the regime. Many of the labor measures enacted during that time are said to be directly attributable to the SITRACHILCO unions, such as the law decreeing payment of a thirteenth-month salary and the 1972 Labor Code.

After the second large strike in the 1960s, the United Fruit Company began leasing land to independent growers. These growers received services from the company and in turn sold their production to it. Today there are 6 independent growers in Bocas on the Atlantic side and 14 in Puerto Armuelles on the Pacific. The laborers of these independent farms formed two new unions, the Sindicato Industrial de Trabajadores de

Productores de Bananeras Independientes (Bocas del Toro) and the Sindicato de Trabajadores de las Bananeras Independientes de Chiriquí (Puerto Armuelles).

Then, after the Guerra del Banano in 1975 between the government and the United Fruit Company, the company sold most of its land back to Panama, who established two corporations to handle the production: COBAPA, or Corporación Bananera del Pacífico, and COBANA, or Corporación Bananera del Atlántico, which came under the umbrella of another corporation known by the acronym of COMUMBANA.

After the 1964 strike and up to 1977 there were no major strikes at the plantations. Since 1977, the situation has been very unstable. In Puerto Armuelles there have been strikes or declarations of intent to strike every year, sometimes three or four times a year. In Bocas, between 1977 and 1978, 13 declarations of intent to strike were submitted to the labor office. These statements are usually concerned with alleged violations of the existing collective agreement.

From the mid-1970s and up to 1978, all the unions representing banana workers formed the Federación Independiente de Sindicatos. Since 1978 there have been some changes, as given in Table 23, with approximate membership in parentheses.

Table 23   Unions Representing Workers in the Banana Plantations: affiliation and membership (in parentheses)

| Puerto Armuelles, Chiriquí | Bocas del Toro |
| --- | --- |
| SITRACHILCO, Chiriqui - CNTP (6,500) | SITRACHILCO, Bocas - CTRP (6,000) |
| Sindicato de Trabajadores de Chiriqui - CNTP (1,400) | Sindicato Industrial de Trabajadores de Productores de Bananeras Independientes - CNTP (800) |
| COBAPA* - CIT (1,200) | COBANA - CNTP (300) |

*This corporation went bankrupt in 1981 and has ceased operations.
Source: Interview with José Nemo Herrera, former union official of SITRACHILCO, Chiriquí, and Director of Labor for Chiriquí Province, Ministerio de Trabajo y Bienestar Social.

# APPENDIX 2

# INTERVIEWS*

Lic. Ricardo Alemán, lawyer and private-sector representative to the tripartite commission that reviewed Ley 95. October 27, 1981.

Dr. Nicolás Ardito Barletta, minister of planning 1971-1978; vice president of the World Bank for Latin America 1978-1982; president of Panama 1984-1985. Washington, D.C. January 6, 1981.

Lic. Rogelio Alvarado, economist for the Sindicato de Industriales (SIP). October 14, 1981.

Sr. Gilberto Ayarza, former SITRACHILCO labor organizer; former secretary general of CTRP. November 13, 1981.

Ing. José Dominador (Kaiser) Bazán, Jr., former president of CONEP; ambassador to the United States. December 17, 1981.

Arq. Marisín Bieberach, Ministerio de Comercio e Industria. November 9, 1981.

Sr. Philip Dean Butcher, former ambassador to Jamaica, secretary general of CTRP 1973-1981. November 24, 1981.

Sr. Santiago Cajar, secretary general of the Typographers' Union. December 15, 1981.

Sr. Guillermo Cantillo Flores, former SITRACHILCO union organizer; labor arbitrator for MITRAB. December 10, 1981.

Sr. Gabriel Castillo, secretary general of CATI. December 11, 1981.

Lic Aurora Corsen de Correa, Ministerio de Planificación y Política Económica. September 1, 1981.

Sr. Walter Durling, president of the Cámara de Comercio e Industrias. September 23, 1981.

Lic. José María Espino, CONEP. September 21, 1981.

Lic. Jorge Fábrega, leading industrial relations lawyer and president of the 1972 Labor Code Commission. August 28, 1981.

Lic. Alfonso Ferrer, legal counsel to SIP. October 14, 1981.

---

* All interviews were conducted in Panama City, Panama, unless otherwise indicated.

Srta. Migdalia Fuentes, editor of *La Prensa*, and Ministerio de Planificación y Política Económica, 1970-1978. October 8, 1981.

Sr. Santana García, director of Asesoría de Programación Sectorial, MITRAB. September 30, 1981.

Lic. Carlos George, labor arbitrator for MITRAB. November 9, 1981.

Sr. Dulcidio González, industrialist and president of CONEP, 1981. October 28, 1981.

Lic. Gustavo Gonzáles, minister of planning 1978-1981, economic adviser to the president, 1981. October 8, 1981.

Sr. José Nemo Herrera, Director General de Trabajo, Chiriquí Province. November 11, 1981.

Sr. Naheli Herrera, secretary general of CPTT. December 4, 1981.

Dr. Carlos Hoffman, industrialist and member of the Board of SIP. October 14, 1981.

Dr. Arturo Hoyos, leading labor lawyer, member of the 1972 Labor Code Commission, director general de trabajo, 1972-1975. Supreme Court Justice, 1990. October 29, 1981.

Lic. Carlos de Icaza, CAPAC. September 16, 1981.

Sr. Ignacio Mallol, businessman. November 9, 1981.

Lic. Fernando Manfredo, minister, Comercio e Industria 1974-1976; presidential chief of staff 1976-1978; administrator (2nd), Panama Canal Commission, 1978-1990. November 19, 1981.

Dr. César Martans, first minister of labor. September 30, 1981.

Srta. Marta Matamoros, founding member of the Federación Sindical de la República de Panamá (FSTRP) and important CNTP leader. November 23, 1981.

Sr. John Medlinger, businessman. October 30, 1981.

Dr. Carlos Mendoza, leading industrial relations lawyer. September 28, 1981.

Sr. José Meneses, secretary general of CNTP. November 17, 1981.

Dr. Rolando Murgas, member of the 1972 Labor Code Commission, minister of labor, 1972-1975. September 18, October 1, December 4, 1981.

Sr. Rolando Ordóñez, secretary general of CIT. November 12, 1981.

Ing. Héctor Ortega, president of CAPAC, 1981. September 16, 1981.

Lic. Oydén Ortega, minister of labor, 1979-1982. December 3, 1981.

Sr. Félix Pardos, president of the Unión Nacional de la Pequeña Industria. September 15, 1981.

Lic. Georgina de Pérez, Ministerio de Comercio e Industrias. October 9, 1981.

Dr. Humberto Ricord, leading labor lawyer; dean, Law School, University of Panama, 1981. September 29, 1981.

Sr. Eduardo Ríos, secretary general of SUNTRACS. November 21, 1981.

Lic. Américo Rivera, industrial relations lawyer; member of the 1972 Labor
   Code Commission; Supreme Court Justice, 1981. October 29, 1981.
Lic. Luis Shirley, member of the 1972 Labor Code Commission; vice-
   minister of labor, 1972-1975. September 1, 1981.
Dr. Carlos Valencia, economist and businessman. October 21, 1981.
Lic. Juan Materno Vásquez, presidential chief of staff, 1968-1972; president
   of the Supreme Court, 1972-1978. November 11, 1981.
Lic. Carlos Iván Zúñiga, leading labor lawyer representative of the
   SITRACHILCO workers in the 1960s and highly respected politi-
   cian. October 16, 1981.

# BIBLIOGRAPHY

## I. NEWSPAPERS

*Crítica*, 1970-1981.
*La Estrella de Panamá*, 1970-1981.
*Matutino*, 1971-1981.
*El Panamá América*, 1970-1977.
*La Prensa*, 1980-1981.
*República*, 1977-1981.

## II. BOOKS AND DOCUMENTS

Achong, Andrés. *Orígenes del movimiento obrero panameño*. Panamá: Centro de Estudios Latinoamericanos "Justo Arosemena." 1980.

Alfaro, Ricardo J. *Panamá: Cincuenta años de república*. Panamá: Edición de la Junta Nacional del Cincuentenario. 1953.

Arroyo Camacho, Dulio. *El sistema de gobierno existente en Panamá luego de las últimas reformas a la Constitución*. Panamá: Litho-Impresora Panamá, S.A. 1979.

Asociación Panameña de Ejecutivos de Empresa. VIII Conferencia Anual de Ejecutivos - CADE. "El empleo: factor prioritario del desarrollo." Panamá: APEDE, 1973.

____. *¿Qué es un CADE?* Panamá. 1980.

Barrera, Eugenio. *La marcha del hambre y la desesperación*. Panamá: Centro de Estudios Latinoamericanos "Justo Arosemena." 1980.

Barry, Tom. *Dollars & Dictators*. Albuquerque: Resource Center. 1982.

Barsallo J., Pedro A. "Consideraciones generales sobre algunas normas procesales del nuevo código de trabajo." *Revista Jurídica Panameña*, no. 2. 1974.

Boulding, Elise et al. *Handbook of International Data on Women*. New York: Sage Publications. 1976.

Bronheim, David. "Relations Between the U.S. and Latin America." *International Affairs*. 46(3): 501-516. 1970.

Cámara Panameña de la Construcción. *Boletín de Promoción*. Panamá: Imprenta Edilito, S.A. 1981.

____. *Estatutos*. Mimeo. Panamá. 1979.

Cardoso, Fernando Henrique, and Enzo Faletto. *Dependencia y desarrollo en América Latina*. Mexico: Siglo Veintiuno. 1969.

Castillo, Jorge. *La actividad bananera en la región occidental de Panamá*. Panamá: CEASPA. 1979.

Castro Herrera, Guillermo. *Panamá, 1977*. Panamá: Centro de Estudios Latinoamericanos "Justo Arosemena." 1978.

Chacón, Boris and Hugo Morgado. *Una política de empleo a través de un plan de urgencia: Implicaciones y perspectivas.* Panamá: MIPPE. 1978.

Chapman, Guillermo. "Factores que afectan la demanda por mano de obra en Panamá." Informe preparado para el Ministerio de Planificación y Política Económica y la Agencia para el Desarrollo Internacional (AID). Panamá: INDESA. 1979.

Collier, David. "Overview of the Bureaucratic-Authoritarian Model." in *The New Authoritarism in Latin America.* Edited by David Collier. Princeton: Princeton University Press. 1979.

Collier, Ruth Berins and David Collier. "Inducements versus Constraints: Disaggregating Corporatism." *American Political Science Review.* 73(1979): 967-986.

Comité Panameño por los Derechos Humanos. *La Caja de Seguro Social al borde de la quiebra.* Panamá. 1981.

Conferencia Episcopal Panameña. "Carta pastoral de la CEP sobre la situación del pais." Mimeo. Panamá. 1978.

Consejo Nacional de la Empresa Privada (CONEP). "Efectos de la Ley 95 de 1976." Mimeo. Panamá. 1979.

_____. *En pocas palabras ... ésto es el CONEP.* Panamá: Coagra. n.d.

_____. "Evaluación crítica del análisis presentado por el Ministerio de Trabajo y Bienestar Social para sustentar el Proyecto de Ley por medio del cual se decreta un aumento general de salarios a los empleados de la empresa privada." Mimeo. Panamá. 1981.

_____. "Observaciones y recomendaciones al Ante-proyecto de Código de Trabajo del 11 de enero de 1968 ante la Comisión Revisora." Mimeo. Panamá. 1971.

_____. "Reunión del CONEP y la Junta Directiva de la Cámara de Comercio e Industrias de Chiriquí." Mimeo. Panamá. 1975.

Correa, Jaime. "Atacar la enfermedad desde la base." *Análisis.* 2(5). 1979.

_____. "¿Qué hacer para el empleo?" *Análisis.* 2(8): 45-46. 1979.

Cuevas, Alexander. *El movimiento inquilinario de 1925.* Panamá: Centro de Estudios Latinoamericanos "Justo Arosemena." 1980.

Dirección de Estadística y Censo. *Panamá en cifras: Años 1970-1975.* Panamá. 1976.

_____. *Panamá en cifras: Años 1976-1980.* Panamá. 1981.

Epica Task Force. *Panamá: Sovereignty for a Land Divided.* Washington, D.C. 1976.

Epstein, Edward C. "Control and Co-optation of the Argentine Labor Movement." *Economic Development and Cultural Change.* 27(3): 445-465. 1979.

Escala González, Virginia, and Elsa Cecilia Meza. *Asegurado: conoce tus derechos.* Panamá: Impresora de la Nación. 1978.

Escobar Bethancourt, Rómulo. *Torrijos: Colonia Americana, No.* Bogotá: Carlos Valencia Editores. 1981.

Espinoza, Dimas, and Jorge E. Visuetti. "Movimiento reinvidicativo del Sindicato de Trabajadores de la Chiriquí Land Co. - Sección de Puerto Armuelles - 1960." Tesis de licenciatura. Panamá: Universidad de Panamá. 1978.

Evans, Peter, et al., eds. *Bringing the State Back In.* New York: Cambridge University Press. 1985.

Fábrega, Jorge, trans. *Labor Code of the Republic of Panama.* (Substantive Provisions). Panamá: Litho-Impresora Panamá. 1974.

_____. *Las convenciones colectivas en Panamá.* Panamá: n.p. 1981.

Fábrega, Jorge, et al. *Código de trabajo con notas, concordancias y leyes complementarias.* 6th ed. Panamá: Litho-Impresora Panamá. 1981.

Fernández y Fernández, Ramón. "Diez años de reforma agraria en Panamá." *Temas agrarios.* Mexico: Fondo de Cultura Económica. 1974.

Figueroa Navarro, Alfredo. *Dominio y sociedad en el Panamá Colombiano (1821-1903).* 2d ed. Bogotá: Ediciones Mundo. 1980.

Franco Muñoz, Hernando. *Movimiento obrero panameño.* Panamá: n.p. 1979.

Gandásegui, Marco Antonio. "La concentración del poder económico en Panamá." in *Panamá, dependencia y liberación*. Edited by Ricaute Soler. 2d ed. Ciudad Universitaria Rodrigo Facio, Costa Rica: EDUCA. 1976.

Gandásegui, Marco Antonio, et al. *Las luchas obreras en Panamá: 1850-1978*. Panamá: Talleres Diálogo. 1980.

García Márquez, Gabriel. "Cuatro preguntas al General Torrijos." Panamá: Ediciones Reforma Educativa. 1975.

George, Carlos J. "La conciliación y el arbitraje en materia laboral y su vigencia en Panamá." Tesis de licenciatura. Panamá: Universidad de Panamá. 1972.

Goldrich, Daniel. "Panamá." in *Political Systems of Latin America*. Edited by Martin C. Needler. Princeton: D. Van Nostrand. 1978.

González C., Ismael. "El salario mínimo en la legislación panameña." Tesis de licenciatura. Panamá: Universidad de Panamá. 1978.

Gramsci, Antonio. *Selections from the Prison Notebooks*. New York: International Publishers. 1980.

Hamilton, Nora. *Limits of State Autonomy*. Princeton: Princeton University Press. 1982.

"¿Hay diálogo? En torno a la Declaración de Boquete." *Dialógo Social*. 65(Mar). 1975.

Herrera, Margarita, Marta Arce, and Mayra Castillo. *Panamá: Los sectores populares y el proletariado*. Panamá: CEASPA. 1979.

Hoyos, Arturo. "Derecho laboral y desarrollo económico: el caso de Panamá." Estudio de derecho laboral en homenaje a Rafael Caldera. Caracas: Editorial Sucre. 1977.

_____. *La reforma laboral. Estudio sobre la Ley 1a. de 17 de marzo de 1986*. Panamá: Arias, Fábrega y Fábrega. 1986.

Imaz, José Luis de. "Neo-Bismarckianism and the Argentine Revolution." in *Models of Political Change in Latin America*. Edited by Paul E. Sigmund. New York: Praeger. 1970.

Investigación y Desarrollo, S. A. (INDESA). "Informe de la encuesta de opiniones y actitudes de inversionistas y empresarios." Informe preparado para el Consejo Nacional de la Empresa Privada (CONEP). Mimeo. Panamá: INDESA. 1976.

_____. "Informe del estudio de productividad preparado para el Consejo Nacional de la Empresa Privada (CONEP)." Mimeo. Panamá: INDESA. 1977.

_____. "Situación de la pequeña empresa en Panamá. Informe preparado para la Agencia para el Desarrollo Internacional (AID)." Mimeo. Panamá: 1980.

Instituto para la Formación de Recursos Humanos. *Seguro educativo: significado y beneficios*. Panamá: Impresora Panamá. 1971.

Jaén Suárez, Omar. *Hombres y ecología en Panamá*. Panamá: Editorial Universitaria. 1981.

_____. *La población del Istmo de Panamá del siglo XVI al siglo XX*. Panamá: Impresora de la Nación. 1978.

Johnson, Harry. "Panama as a Regional Financial Center: a Preliminary Analysis of Development Contribution." *Economic Development and Cultural Change*. 24(Jan). 1976.

Jordan, Hamilton. *Crisis*. New York: Putnam Sons. 1982.

Jované, Juan, Jorge Castillo, and Julio Manduley. "La dinámica agrícola en los últimos años en la República de Panamá." Heredia, Costa Rica: n.p. 1976.

*Jurisprudencia laboral*. Panamá: Universidad de Panamá, Centro de Investigaciones Jurídicas. 1981.

Krasner, Stephen. *Defending the National Interest*. Princeton: Princeton University Press. 1978.

LaFeber, Walter. *The Panamá Canal: The Crisis in Historical Perspective*. Expanded ed. Oxford: Oxford University Press. 1979.

Leis, Raul Alberto. *Colón en el ojo de la tormenta*. Panamá: CEASPA. 1979.

_____. *La ciudad y los pobres: las clases sociales en la ciudad transitista*. Panamá: CEASPA. 1979.

"Ley 95 o revisión al código." *Análisis*. 8(1). 1981.

Liss, Sheldon B. "Panamá." in *Political Parties of the Americas*. Edited by Robert J. Alexander. New York: Greenwood Press. 1982.

Looney, Robert E. *The Economic Development of Panamá: The Impact of World Inflation*. New York: Praeger. 1976.

Manduley, Julio. "Panamá: Dependent Capitalism and Beyond." *Latin American Perspectives*. 8:2(1980): 57-74.

Marx, Karl. *The Eighteenth Brumaire of Louis Bonaparte*. New York: International Publishers. 1963.

Matamoros, Marta. *Huelgas ilegales: Cuando las huelgas simpre eran ilegales*. Panamá: n.p., n.d.

Merrill, William C., et al. *Panamá's Economic Development: The Role of Agriculture*. Ames: Iowa State University Press. 1975

Miller, Robert Howard. "Military Government and Approaches to National Development: A Comparative Analysis of the Peruvian and Panamanian Experience." Unpublished Ph.D. dissertation. Miami: University of Miami. 1975.

Miliband, Ralph. "The Capitalist State: Reply to Nicos Poulantzas." *New Left Review*. 59(1970): 53-60.

_____. *The State in Capitalist Society*. New York: Basic Books. 1969.

Ministerio de Planificación y Política Económica. "Evolución, problemática, perspectivas y lineamientos del empleo: 1970-1985." Panamá: 1980.

_____. *Estrategias para el desarrollo nacional 1970-1980: Visión y realización nueve años después*. Panamá: MIPPE. 1978.

_____. *Informe económico de 1970*. Panamá: MIPPE. 1975.

_____. "Proyecto nacional de desarrollo de Panamá." Mimeo. Panamá. 1980.

Ministerio de Trabajo y Bienestar Social. *Estadísticas laborales, 1970-1973; 1974-1976; 1975-1978; 1979-1980*. Panamá.

_____. "Explicación sobre la interpretación y aplicación de la ley de aumentos de salarios para los trabajadores de la empresa privada." Mimeo. Panamá. 1981.

_____. *Memoria*. Panamá. 1970-1981.

_____. Asesoría de Programación Sectorial. *Boletín informativo*. Mimeo. Panamá. 1980.

_____. Dirección Nacional del Empleo. "Balance de los programas de mano de obra 1980-1981." Panamá. 1981.

Mora M., Lorenzo. *Síntesis histórica del movimiento obrero panameño*. Panamá: Instituto Superior de Estudios Sindicales. 1979.

Muhtar, Ezequiel. *La mordida*. Miami: Editorial Istmo. 1976.

Murgas, Rolando. *El código de trabajo y los descansos*. Panamá: Imprenta Tribunal Electoral. n.d.

_____. "Panamá." in *La intervención del estado en las relaciones industriales en la década de los 80*. Madrid: Insituto de Estudios Sociales. 1982.

Navas, J. F. "Aumento general de salarios--ilusión o realidad." *Análisis*. 3(1): 33-34. 1981.

Nordlinger, Eric. *On the Autonomy of the Democratic State*. Cambridge: Harvard University Press. 1981.

Nuñez Soto, Orlando and Carmen Guevara. "Desarrollo y contradicciones del proceso panameño." *Tareas*. 41(1978): 25-63.

O'Donnell, Guillermo A. *Modernization and Bureaucratic-Authoritarianism: Studies in South American Politics*. Berkeley: Institute of International Studies, University of California. 1973.

Ortega Durán, Oydén. "Intervención del Lic. Oydén Ortega Durán, Ministro del Trabajo y Bienestar Social en el Seminario 'El servidor público frente a la realidad nacional e internacional panameña.'" Mimeo. Panamá: n.p.

Padilla, Salomón and Hugo Vargas. *El financiamiento público externo en Panamá y sus implicaciones económicas*. Panamá: Centro de Estudios Latinoamericanos "Justo Arosemena." 1978.

Partido Revolucionario Democrático (PRD). "El pensamiento político del General Omar Torrijos Herrera y el Partido Revolucionario Democrático." Mimeo. Panamá: Ediciones PRD. n.d.

Pascual, Juan. "Discusión laboral debe ser apolítica." *Análisis*. 3(1). 1981.

Pereira, Renato. *Panamá: fuerzas armadas y política*. Panamá: Ediciones Nueva Universidad. 1979.

Pino de Toledo, Elida and Gustavo Alvarado. "El movimiento sindical panameño y su incidencia socio-económica y política." Tesis de licenciatura. Panamá: Universidad de Panamá. 1975.

Pinzón, Julio César. "Establecer conjuntamente una política de pleno empleo." *Análisis*. 1(5). 1979.

Pippin, Larry LaRae. *The Remon Era: An Analysis of a Decade of Events in Panama (1947-1957)*. Stanford: Institute of Hispanic American and Luso-Brazilian Studies. 1964.

Porras, Demetrio A. *Problemas vitales panameños*. Panamá: Ministerio de Educación, Departamento de Bellas Artes y Publicaciones. 1960.

Poulantzas, Nicos. *Fascism and Dictatorship*. London: Verso Editions. 1979.

_____. *Political Power and Social Classes*. London: New Left Books. 1973.

_____. *State, Power, Socialism*. London: New Left Books. 1978.

Programa Regional del Empleo para Panamá y el Caribe (PREALC). "La devolución del canal de Panamá y su efecto sobre el empleo." Geneva: ILO/Documento de Trabajo PREALC/195. 1980.

_____. "Efectos del código del trabajo sobre el empleo, la productividad, los costos y la inversión en Panamá." Geneva: ILO/Documento de Trabajo PREALC/156. 1978.

_____. "Panamá: Estrategia de necesidades básicas y empleo." Geneva: ILO/Documento de Trabajo PREALC/189. 1980.

_____. "Panamá: Instrumentos del incentivo al desarrollo industrial y su efecto en el empleo." Geneva: ILO/Documento de Trabajo PREALC/179. 1980.

_____. *Situación y perspectiva del empleo en Panamá*. Geneva: ILO. 1974.

Purcell, Susan Kaufman. *The Mexican Profit-Sharing Decision*. Berkeley: University of California Press. 1975.

Quintero, Iván. *El Sindicato General de Trabajadores*. Panamá: Centro de Estudios Latinoamericanos "Justo Arosemena." 1979.

Reyes, Herasto. *Historia de San Miguelito*. Panamá: Centro de Comunicación Popular. 1981.

Richardson, Neil R. *Foreign Policy and Economic Dependence*. Austin: University of Texas Press. 1978.

Ricord, Humberto E. "El código de 1972: cambio radical en la legislación laboral panameña." *Revista Jurídica Panameña*. 2(1974): 140-154.

_____. "Lecciones de derecho laboral panameño." in *Apuntes de derecho del trabajo*. Edited by Jorge Fábrega. Panamá: n.p. 1976.

_____. "El sistema panameño de riesgos profesionales." *Revista Jurídica Panameña*. 1(1973): 116-141.

Ricord, Humberto E., et al. *Panamá y la frutera*. Panamá: Editorial Universitaria. 1973.

Ropp, Stephen C. "In Search of the New Soldier: Junior Officers and the Prospects of Social Reform in Panama, Honduras and Nicaragua." Unpublished Ph.D. dissertation. Riverside: University of California at Riverside. 1972.

____. "Leadership and Political Transformation in Panama: Two Levels of Regime Crisis." in *Central America: Crisis and Adaptation*. Edited by Steve C. Ropp and James A. Morris. Albuquerque: University of New Mexico Press. 1984.

____. *Panamanian Politics: From Guarded Nation to National Guard*. New York: Praeger. 1982.

Rouquie, Alain. "L'Hypothese 'bonapartiste' et l'emergence des systemes politiques semi-competitifs." *Revue Française de Science Politique*. 25(1975): 1099-1109.

Saavedra, A. *Una encuesta a los trabajadores de la Ciudad de Panamá*. Panamá: Centro de Estudios Latinoamericanos "Justo Arosemena." 1979.

Sahota, Gian. "Public Expenditure and Income Distribution in Panama." Informe preparado para el Ministerio de Planificación y Política Económica y la Agencia Internacional de Desarrollo. Mimeo. Panamá. 1972.

Sindicato de Industriales de Panamá (SIP). *El banco de convenciones colectivas del Sindicato de Industriales de Panamá*. Panamá: Imprenta Los Angeles. 1980.

Small, Janina M. "Las Juntas de Conciliación y Decisión, un mito del derecho panameño." Tesis de licenciatura. Panamá: Universidad de Panamá. 1977.

Sossa, José Antonio. *Imperialismos, fuerzas armadas y partidos políticos en Panamá*. Panamá: Ediciones Documento. 1977.

____. "Relaciones obrero-patronales y situación del sindicalismo." Mimeo. Panamá: n.p. 1981.

Sousa, Herbet. "Notas acerca de la situación socio-política de Panamá." *Tareas*. 35(1976):7-42.

Stallings, Barbara. "International Lending and the Relative Autonomy of the State: A Case Study of Twentieth-Century Peru." *Politics & Society*. 14:3(1985): 260-280.

Stepan, Alfred. *The State and Society: Peru in Comparative Perspective*. Princeton: Princeton University Press. 1978.

Stephens, Evelyne Huber. "The Peruvian Military Government, Labor Mobilization, and the Political Strength of the Left." *Latin American Research Review* 18:2(1983): 57-93.

____. *The Politics of Workers Participation*. New York: Academic Press. 1980.

Therborn, Goran. "The Travail of Latin American Democracy." *New Left Review*. 113-114(1979).

Tómlinson Hernández, Everardo E. *El poder político en Panamá*. Panamá: Tribuna Electoral. 1977.

Torres Abrego, José E. "Panamá: efectos del régimen de Torrijos en la estructura económica." *Comercio Exterior*. 32(1): 56-59. 1982.

Torres, Aureliano. "Cronología de una reforma." *Diálogo Social*. 86-87(1977): 6-7.

Torrijos H., Omar. *La batalla de Panamá*. Buenos Aires: EUDEBA, 1973.

____. "Ideas en borrador." *Línea 2000*. 1:2(1981): 13-22.

Trimberger, Ellen Kay. *Revolution from Above: Military Bureaucrats and Development in Japan, Turkey, Egypt and Peru*. New Brunswick: Transaction Books. 1978.

Turner, Jorge. *Raíz, historia y destino de los obreros panameños*. Mexico: UNAM, Insituto de Investigaciones Sociales. 1979.

Unión Nacional de Pequeñas Industrias. *Boletín Informativo*. Panamá: n.d.

Vásquez, Juan Materno. "La posición del estado panameño frente a la cuestión social: una exposición sobre la filosofía del código de trabajo panameño." *Revista Jurídica Panameña*. 2(1974): 135-139.

Veces, María P. *Apuntes socio-económicos de la provincia de Chiriquí*. Panamá: CEASPA. 1978.

Walker, Bobby D. "La industria bananera en Panamá." *Revista Diplomática*. September (1981): 72-76.

Wiarda, Howard J. "Corporative Origins of the Iberian and LatinAmerican Labor Relations Systems." *Studies in Comparative International Development*. 13:1(1978): 3-37.

____. "The Latin American Development Process and the New Developmental Alternatives: Military 'Nasserism' and 'Dictatorships with Popular Support.'" *Western Political Quarterly.* 25(3): 464-490. 1972.

Zúñiga, Carlos Iván. "Las elecciones presidenciales de 1968." *Tareas.* Jun-Oct(1974): 57-69.

Zúñiga, Gloria. "El despido: exposición teórica y estudio de su interpretación en el código de trabajo." Tesis de licenciatura. Panamá: Universidad Santa María la Antigua. 1974.

# INDEX

# LABOR AND POLITICS IN PANAMA
## The Torrijos Years
Sharon Phillipps Collazos

Labor law reforms introduced in Panama during the Torrijos administration (1968–1981) were a radical departure from past authoritarian agendas that had benefited only a small, entrenched elite. Offering a historical analysis of the enactment and implementation of labor policy in those years, Dr. Phillipps Collazos presents a penetrating study of the power relations among Panama's political elite, the business sector, and labor. The author argues that the 1972 Labor Code, which exemplified the Torrijos regime's reformist nature, lent the regime popular support and a measure of legitimacy. The business sector, however, blamed the Labor Code for most of the economic woes experienced during the mid-1970s, including widespread unemployment. By manipulating their considerable economic assets and waging a fierce antigovernment campaign both in Panama and in the United States at the time of the Canal Treaty negotiations, the members of the business sector were able to have the Labor Code amended and significantly weakened.

In light of the recent upheaval in Panama, this study is important because it provides a critical profile of Panama's political elite and analyzes the country's fragile political institutions. Though the Torrijos administration provided an opening for the greater enfranchisement of the working classes, the Noriega years—characterized by greed and plunder—obliterated most of Torrijos's reforms and set the stage for the return of the traditional ruling class.

Sharon Phillipps Collazos, former coordinator of the Center for Latin American Studies at Stanford University, is a development consultant.

---

For order and other information, please write to:
**WESTVIEW PRESS**
5500 Central Avenue
Boulder, Colorado 80301

ISBN 0-8133-8115-0

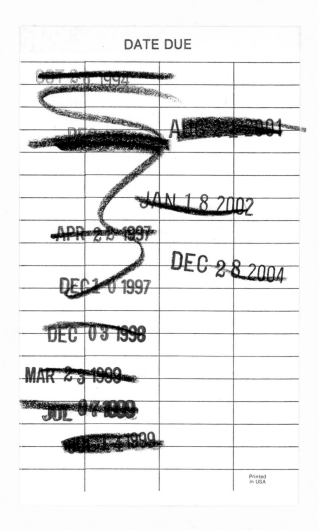

## DATE DUE

OCT 3 0 1994

A      2001

JAN 1 8 2002

APR 2 3 1997

DEC 2 8 2004

DEC 1 0 1997

DEC 0 3 1998

MAR 2 3 1999

JUL 0 7 1999

1999